DATE DUE

DEMCO 38-296

Innovative Applications of Artificial Intelligence 3

Innovative Applications of Artificial Intelligence 3

Proceedings of the IAAI-91 Conference

Edited by Reid G. Smith and A. Carlisle Scott

Q334 .I5433 1991
Innovative applications of
artificial intelligence 3 :
proceedings of the IAAI-91
conference

be reproduced in
ans (including
age and retrieval)
her.

ss, Massachusetts
usetts, and London,
England.

ISBN 0-262-68068-8

The chapter, "Intelligent Decision Support for Assembly System Design," (Hernandez et al.) was funded by the Defense Advanced Research Projects Agency, contract MDA972-88-C-0027, and was approved for public release with unlimited distribution under OASD(PA) 2/7/91.

Trademarks

The trademarked terms that appear throughout this book are used in an editorial nature only to the benefit of the trademark owner. No infringement of any trademarked terms is intended.

ADS™ is a registered trademark of Aion Corporation. AirBus® is a register mark of AirBus Industries. SABRE® and American Airlines® are register marks and AA™, AAdvantage™, and FOS™ are registered trademarks of AMR Corporation. Macintosh® and Macintosh II are registered trademarks of Apple Computer, Inc. UNIX™, LMOS™, MLT™, LEX™, and YACC™ are registered trademarks of AT&T. Boeing® is a register mark of Boeing Aircraft Corporation. TURBO BASIC, Turbo C, and Turbo C++ are registered trademarks of Borland International, Inc. DEC™, VAX™, CANASTA™, and VMS™ are registered trademarks of Digital Equipment Corporation. Framemaker™ is a registered trademark of Frame Technology. Golden Common Lisp™, GoldWorks™, Anvil 1000™, Autocad™, AutoLisp™, and muLisp™ are registered trademarks of Goldhill Computers, Inc. IBM® is a register mark and MVS™, PC™, Informix™, and X Window System™ are registered trademarks of IBM. ART™ and ART-IM™ are registered trademarks of Inference Corp. 386™ is a registered trademark of Intel Corporation. KEE™ is a registered trademark of Intellicorp. McDonnel Douglas® is a register mark of McDonnel Douglas Corporation. Microsoft® is a register mark and Windows™ and Word™ are registered trademarks of Microsoft Corporation. Nexpert Object™ is a registered trademark of Neuron Data, Inc. NYNEX MAX is a registered trademark of NYNEX. TELON ™ is a registered trademark of Pansophic Systems Inc. SAIC® is a register mark of Science Applications International Corporation. I-DEAS™ and PEARL™ are registered trademarks of SDRC, Inc. Sunlink™, Sunview™, and SparcStation™ are registered trademarks of Sun Microsystems. Symbolics® is a register mark of Symbolics Inc. MicroExplorer™ is a registered trademark of Texas Instruments. Grammatik™ is a registered trademark of Wang Laboratories.

Contents

Diagnosis

Engineering & Manufacturing

Failure Analysis

Finance

Preface

Innovative Applications of Artificial Intelligence 3 is the 1991 addition to the IAAI series.

This series aims to promote applications of the highest caliber in AI. To be included, a contribution must demonstrate innovation from a technical, economical, managerial, or application domain perspective. It must also represent a successful application in actual use in an operational environment. Each book in the series is a casebook for the businessperson—showing in a variety of domains what can be done with the current technology as well as practical problems that arise in its application.

As in many computational disciplines, research in AI is driven by applications—especially those pressing on the frontiers of what we know how to design and implement. By highlighting both the successes and the problems actually faced by the appliers of today's AI technology, the IAAI series aims to suggest areas ripe for research.

In addition to describing the application domains of their systems, how the systems operate, and the AI technology they use, authors are asked to cover a variety of other dimensions. These include *payoff,* in terms of competitive advantage gained, enhanced quality or productivity; *cost* of development and deployment in terms of time, personnel, and equipment; mechanisms by which *validation* of performance has been achieved; and *maintenance,* including automated knowledge-base update in dynamic environments.

Given that this is the third book in the IAAI series, it is interesting to examine the entire collection, looking for visible trends and changes. In doing this, we noticed the following points:

We tend to see AI technology used in situations where data rate, time pressure, problem complexity, requisite knowledge, or the dynamic nature of the task environment overwhelm humans. "The Application of Artificial Intelligence in the Field of Chemical Regulation" (page 55), and "AES: SunAmerica's Appointment Expert System" (page 233), are two examples. "MOCA—A Knowledge-Based System for Airline Maintenance Scheduling" (page 21), is a third example. In addition, this chapter demonstrates the care with which new technology must be introduced into the workplace, and the understanding required of the existing social context.

In many situations, AI technology is being used to make inferences based on mining the information held in corporate databases. "Meeting a Competitive Challenge in the Frequent Flyer Competition" (page 11), is one such example.

The areas of finance and engineering/manufacturing each contribute to account for approximately 20 percent of the contributions. Something new in IAAI-3 is a collection of three applications that indicate extensive use of AI technology by commercial airlines (pages 3-37).

The vast majority of the systems can be described as expert systems. As in past years, a few additional AI technologies are presented in IAAI 3. These include natural language ("Automatic Letter Composition for Customer Service," page 67); vision ("The Thallium Diagnostic Workstation," page 105—also the first medical application in the series); machine learning ("QDES: Quality-Design Expert System for Steel Products," page 177), and case-based reasoning ("A Case-Based Reasoning Solution to the Problem of Redundant Resolutions of Nonconformances in Large-Scale Manufacturing," page 121).

Systems tend to be built on top of shells, either vendor-supplied or developed along with the applications, with an eye to reuse in subsequent projects. The most popular shells are rule based, although many include support for object-oriented programming.

Noteworthy is the rise of C and C++. In 1989, almost all reported systems were based on Lisp. By 1991 there was an even balance. The practice continues of developing systems on top of one programming languages, and then porting them to another for production use.

Another trend is increased use of personal computers and engineering workstations as development and delivery platforms. This year they have overtaken AI workstations in popularity.

Most developers note payoff in terms of *quality* of products, services, or decisions. Almost as common is savings in time or money. Some authors note that AI systems have allowed them to head off an increased number of personnel that otherwise should have kept pace with business growth.

On a discouraging note, application developers continue to be forced to spend large fractions of their time coping with the unfortunate and grim realities of integrated computing in today's world. While we may dream that human energy will be concentrated almost exclusively on capturing, representing, and applying knowledge to business problems, careful reading of the chapters in this book reveals the darker picture. Far too much talent and time is dissipated in piecing together, rewriting, or force-fitting low-level components not designed for evolution.

On a brighter note, we are awash in opportunities and challenges for improving information technology in the future!

To be sure, the above trends are important and representative of the "here and now" of AI applications. However, in our view, there is one common theme that stands out in IAAI 3: Almost all applications are integrated with or embedded in the very core of the information systems used in today's business environment. They are intimately connected with the mainline company databases, financial systems, design systems, and manufacturing facilities. We believe this is a striking indication that AI tools have become peers among the traditional computational tools in the business toolbox.

Reid Smith   Carlisle Scott
Program Chair   *Program Cochair*

Airlines & Scheduling

Auditing Airline Passenger Tickets
Northwest Airlines & Andersen Consulting

Frequent Flyer Competition
American Airlines

MOCA
American Airlines & Inference Corporation

SYLLABUS
Scientia Ltd.

An Expert Auditing System for Airline Passenger Tickets

Andrew J. Valles and Joseph A. VanLoy

The passenger revenue accounting (PRA) system has the monumental task of accounting for each of the 60,000 or so tickets that Northwest Airlines sells each day. One function of PRA is to audit each ticket to ensure that the travel agent or Northwest ticket station that sold the ticket collected the correct fare and claimed the correct commission.

The fare and commission audit expert system performs the difficult task of comparing each item on the ticket against the diverse and complex rules of airline fares and commission programs to detect any discrepancies. Discrepancies are flagged, and detailed remarks are created by the expert system for review by a revenue accounting staff member.

Audit System Objectives

There are many reasons for implementing the audit functions in an expert system. The restrictions of fare audit and the conditions of commission audit are rule based. The audit process has to deal with incomplete data received from the electronic sales sources. Commission audit must explore all possibilities to award commissions.

Audit functions are handled by two completely separate knowledge bases: the fare audit knowledge base and the commission audit knowledge base.

Fare Audit

Before airline deregulation, the amount of money one person spent for a coach class seat was exactly the same as every other passenger. This situation, of course, is no longer true. A passenger might well spend a different amount for a flight than the passenger seated across the aisle. Each different price category, along with its associated restrictions, is known as a *fare*.

One of the difficulties in auditing fares is the large number of diverse restrictions that can be placed on a fare. These restrictions range from a simple *advance purchase restriction* (for example, this fare must be purchased at least 14 days before departure) to a more complex *combinability restriction* (for example, this fare cannot be combined with any other fare unless service for each flight segment is provided by the same carrier).

The volume of fares was also a system concern because at any given time, a *market* (origin–destination city pair) can have as many as 100 different fares for a single airline. Also, an airline can change the restrictions for as many as 100,000 fares in a single day, making maintenance of the system a definite concern.

Auditing every fare sold by both travel agents and airline ticket offices offers definite benefits, the greatest benefit being the ability to monitor ticket sales to ensure that fares are sold without violating specified restrictions. Selling travel agencies and Northwest ticket stations are notified of discrepancies and, when appropriate, assisted with ways to avoid future mistakes.

The Fare Audit Knowledge Base

The fare audit knowledge base is fed from two sources (figure 1). The first source is the electronic transmission of ticket sales information from clearinghouses located worldwide. All airline ticket sales are reported to the appropriate regional clearinghouse. Every airline receives periodic transmissions from each clearinghouse of its ticket sale information. This information reveals the place the ticket was sold, the fare that was used, the date of sale, and the flight information. The second source of data is the fare database. This database is formed from daily transmissions from the Airline Tariff Publishing Company (ATPCO). Federal law requires airlines that fly to, from, or within the United States to file their fares with ATPCO. International airlines file

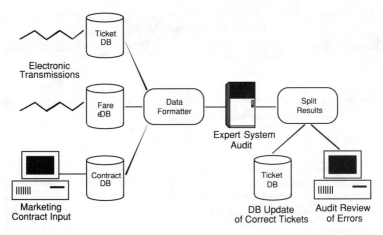

Figure 1. Audit Process Flow.

fares with ATPCO voluntarily. Therefore, this database contains historical information on nearly every airline fare. Before a ticket is fed into the fare audit knowledge base, a C program retrieves the restrictions for each fare found on the ticket. The restrictions are then formatted by this program and sent to the knowledge base along with the ticket sale information.

Each fare restriction that can be specified falls into a single category (such as advance purchase or combinability). The knowledge base has approximately 250 rules. These rules pertain to each restriction found within a category. The rule-based nature of the knowledge base allows any combination of the restrictions to be checked without relying on another restriction to be specified. This approach makes the knowledge base static in nature: The only changes that are required will be prompted from changes in how the fares are filed with ATPCO. ATPCO rarely changes the method for filing fares.

The categories of fare restrictions can be used in conjunction to form a single meaning (for example, this fare must be used on flight 142, or it must only be used on Monday). Therefore, after all the categories are audited, a final examination of the data must be completed to see if any of the category restrictions were not met.

The knowledge base checks the restrictions and, if errors are found, puts out a textual message stating what is in error (for example, "This fare must be purchased 14 days before departure but was only purchased 6 days before departure."). These messages will appear directly on a memo to the selling agent or airline station, notifying it of the discrepancy (figure 2).

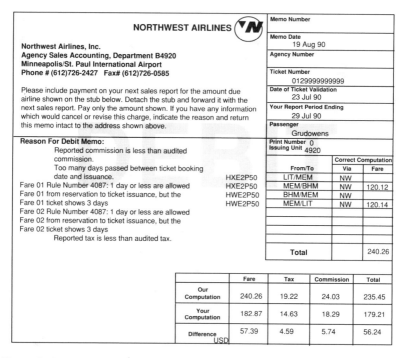

Figure 2. Sample Discrepancy Memo.

Commission Audit

Airline commissions are much the same as commissions in other industries. A *commission* is paid to a travel agent in exchange for the agent selling a ticket that includes travel on this airline. Northwest Airlines ticket stations do not receive commissions; therefore, a commission audit is not performed on tickets sold by these stations.

There are several difficulties with auditing commissions. First, Northwest Airlines has nearly 60,000 tickets sold each day by travel agents throughout the world. Most of these tickets are available for commissions; so, the volume of tickets that must go through the audit is large.

Second, Northwest has more than 40,000 commission programs with travel agents. These programs can specify a large number of conditions for payment. Some commission (or marketing) programs state the entire ticket must be flown on Northwest Airlines; others state commissions are only paid on transpacific flights; and still others state only certain flight, date, and market combinations are available for commissions. Agents do not specify what commission programs they are claiming payment for when reporting commissions, only the amount of commission they are taking. Therefore, determining what commission programs a ticket might be eligible for made commission audit difficult.

Auditing commissions allows Northwest Airlines to correctly identify what commission programs are found on a ticket and perform the appropriate accounting. It also shows the programs to which agents are responding and allows the airline to verify that commissions being taken by an agent were earned. The system also identifies commissions that agents are eligible for that they did not originally claim.

The Commission Audit Knowledge Base

The commission audit knowledge base is also fed from two sources (figure 1). The first source is the same daily electronic transmission of ticket sales that the fare audit receives. The second source of data is the marketing contract database. This database contains all the commission programs between Northwest and travel agents. The Northwest marketing department maintains this database through a separate graphic user interface. This interface allows the user to specify a condition about any item of data available on the ticket. The user can also combine conditions by using various operators (for example, "ALL flight coupons must be on flight 10 OR 11," "ONE OR MORE flight coupons must be on flight 30"). These commission programs are retrieved by a c program based on selection criteria from each ticket. The ticket sale information and associated commission programs are formatted and sent to the knowledge base.

Although fare rules fit into distinct categories, the commission programs have conditions that are much more complex. For example, a commission condition might state "Each flight segment must be flown on Northwest, and flight segment 2 cannot occur on Wednesday, and one or more flight segments must be on flight 48." Such conditions generate hundreds of thousands of possible combinations, making it prohibitive to code an expert system rule for each possible combination. The solution to this problem was to implement the knowledge base with a generic set of rules. Conditions are placed into categories that identify the type of comparison to be performed. A set of rules was then written for each of the categories of comparisons. Operators (that is, All, None, One, or More) are then applied to the results of this rule set to determine whether the condition was satisfied by the ticket. This approach allowed for a minimal number of rules to check all possible combinations of restrictions. The commission audit knowledge base contains approximately 350 rules.

Some commission programs state certain conditions that must occur in a specific order. For example, a program might specify that the ticket must first contain travel from New York to Tokyo. However, a ticket with the itinerary of New York–Los Angeles–Honolulu–Tokyo would still qualify for the commission. Because the commission program did not specifically exclude this travel, the ticket must qualify for the commission. The job of sequentially processing the itinerary (the ticket must still include travel from New York to Tokyo) but allowing for opportunistic rule firings (recognizing that the additional travel to Los Angeles and Honolulu is acceptable) was a sizable task. By using a set of control facts for both the ticket and commission program information, the knowledge base was able to procedurally step through such conditions and still tolerate some deviation. The commission audit knowledge base also has to cope with occasional missing or inconsistent data from the electronic transmissions. If the data can be interpreted in more than one way, all possibilities are explored to determine whether the ticket satisfies the conditions. As long as one possibility satisfies the condition, the ticket is still eligible for the commission.

Once the knowledge base completes the audit process, all eligible commissions for the ticket are output to a C program. This program then updates the database and notes any discrepancy between the commission amount determined by the knowledge base and the amount claimed by the travel agent. All discrepancies are reviewed before any action is taken.

Implementation

The criteria for choosing an expert system shell specified that the shell must (1) be rule based, (2) run on a Sun platform, (3) operate in batch mode, (4) handle text manipulation, (5) be a production release (no alpha or beta test versions were considered), and (6) be supported by an established company. The package that best fit these criteria was ART (automated reasoning tool), an expert system tool by Inference Corporation. Because ART allows suppression of the graphic user interface, it facilitated the batch implementation of the knowledge bases. The text-manipulation requirements of fare audit required extensive string manipulation in Lisp. ART allowed for simple function calls to native Lisp to format text messages for output.

The auditing functions that the knowledge bases perform are not limited to tickets sold by Northwest Airlines. Without any modification of the knowledge bases, the system can audit anyother airline's passenger tickets. The fare audit knowledge base can audit tickets from any airline that files its fares with ATPCO. Because commission programs are specific to a given airline and are not public information, the database that stores these programs would need to be created for each airline. Once the database was created, the commission audit knowledge base could audit any airline's commission programs.

Deployment

The expert system was implemented as a production release on 21 May 1990. The audits are currently running nightly on Sun 4/490 servers. The effort to design and program the knowledge bases used 3 full-time knowledge engineers for approximately 1 year. The payoff for the system is expected to be between $10 and $30 million dollars a year. This amount is a combination of savings resulting from the reduction or elimination of unprofitable commission programs, fewer errors made by agents when calculating fares and claiming commissions, and the automation of the audit process.

Maintenance

The fare and commission audit expert system was designed to require a minimum amount of maintenance. Currently, one knowledge engineer, who is not one of the original designers of the system, is supporting the system. The generic implementation of the commission audit knowledge base and the static fare audit categories accomplished their objective. To date, there have been no updates to the system because of knowledge changes.

Conclusion

A complete audit of passenger tickets had never been attempted at Northwest Airlines. The sheer volume and complexity of the data made attempts at automation in a conventional way unthinkable. The fare and commission audit expert system made possible what was once thought to be impossible. The successful integration of the expert system into the audit process allowed for greater flexibility and lower maintenance than originally anticipated.

Acknowledgments

The authors want to acknowledge the hard work and dedication of all the members of the PRA project staff. Special thanks to the PRA audit team for its assistance in integrating the expert system.

Meeting a Competitive Challenge in the Frequent Flyer Competition

Brian Ebersold

In January 1990, a major airline made a promotional offering to its frequent flyer members: "Fly three round trips from a hub city, and earn a free round-trip pass." American Airlines, wanting to gain a competitive edge, reacted rapidly by offering its frequent flyer customers a more progressive offering. Marketing offered a free round-trip domestic pass to any AAdvantage customer flying three round trips anywhere in the entire American Airlines route network, the awards to be mailed in May 1990. Round-trip identification had not previously been solved by a computer automation method because of complexities introduced by inconsistent or missing data. Historically, airlines have based the calculation of frequent flyer awards on the number of segments, segment miles flown, or specific (that is, hub) city activity. Offering round-trip promotions held the potential for opening a new era in frequent flyer competition and tipping the edge toward the airline that could make the offer.

In late January 1990, the Sabre Computer Services department initiated a joint effort (traditional data processing staff and knowledge based systems staff) aimed toward developing a system that could identify round trips. This system, a response to a competitive market situation, was intended for use against the frequent flyer customer database. The effort consisted of the traditional application development support group defining and developing the methodologies for the extraction of data and the compilation of award certificates, and a knowledge engineer from the knowledge system group developing an expert system solution for the round-trip identification problem.

Ultimately, an expert system that resolved the round-trip identification task was designed, developed, and implemented by the May 1990 deadline. The problem required the pattern processing of, and inferencing on, nearly 10 million data records. The objective, automating the identification and classification of a variety of round-trip types and minimizing a need for human intervention, was achieved.

Problem Statement

The marketing department is supported by a dedicated data processing support staff that in the past has provided exclusive service to the user's data processing requirements. In January 1990, the staff members were faced with a problem of enormous proportions, with a short time in which to respond. In short, they needed to develop and deliver a system that could process 10 million customer records with greater than 98 percent accuracy in less than $3\frac{1}{2}$ months. Within 3 months, the promotion would be over, and customers would be anticipating the delivery of their travel awards. The initial forecast by the marketing department was that 7 to 9 million flight segments would be traveled by frequent flyer members during the 3-month period (the actual number of segments flown was 10 million). Within this short time period, a suitable round-trip strategy would need to be defined, developed, and implemented.

The data processing staff supporting this marketing group is a conventional application development group of medium size (10 to 12 people). Typically, staff member time is spent developing methods to perform extracts from mainframe DB2 files and compiling the results in other DB2 or flat-file output. The output files generate the activity and award reports that are used by the frequent flyer program and sent to the customers. The current promotion would utilize the majority of the programmer resources in developing the extraction and award software. Data processing estimated the time required to design and build the round-trip identification and categorization software at 10 months but only if resources (staff) were available to support the development effort. A decision was made to proceed with a radical departure from the past and incorporate an expert system solution.

A developer from the knowledge system group was assigned to examine the round-trip identification and classification problem. Initially, a similarity with another expert system, one that identified markets, was assumed. An initial prototype was completed within 24 hours and a determination made that although round trips were not similar to markets (in the context of frequent flyer travel), the problem showed the potential for incorporating a rule-based solution. A second prototype, completed within 2 weeks, confirmed that an expert system was capable of identifying and classifying the majority of the segments in question. This prototype ran against actual frequent flyer member data and classified the segments into 1 of the 4 or 5 round-trip types that were then currently known. Another important result of the prototyping effort was discerning that a delivery time of 2½ months was feasible. The primary issues raised during prototyping were processing requirements and hardware capabilities.

The definition of a round trip is not as simple as flying from point A to point B and back again. A flight segment in the airline industry is often referred to as a *leg*. A pure *round trip* is one in which all the legs flown during an itinerary can be linked in a sequential order, leaving from, and returning to, point A (figure 1).

The *open jaw* (from the appearance of the itinerary when drawn on a piece of paper) is a second type of round trip that is ambiguous and less self evident: A customer visits a number of cities during the course of his(her) itinerary, and the possibility exists that either the data for one or more of legs are not reported in a timely manner, or a flight originally booked was not taken (that is, one or more segments of a pure round trip is missing).

Linking the open jaw segments posed the greatest challenge in the round-trip identification problem. Specifically, when a customer had a number of open jaw itineraries that occurred sequentially in his(her) account record, it was difficult to determine when one trip ended, and a new one began. Dates could not necessarily be used as a constraining factor because of the wide range of travel dates that were eligible to qualify for the round-trip promotion (for example, travel out on the first day of the promotion and back on the last day of the promotion could qualify as a round trip). Reservation numbers (record locaters) also could not be used exclusively to constrain the problem because the possibility of a customer booking a flight out and back at different times (with different record locaters) was real.

The following distinct characteristics of this problem lent themselves toward using an expert system solution:

First, the problem had a well-defined and limited scope (classify all flights for an individual account activity from 15 January to 15 April). In addition, there was a drop-dead date (15 May) limiting how far the

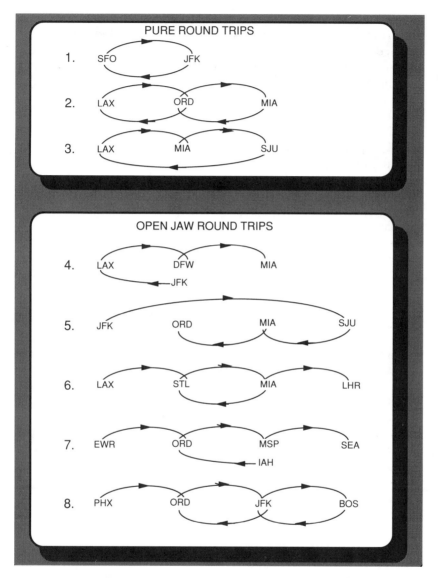

Figure 1. Round-Trip Types.

customer and developers could press the breadth and depth of the knowledge modeling.

Second, distinguishing patterns were evident in the data when flight legs were linked.

Third, there was a distinct concept of what the answers should look like (although some round-trip characteristics were formulated just prior to deployment).

The primary issues encountered were (1) the accurate capture of the business rules (because this problem was new, previous specific expertise didn't exist); (2) processing time (the volume [10 million] of records would require deployment in a mainframe environment, and the knowledge system group had no previous experience with mainframe expert systems); (3) high accuracy (a 1 percent error rate could generate 10,000 inquiry calls; operations would potentially be incapable of handling a rate greater than 2 percent); (4) fragmented data resources residing in a number of different environments, including realtime and commercial processing mainframes (figure 2); and (5) rapid development to leave adequate time for system test and integration.

Approach

This system was developed on an IBM/PS2 Model-80 personal computer and ported directly to an IBM 3090 mainframe. The development profile fits that of the rapid application development model. For example, four distinct prototypes were developed, all somewhat similar but using significant strategy changes or enhancements. The customer was constantly revisited with the processing results for knowledge validation and refinement. The business rules modeled during these iterative processes became more distinct and simple as the knowledge-acquisition and knowledge validation phases proceeded.

The ART-IM expert system shell was chosen as the development and, ultimately, the deployment environment. The knowledge engineer who developed the expert system was familiar with the ART-IM development environment. The ART-IM tool seemed to be a fairly good match for the data representation (frames) and inferencing technique (rules). Also influencing the decision was the fact that Inference Corporation had a mainframe tool available that allowed portability from the personal computer development environment.

By working interactively with the customer, the business rules were modeled. By comparing the results they expected with the results given by the expert system (running against a control data set), the differences narrowed. The criteria for the types of round trips that hold the greatest significance were prioritized; this information was then incorporated in the rule base so that the expert system would seek the patterns of greatest significance first.

Recognizing the (itinerary) topographies (figure 1) that would possibly qualify as round trips was the single greatest problem in solving the

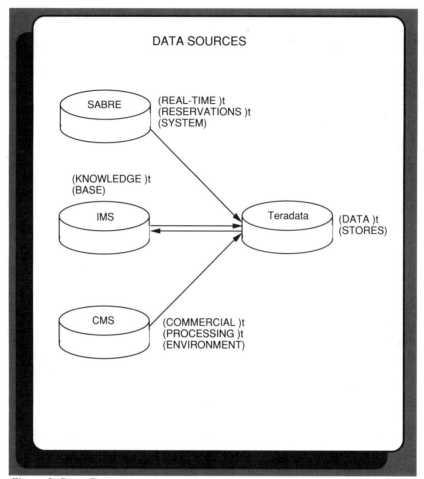

Figure 2. Data Resources.

identification and categorization problem. The two distinct superclasses of round trips, pure and open jaw, contain eight subclasses, which were eventually identified by the customer and the expert system. Each account was individually resolved using a combination of date, reservation number, chronology, and airport constraints. The result was an account activity log for the flyer that categorized and classified all the flight activity.

The system was designed to use the minimal number of rule firings to resolve each flyer account. Rule firings were at a premium because of the magnitude of data that required processing. A total of 20 rules were deployed, many of which were complex and multifunctional.

Most of the configuration parameters are user definable and picked up by the system as variables. This approach empowered the user greater flexibility to modify system behavior (either liberalize or constrain the expected solutions).

Fixed-format data files residing on the mainframe provided the simplest way to interface the data to the knowledge base. Data initially came from a variety of databases and a real-time reservation system, then were compiled into the knowledge base data-input files. A joint decision was made by knowledge systems and data processing to create files with a working set size of 450,000 customer records each, making a total of 22 input files.

Analysis

The analysis is performed in four basic phases: The first phase establishes a chronology for the occurrence of events (flight segments) (figure 3). The second phase ties the plausible events based on origin, connection city, or destination points. The third phase classifies the event strings based on the topography by using pattern-matching heuristics. Pure topographies have the highest confidence, thus the highest priority. Open jaws have lower confidence and precedence values (figure 4). The fourth and final phase disconnects illogical solutions and reinstates the second phase using an altered group of events. When inferencing is concluded, all flight segments in the account are grouped or categorized.

Development Cost

The internal development costs were calculated at approximately $62,000 for the knowledge engineer to develop and deploy the expert system and $150,000 for the data processing programmers compiling the data sources and developing the software to perform the award identification. The total cost was approximately $212,000.

System Use

This application has been in use since May 1990. Its initial run was against a full 10 million customer records and took approximately 122 hours of central processing unit time on an IBM 3090 computer. It was subsequently run as a monthly batch process until the promotion expired, allowing the expert system to reevaluate customer accounts with previously missing or unaccounted-for flight activity data. The reevalua-

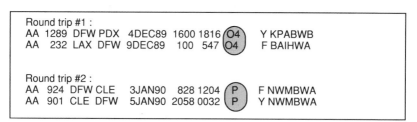

Figure 3. Sequencing.

```
Round trip #1 :
AA  1289  DFW PDX  4DEC89  1600 1816 (O4)   Y KPABWB
AA   232  LAX DFW  9DEC89   100  547 (O4)   F BAIHWA


Round trip #2 :
AA  924  DFW CLE   3JAN90   828 1204 (P)    F NWMBWA
AA  901  CLE DFW   5JAN90  2058 0032 (P)    Y NWMBWA
```

Figure 4. Categorizing.

tion runs were only applied against frequent flyer records with effected data and typically ran in minutes.

Payoff

The revenue implications for this effort are difficult to calculate. One would need to determine the revenue damage that would have occurred if the competitive offering had not been responded to. However, American Airlines did post its best first-quarter revenue results in the company's history, and the number of segments flown during the qualifying period was 10 percent more than had been forecast by the marketing department.

Planned future use seems assured. Airline marketing is cyclical by nature, and it typically makes use of all the available marketing options at its disposal. Knowledge of what a round trip is has now been codified, and the expert system can be called on to assure this knowledge is applied (on demand) in a consistent fashion; otherwise, the application of the round-trip policies would be subject to the individual interpretation of each customer service agent. Marketing has a unique and powerful new tool that they can leverage to offer travelers attractive new incentives for brand loyalty. Provisions for future enhancements, notably an account fraud-abuse strategy, were also incorporated into the system design. This benefit also results from the pattern processing and rule techniques used.

Conclusions

This mainframe expert system project produced the following significant results for American Airlines: (1) Round trips can now be identified and categorized for the frequent flyer program. (2) The use of an expert system shell was proven to be a dramatic productivity enhancer, with a reduced personnel requirement to deploy and maintain an application. (3) An expert system was successfully developed on a workstation platform and deployed on the mainframe (the development could have been accomplished entirely on the mainframe). (4) The system required minimal maintenance interventions by the developer or data processing staff. The scope of the knowledge domain was correct, and the flexibility to manipulate the results was incorporated into the design. (5) Marketing can offer more competitive incentive programs now that the automated round-trip system is in place. A situation occurred in late 1990 when another competitor made a promotional offering to its customers. This promotion was based on six completed segments of travel being awarded a free trip for future travel. American Airlines was able to respond with a promotional offering that included round trips or one-way trips (a subset of round trips), the award to be based on the most favorable conditions for the passenger.

Prolog

The round-trip identification expert system continues to be used in support of marketing's promotional offerings in the frequent flyer program. No significant changes or modifications have been made to the core knowledge base, although some heuristics were modified to support different strategies applied during the account processing. At the time of the initial writing of this chapter, the application had been used to support one promotion. Since this time, in the spring of 1991, another competitive response promotion implemented by marketing made use of the round-trip expert system.

Acknowledgments

My thanks go to the following individuals: Chuck Harvey, Data Dallas Inc.; George Geotz, director, AAdvantage Customer Services, American Airlines; and Mark Reynolds, Tim Robe, and Pippa Hearn, Sabre Computer Services, American Airlines.

MOCA—A Knowledge-Based System for Airline Maintenance Scheduling

Scott Smits and Dave Pracht

American Airlines currently operates in excess of 550 aircraft and flies over 2200 scheduled flights a day to over 160 destinations worldwide. Maintenance planning in a route network of American's magnitude is a complex, decision-intensive task that is managed at the Maintenance Operations Center (MOC) in Tulsa, Oklahoma.

The employees in this center are responsible for planning all maintenance on aircraft owned or leased by American Airlines. This planning problem grows in complexity with the dynamic nature of American's fleet: On average, an aircraft remains on its current routing for only one to three days before a change in the routing occurs. The aircraft routing might change as a direct result of weather, crew constraints, unanticipated maintenance, air traffic control restrictions, or other events. Making certain that all aircraft receive their maintenance on time in such a dynamic environment is a difficult and time-consuming task.

American's fleet is heterogeneous by nature, with aircraft of multiple types from multiple vendors. These aircraft are split into two body types (wide and narrow) and are organized into four distinct groupings (or subfleets) for the purpose of maintenance scheduling. These subfleets are managed at "desks" within the operations center and are organized as follows:

MD-80 Desk: All McDonnell Douglas Super-80 aircraft
727 Desk: All Boeing 727-100 or 200 model aircraft
Wide-Body Desk 1:   All McDonnell Douglas DC-10 models
Wide-Body Desk 2:   All Boeing 767, 757, and AirBus models

The process of routing aircraft for maintenance has evolved over the years but until recently was still a manual process, involving many large paper documents, that was the responsibility of the Maintenance Operations Center controllers. Historically, as a desk grew, the operation center had to add controllers to route the aircraft. The MD-80 fleet, which was American's first pure fleet and was planned to be over 200 aircraft, was projected to grow too large for the controllers to manually route the aircraft. It would have been difficult to further divide the fleet without adding personnel, possibly lowering productivity in the area, and increasing the exposure of unskilled controllers.

The automation approach chosen was to build an expert system application called the maintenance operations controller adviser (MOCA). MOCA is a knowledge-based system that automates the previously manual planning and document maintenance (paperwork) tasks. MOCA was implemented as an operational system in April 1990 for the MD-80 desk. A 727 implementation is targeted for mid-1991, with wide-body implementations planned by the end of 1991.

Operational Environment

The Maintenance Operations Center comprises several different organizations, numerous telephones, speakers, paper documents, and people, all performing their part of a global task to safely route aircraft for maintenance requirements. Figure 1 presents a high-level overview of the center's current environment.

The grey shaded area in the figure represents the span of control of the controller and the decisions and data elements contained within this span. This environment is described in the following sections. Each section refers to pre- and post-MOCA implementations.

The FOS System

The flight operations system (FOS) is a near real-time transaction-processing system that contains all information pertinent to the daily airline operation. FOS is used to control, communicate, and track the execution of the daily plan. This system maintains information such as flight schedules, maintenance information, and aircraft assignments.

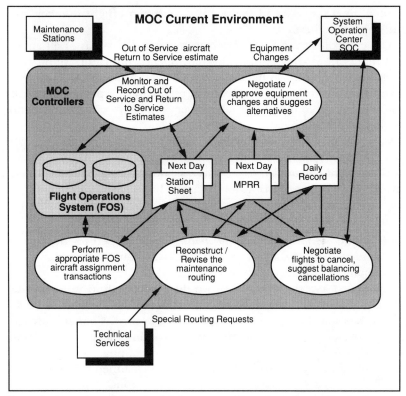

Figure 1. Overview of Current Maintenance Operations Center Environment.

MOCA connects to, receives data from, and sends data to FOS. The method in which this communications link is established is detailed in System Architecture.

Paper Documents

Hard-copy documents were heavily relied on to perform the tracking and planning functions performed by the maintenance operation controllers. The paper documents are replicas of the information that could be retrieved through transactions from the FOS system. The paper documents are described in the following subsections.

Station Sheets. The *station sheets* are large double-sided documents that represent the current aircraft routings by fleet type for all flights flown in a single day. The MD-80 desk maintains two sets of sheets, one for the current day and one for the next day. The station sheets are organized by stations-cities, showing inbound flight number, date and time, aircraft assigned, a maintenance indicator if the aircraft is on a routing, next sequence of flights to fly, outbound flight number, date, and departure time.

The controllers use these sheets to monitor the status of all aircraft and flights flown throughout the day. Special indicators show which aircraft are currently on maintenance-planned routings. All changes or events that occur during the day must manually be updated on the station sheets. It is common to change over 30 percent of the information on these sheets each day.

MOCA electronically automates the station sheets in the form of periodic updates from FOS and controllers' acceptance of routing alternatives that were created by MOCA. This task alone can save the controllers one to three hours of work during an eight-hour shift, depending on the work load. The automation of this task is achieved through an interactive user-friendly interface.

MPRR. The *maintenance planned routing record* is used to indicate the planned routing for all the aircraft that are currently planned for maintenance within the next seven days.

Prior to MOCA, the controllers would manually find valid routings when planning an aircraft for maintenance. Once a valid route was found, it would be written on this routing record. Changes affecting the routing would necessitate manually rerouting the aircraft for maintenance as well as manually erasing the old routings and writing the new routing on the sheets of the maintenance planned routing record.

MOCA automates the task of maintaining the routing record by automatically generating it as maintenance routings created by MOCA are accepted by the controllers. Planned routings that are dynamically affected are automatically deleted from the record by MOCA. The automation of this task allows the controllers to maintain routings for as many as seven days instead of the previous three to four days with the manual method.

Daily Record. The *daily record* is used by the controllers as a snapshot of the current planned maintenance events. This sheet shows the terminating station-city for this night by aircraft and whether the aircraft is currently on a planned maintenance routing. Changes to an aircraft routing were also manually maintained by the controllers prior to MOCA. MOCA automates this task by dynamically updating the daily record as changes are made in the system.

Higher Ops. A fourth document, not shown in figure 1, is a weekly computer printout referred to as the *higher ops*, which lists all maintenance requirements for aircraft and the type of maintenance to be performed. Maintenance routings are generated based on the requirements listed in the higher ops document. Requirements includes both routine and nonroutine maintenance. MOCA currently automates the higher ops sheets for the most important routine maintenance associated with the aircraft type.

Note: All paper documents previously used in the Maintenance Operations Center were replaced by the MOCA system with the exception of the higher ops.

Controller Tasks

The ovals shown in figure 1 represent some of the daily tasks handled by the controllers. The arrows in the figure represent analysis of information on the paper documents or in FOS to make the appropriate decisions.

Each day, the controllers must plan new routings for aircraft; replan maintenance routings that were affected; and react to dynamic events such as weather, delayed flights, cancellations, out-of-service aircraft, or other scheduling-related problems. Any or all of these dynamic events can cause problems to the current planned routings of the aircraft. As much as 75 percent of the fleet can be on some type of maintenance routing. On an average day, a controller needs to route approximately 60 to 100 aircraft on the MD-80 desk. When routings are modified from the aircraft's current route, changes must be made in FOS; prior to MOCA, these changes were made on the paper documents.

For example, if a severe weather problem was affecting one of the major airports, the controller might not be able to manually maintain all the routing changes for the next seven days. Many of the paper documents become unusable, and the controller is forced to use the first route found that satisfies the maintenance requirement rather than continue to look for a near-optimal solution. If the routing is not needed in the next one or two days, it can be deferred until there is enough time to perform all the routing changes. MOCA allows the controllers to maintain their routings for as many as seven days and create new routings much faster than previously possible during irregular operations.

External Influences

The boxes outside the grey shaded area in figure 1 represent other operating entities of the airline that affect the maintenance routings created by the Maintenance Operations Center.

The Systems Operation Center is responsible for the daily operation of the airline. The dispatchers working in this environment have the final word on events that affect the daily operation of the airline. For example, if weather problems at the Dallas–Fort Worth (DFW) Airport affect the number of takeoffs and landings that can occur, the dispatchers in this center are responsible for determining which flights to divert to other airports or cancel.

Operational problems accumulate and cause problems for the maintenance operation controllers because the aircraft that are affected in the more global running of the airline might be on maintenance routings. These aircraft would have to be replanned by the controllers to ensure maintenance is received. The system and maintenance operation centers communicate constantly in trying to minimize disturbances and maintain the most effective combinations of routings. MOCA has been a tremendous benefit to both centers for irregular operations, assisting in determining which would be the best aircraft to use for a particular flight and which aircraft are not currently assigned to a flight in an airport.

Project Justification

Several attempts had been made to automate this process of planning aircraft for maintenance using traditional operation research and conventional programming techniques. All these attempts were unsuccessful because of the complexity of the problem. A prototype system built over a three-month period from December 1987 to February 1988 successfully validated that a knowledge-based system approach could be used to solve the planning problem. The functions demonstrated accounted for about 10 percent of the total solution.

The prototype was followed by an additional feasibility study beginning in late February 1988 and continuing through April. The feasibility study determined the time frame, personnel, and best approach required to build the MOCA system. It was decided that because of the growth plan of the airline and, specifically, the MD-80 fleet, that the knowledge systems group at American Airlines should first address building a solution for the MD-80 desk followed by phased-in approaches for the other fleets.

The project was fully funded as an operational necessity required to successfully maintain the current growth plan of the airline. A cost-benefit analysis showed that not having to hire additional personnel could, alone, over a five-year period pay for the system. In addition, the manual process was clearly becoming overwhelming, even for the most qualified maintenance operation controllers.

The feasibility study also defined two potential improvements that the system could provide for the current operation: (1) a reduction in the number of *flight breaks* (switching two aircraft assigned to direct flights at an intermediate station) that were scheduled by the controllers and (2) an increase in the *yield* (a comparison of the time remaining to perform a maintenance check with the time allowed to perform this check) for maintenance checks.

The feasibility study clearly indicated a knowledge-based system was a good approach to solving the controllers' planning problem. Three other factors were involved in the decision:

First, a knowledge-based system solution would add consistency to the controllers' decision-making process. Knowledge acquisition allowed us to capture the heuristics of the best controllers in regard to routing aircraft for maintenance. A better standard could be maintained and implemented by the knowledge-based system.

Second, a knowledge-based system could broaden the decision-making parameters. A computer can more easily generate thousands of potential routes for planning aircraft for maintenance routings. Even the best controllers often stopped once a valid solution was found.

A knowledge-based system approach with a user-friendly, reliable, and interactive interface automates the routine aspects of the controllers' jobs. Automating the manual paperwork process allowed the controllers to save many hours of propagation work: copying, erasing, and modifying information on the paper documents when changes were necessary.

System Description

The MOCA project was divided into a set of modules, each responsible for its own unique function. Figure 2 shows a functional diagram of the MOCA system. The MOCA solution was provided by tightly integrating the modules, providing the following functions:

First is FOS communications and database access, including provisions for terminal emulation, system initialization, and recovery.

Second is daily plan generation and maintenance. This module controls the startup and initialization of the knowledge base, the parsing of the data into structures, the update mechanism, and the initial generation of the aircraft normal routings.

Third is the *planning module*, which is responsible for the resolution of all planning goals presented to it.

Fourth is the *dynamic changes module*, which is responsible for resolving problems with the aircraft routings caused by System Operations Center requests, canceled flights, *out-of-type events* (using aircraft from a different fleet type), or special maintenance requests.

Fifth is the *impact analysis module*, which suggests a list of possible solutions and an explanation of the differences between solutions when routing aircraft for maintenance.

Sixth is the user interface, which presents the information to the user and allows the user to input and request information from the knowledge base, including hard-copy capabilities.

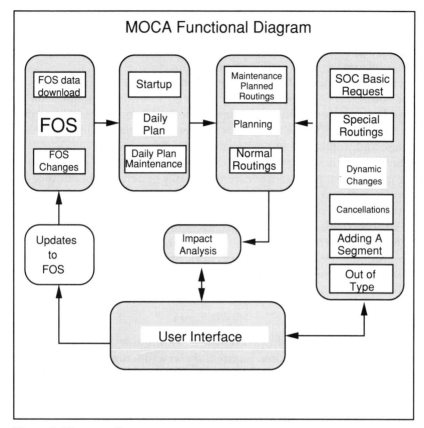

Figure 2. The MOCA System.

System Architecture

This section describes the MOCA system architecture. We discuss the hardware and software environment, the FOS connectivity and data access, the local database, the user interface, and planning.

Hardware and Software Environment

MOCA was developed on the Texas Instruments MicroExplorer workstation, using ART from Inference Corporation. The MicroExplorer is built on a Macintosh II, using an additional Lisp coprocessor board. The Macintosh was connected to FOS through a specialized communications board developed for American Airlines.

FOS Connectivity

Perhaps the most challenging function provided on the system integration side was physically connecting a Macintosh with a Lisp coprocessor board to the transaction-processing facility host-based environment. The following tasks were completed for the MOCA project:

We used an AirLine Control (ALC) connectivity board to connect the Macintosh II to the host transaction-processing facility. The ALC board was supplied by Innosys and was in its beta form at the start of the project. The board would reside on a gateway machine, allowing 16 other devices to connect to the host through the gateway machine. This same board would also provide SABRE terminal emulation on the Macintosh II platform. The ALC board provided a hardware and software solution, allowing the 6-bit ALC protocol on the host transaction-processing facility to be converted to an 8-bit protocol on the Macintosh side, with additional low-level error checking being performed.

An application was written allowing the Macintosh to communicate, send, and retrieve information through the buffer on the gateway machine. This application was written in C and ran on the Macintosh processor as opposed to the Lisp coprocessor. Finally, remote procedure calls from the MicroExplorer Lisp side and the communications application allowed the data to be parsed and asserted into the MOCA knowledge base.

Access to FOS Data

A mechanism was built that allowed a large data source to be retrieved from the host system and maintained on the local Macintosh machine. A time-stamping mechanism was also required, only allowing updates of changes to the requested data from FOS to be sent since the last time stamp.

Two special transactions were written in the transaction-processing facility that allowed a calling application to request flight-specific or aircraft-specific data from the host transaction-processing system.

MOCA sends a request to receive the initial flight- and aircraft-specific data downloaded during system initialization. It then periodically sends a request with a time stamp to receive all data that have changed since the last update.

The download and update mechanism greatly reduces the number of transactions that would typically have been sent to the transaction-processing host because the same data are on the local machine and can be accessed through the user interface. Prior to MOCA, hundreds of transaction-processing facility transactions were requested each day by each controller.

Local Database

MOCA maintains a local in-core data store that is both a subset of the

FOS database and an extension, providing additional data required for the user interface and planning capabilities. This local data store contains the information MOCA uses to present the current state of the MD-80 fleet to the user as well as all information needed to route aircraft. At program initiation, MOCA downloads seven days of flight data from FOS as well as data on all aircraft within the fleet. During operation, MOCA receives updates from FOS every five minutes that consist of all modifications made to the FOS database that affect any record previously downloaded, for example, updated flight status, departure times, or aircraft flying hours.

User Interface

The man-machine interface automated a complex task by using a highly interactive, yet easy-to-use mouse-driven interface. The user interface consists of over 20 tables of information, allowing the user to browse through different views of the information contained in the local database.

The user interface was designed and built to be reliable, interactive, and user friendly. The data displayed on the screen are automatically changed as an update from FOS makes modifications. The users are presented with the information on overlaying tables that were specifically designed to optimize the amount of data shown but maintain the related tables that are required for simultaneous display. The users can modify several of the tables to obtain information about the fleet in multiple ways, allowing the user maximum utility from the displays.

Flexibility became more evident as the system was initially rolled out. The users gave feedback to the knowledge engineers on ways to improve the type of information they wanted to see displayed on the screen (sorting data, viewing information through multiple approaches, and so on, became important to the users). Because the data are available through the knowledge base, the knowledge engineers were able to build accessor functions that display different views of the data to the users.

Planning

Each aircraft within the fleet has requirements for scheduled and un-scheduled (routine and nonroutine) maintenance and is assigned to fly a particular set of routes. It is the responsibility of the Maintenance Operations Center controller to make certain that all maintenance requirements for each aircraft are met, making changes to the routing of the aircraft if necessary.

This task requires the ability to generate aircraft routings in a rapidly changing, dynamic environment. MOCA uses a modified A* search algorithm to search the state space of all possible routing combinations looking for a minimal cost solution. This technique was chosen because it can find solutions quickly and efficiently, even when the search space is large, as is the case with the set of all routes that a fleet of aircraft might fly.

The planning module seeks to model the objects and relationships that are necessary for the controller's task of routing aircraft. The objects modeled include aircraft, flight leg segments, maintenance capabilities, requirements and assignments. Each database object is implemented as a Lisp structure. Garbage-free data structures were created for all objects to reduce the need for MOCA to interrupt processing to reclaim garbage memory.

MOCA maintains a list of aircraft that need planning for maintenance, which is displayed to the controllers through the user interface. From this list, the controller selects an aircraft to plan. MOCA then sets up an internal list of tasks it must perform called *planning goals*. These goals correspond to the maintenance requirements of the basic data model. An example goal might be to find a route that will get an aircraft to the Chicago O'Hare (ORD) airport for a B-check within three days.

The A* search utilizes a best-first methodology to apply the most promising routing modification operators to the current state of the database to arrive at a solution based on the current set of goals. An example state-space search operator would be to swap two aircraft (placing one on the other aircraft's outbound flight) when their routings meet each other at approximately the same time in the same station. The application of this operator might allow the aircraft to satisfy its maintenance requirement goal, or additional or alternative operators can be applied. A cost-estimating function is applied against each of the operations available to determine the lowest-cost operator to apply. Examples of costing parameters used in the search include overnight ground time, early or late termination in a station, early or late origin, delay, overbooking of maintenance capabilities, or use of spare aircraft to satisfy a routing. All these costs can affect the routing solution.

Each modification to the database through the use of these operators creates a new child state within MOCA. The new state is identical to the parent state in every way except for the modifications made by applying the operator. Each new state is evaluated, and the lowest-cost operators are applied to the current state until all the planning goals are satisfied. If an operator can be applied to a previously generated state that results in a lower cost, MOCA redirects its search to the other state.

A simple example of the use of the planning algorithm is shown in figure 3. The initial state contains the routings for aircraft 400 and 401. A goal was generated to find a route to get aircraft 400 to Chicago O'Hare (ORD) for maintenance. The child state, or swap state,

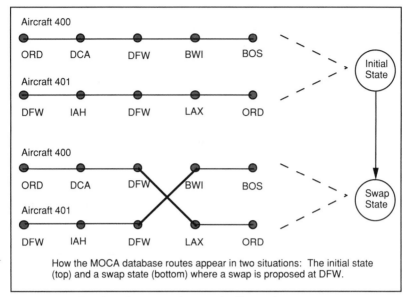

How the MOCA database routes appear in two situations: The initial state (top) and a swap state (bottom) where a swap is proposed at DFW.

Figure 3. The Use of the Planning System: An Example.

demonstrates a swap operator being applied to the two aircraft at the Dallas-Ft.Worth (DFW) airport. The goal is now satisfied because aircraft 400 will be at ORD.

When MOCA determines a suitable solution to the current planning goal, the proposed routing is presented, along with the current routing, for the user's approval. The user can elect to have MOCA continue to search for additional routings that satisfy the planning goals or can select any of the generated solutions for acceptance.

The basic routing heuristics used in the planning algorithm are not likely to change significantly. However, the cost associated with the operators used in the search could change, and these changes were anticipated by making the object representation for the costing functions modifiable. An extension of the user interface could be added to allow the users to modify the cost associated with key operators, such as flight breaks and delays.

Deployment

Several factors directed the approach for deploying the MOCA system for use by the maintenance operation controllers. First, the users were not computer literate. Over 80 percent of the controllers were unfamiliar with a mouse or a window-oriented interface. Second, the system was going to automate the manual process currently in place. Third, it was difficult to get dedicated training time with the controllers outside normal working hours because of shift rotation and overtime allotment. Fourth, inadequate test systems in place at American Airlines did not allow sufficient testing of each incremental release of the system. The combination of these four items required a phased-in approach, with a lot of cooperation from the controllers. Complete deployment of the system took several months, in the phases described in the following paragraphs:

Phase 1: The first phase of training replaced the current ICOT, or dumb, terminal with a Macintosh II with a 19-inch monitor running an ICOT terminal emulation program. This step allowed the controllers to become familiar with the look and feel of the screen, keyboard, and, most importantly, the mouse without greatly affecting their daily job functions. Each controller was given a two-hour overview of the terminal emulation software, including the execution of the program, windowing features, use of the mouse, and function-key definition. The controllers used the terminal emulation software for several months before MOCA went into operation.

Phase 2: The second phase involved placing a functional version of the MOCA software on the Macintosh II, allowing the controllers to browse through the functions provided by the MOCA system. The controllers went through 3 two-hour sessions with knowledge engineers to become familiar with the different browsing capabilities. This process involved coverage 24 hours a day for 1 week by the knowledge engineers in the Maintenance Operations Center to answer questions.

Phase 3: During the third phase, the controllers made aircraft assignments through MOCA. This step allowed them to link 1 or 2 aircraft to different outbound or originating flights. This step also required 24-hour coverage for a 1-week period.

Phase 4: The final phase of training involved a 1-day class on the planning functions of the MOCA system, including distribution of user manuals to all the controllers. This training was followed by 6 weeks, 24 hours a day, of on-the-job training for the controllers. The knowledge engineers worked directly with the controllers to convert the process from manual to automated.

This phased-in approach allowed the knowledge engineers to modify or extend the features of the system as requirements changed or as extensions were needed for successful operation and deployment. During each of these phases, occasional bug fixes to the operational system were made when errors occurred.

The controllers now use the system 24 hours a day, 7 days a week, to perform the entire planning process. On an average day, the controllers can plan or replan more than 60 aircraft.

User Acceptance

It was important to the success of the project that the controllers felt they had a tool that was both easy to use and solved their problem. The amount of experience of the controllers in routing aircraft varied from several months to many years. Not many of the controllers trained for the MD-80 desk were familiar with a window-oriented, mouse-driven interface.

The MOCA system was required to provide the following capabilities:

First, it must be as easy to use MOCA as it is to manually perform the task. This capability could only be proven over time as the controllers began to realize the true impact and benefits of the system. The system was designed and built around the idea that the manual propagation with the paper documents would be avoided with the MOCA system.

Second, the system must be reliable. The FOS system operates with greater than 99 percent reliability and was almost always available to the controllers. MOCA provides a similar reliability and is available to the controllers when FOS is not operational.

Third, maintenance-planning solutions must be provided in a timely manner. Much of the acceptance of the MOCA system depended on the amount of time MOCA took to find a valid route. The controllers required that MOCA be able to route aircraft fast enough to maintain the fleet in the worst periods of operations (for example, severe weather operations). Response time has been adequate and continues to improve. By automating many of their manual operations, MOCA has provided the controllers with more time to handle irregular operations.

Fourth, the solutions provided must be equal in quality to the routings provided by the controllers. About 95 percent of the first routes found while routing A-checks (the most common routine maintenance check) in MOCA are accepted by the controllers today. Additionally, the MOCA system has not missed any routine maintenance since it was implemented.

Fifth, the system must be able to handle data-consistency problems. The FOS database contained inconsistencies such as flights without aircraft assigned, two aircraft assigned to the same flight, and disjointed flight segment connections. MOCA has been able to maintain a consistent and complete local database despite these problems. MOCA is able to react to external events such as cancellations, diversions, and so on, sometimes even before the Maintenance Operations Center is contacted by the System Operations Center or the maintenance bases.

To summarize, MOCA allows the controllers to view their world in a much more consistent manner. They have access to many different views of the current operating environment with a single keystroke or click of the mouse. The controllers feel they have a system that does indeed solve and, in some instances, go beyond the initial business requirements. Most importantly, the controllers are using the system.

Innovations

The MOCA project was innovative in its approach, and its success is significant to both the AI industry and American Airlines Sabre Computer Systems. The following paragraphs summarize the significant innovations.

Other techniques in both operations research and conventional programming approaches had failed. MOCA was American Airlines' first use of AI techniques to route aircraft within the company.

The Maintenance Operations Center is considered a mission-critical, mainstream business function within the airline. Using AI technologies such as a data-directed, best-first search and a tightly integrated graphic interface, MOCA has allowed American to enhance its efforts by automating its maintenance operations.

By using an efficient search algorithm, MOCA is able to evaluate more potential solutions than the controllers in a shorter amount of time. MOCA provides a higher level of consistency for the planning problem. The system is also able to provide multiple exchanges of aircraft routings (multiple swaps), which is difficult for a human to do because of the increased information that must be evaluated and maintained.

The system would not have been able to successfully perform without a highly interactive, user-friendly means to determine the current status of all aircraft and flights within the fleet. This interface had to be integrated into the planning capabilities to allow the controllers to browse through the current status of the fleet while MOCA provided modifications to the current routings.

MOCA was also innovative within the Sabre Computer Systems organization in that it solved some difficult system integration problems, including connecting a Lisp-based machine to a transaction-processing facility and maintaining a large data source of information on the local machine.

Benefits

First and foremost, MOCA's successful implementation allowed the American Airlines fleet to grow and the Maintenance Operations Center to better address its planning problem. The controllers themselves believe MOCA is capable of routing aircraft more consistently and efficiently than previously routed using the manual method, especially during adverse or irregular operations.

Besides the benefit of eliminating all paper documents, which has saved the controllers many hours of labor, MOCA has had an impact on the operation of the airline in three other distinct areas:

First, the system has resulted in a reduction in the number of flight breaks. Flight breaks occur when an aircraft has to deviate from its normal operating schedule to satisfy some other external constraint. Some of the reasons for a flight break include air traffic control delays, crew scheduling problems, cancellations or diversions because of weather, or maintenance-related problems with the equipment. The airline understands that flight breaks cause a significant delay in the normal operation of the airline. The airline must react to such problems as additional baggage and freight handling, passenger connections, and crew changes. All these factors increase the cost of providing the daily service.

In regard to MOCA, the controllers have expressed that when planning an aircraft for its maintenance routing, there is a significant reduction in the number of scheduled flight breaks. This reduction can primarily be attributed to the fact that MOCA can view many more possible swap alternatives than the human controller.

Second, the system has produced an increase in the *A-check yield* (the average number of hours the aircraft flies before receiving its next A-check). Since April 1990, the A-check yield for the MD-80 fleet has increased by about 10 percent. Increasing the yield should allow the Maintenance Operations Center to perform more maintenance checks without having to add additional personnel.

Third, the system has allowed the size of the fleets handled by the Maintenance Operations Center to grow without proportionately increasing the amount of personnel. Prior to MOCA, plans called for the implementation of seven controller desks by the end of 1992. Each desk would require a minimum of three full-time people and one vacation relief person to be trained in the area. With MOCA, it is realistic to keep the Maintenance Operation Center at its current staffing of four desks.

Summary

Using AI technologies, MOCA has allowed American Airlines to expand its operations by automating a critical business operation that had become increasingly complex and people intensive. Operating a well-maintained fleet of aircraft while providing outstanding service to its customers is the highest priority for American. Without the assistance of an automated computer system, the controllers would have had a more difficult time in providing all the routings necessary for the expansion of the MD-80 fleet. MOCA is able to provide new routings and maintain consistency with the existing routings. In addition, MOCA uniquely combines this routing capability with an interactive, user-friendly means of determining the current status of all aircraft and flights within the fleet. This combination has provided a mission-critical system that operates in real time at the heart of American Airlines' business.

Acknowledgments

Thank you to our experts: Bob Bewley and Bob Ranck, the American Airlines knowledge engineers; Mark Fugate, Mark Kridner, Purna Mishra, Sridhar Rajamani, Kanna Rajan, A. C. Reddy, Knowledge Systems Manager Lynden Tennison, and the Inference knowledge engineers; and Dave Adam, Dave Coles, Sherry Walden, and Peter Holtzman.

The Development of SYLLABUS—An Interactive, Constraint-Based Scheduler for Schools and Colleges

Rick Evertsz

In most schools and colleges, producing a timetable is a task that is dreaded by those charged with annually creating it. In schools in particular, it can be difficult to produce any solution at all because teaching resources are usually stretched to the limit. This situation is made more difficult by the fact that the person making up the timetable must not only produce a valid solution but one that is of good quality.

A large number of judgmental factors are involved in producing a good-quality timetable. Some of these are educational (for example, it is undesirable for a group of pupils to have a Spanish lesson immediately following a German one), others pertain to the work conditions of the staff (for example, the teaching load should be distributed evenly through the day so that no teacher has a long, contiguous block of lessons), and others are political (for example, a senior teacher should not end up with fewer free periods than a more junior one). These qualitative factors make an already difficult problem time consuming indeed.

For a medium-sized school (about 1,000 pupils), even a veteran at the task takes several weeks to produce a satisfactory timetable. Despite this great investment in time and concentration, the timetable will inevitably contain errors, such as requiring a teacher to be in two places at once. Tight resources, together with the need to juggle many qualitative factors, means that the person creating the timetable only has one shot at producing a solution: The timetable is effectively set in concrete and is only amenable to minor modification. Because of the time-consuming nature of manually producing a timetable, there is no opportunity to try alternative scenarios that might enable cost savings or late extensions to the curriculum.

With the advent of greater access to digital computers, attempts began in the seventies to solve this problem by computer. Given the difficulty of manually producing a timetable, one would expect a computer-based timetable program to be a godsend. Early computer-based timetable programs ran on mainframe computers: The school would send its requirement to the administrative center, which would enter the data and run the timetable program overnight. The resulting timetable was usually unsatisfactory because it violated constraints that were important to the school. As a result, school timetable programs got a bad name for themselves. As far as schools were concerned, computers were incapable of producing a solution of the quality achieved by humans performing the same task.

Previous timetable systems have been based on operations research techniques. Although able to generate solutions, the main failing of this approach is the lack of control available to the user. The only way to alter the solution is to change some of the numeric parameters that control the priority of the various factors. This approach is fairly hit or miss because it is never clear what effect altering some numeric value will have on the overall solution. Based as they are on mathematical programming methods, such timetable programs are difficult to control because their processing is completely opaque to the user.

In contrast, AI approaches to problem solving are characterized by their reliance on symbolic, rather than numeric, methods. This technique makes it much easier for a program to communicate its problem-solving rationale to the user. The application of AI to scheduling has a relatively short history, only starting to gather momentum in the mid-eighties (for example, Fox and Smith [1984] and Keng, Yun, and Rossi [1988]). Constraint-satisfaction problem techniques (in particular) seem to offer a powerful way of solving scheduling problems (compare Dincbas, Simonis, and Van Hentenryck [1988] and Keng and Yun [1989]). SYLLABUS uses a constraint-satisfaction problem approach to producing timetables, rarely fails to produce a timetable, and can usually detect such cases before it begins scheduling. However, it is common for operations research–based timetable programs to only manage to produce a timetable for some 90 percent of the curriculum, leaving the user to manually insert the remaining lessons. Unfortunately, these lessons are typically the hardest to fit; so, the machine is only solving the simple part of the problem.

The School Timetable Problem

It comes as a surprise to many who are familiar with scheduling problems to learn that in practice, the setting up of school timetables is one of the hardest problems to solve. The main reason is that school resources are about as tightly stretched as they can be without also facing an insoluble timetable problem (for example, one 1600-pupil school, for which SYLLABUS successfully produced a timetable, had 98 percent use of its mathematics teachers). There is also a large degree of interaction between timetable resources: Teachers can teach a range of subjects (in some order of preference), and rooms can have more than one possible use. Therefore, in assigning a mathematics-French teacher to a mathematics lesson, the person producing the timetable must be wary of the fact that s/he might no longer be able to allocate enough teachers to the remaining French lessons. Assessing the ramifications of such assignments is not easy, and as a result, injudicious choices early on can lead to much backtracking.

A particular thorn in the side of those producing a timetable is the option group, which is designed to provide the pupil with greater curricular choices and is used extensively in the upper school. An *option group* is a composite lesson consisting of a set of subjects (options) offered to a set of classes (groups of pupils). Each pupil in each class makes a choice from those subjects offered in the option group and joins the pupils from the other classes who chose the same option. A typical option group is as follows:

Classes:	4A, 4B, 4C, 4D, 4E, 4F, 4G, 4H
Subjects:	Biology, Chemistry, English, Economics, French, Geography, History, Latin, Mathematics, and Physics

Some children from each of the 8 classes might take biology, whereas other children from these classes might study physics. This problem can be hard to solve in a timetable. The person developing the timetable must find a time slot (possibly several periods in length) where all 8 classes are free, and 10 teachers of the appropriate kind are available, as are 10 suitable rooms (for example, the science lessons typically require an appropriate laboratory). As the timetable process unfolds, these lessons become more and more difficult to place. The assignment of option groups is further complicated by the fact that there is a lot of interaction between them. For example, the previous option group would have to be assigned to a time slot that, through the available resources, enables the classes 4A to 4H to have the same teacher throughout the week.

In summary, the high demand for teaching resources, together with the complex interactions caused by option groups, makes school timetable production a difficult scheduling problem. This already difficult problem is further complicated by the need to satisfy the many qualitative factors that a school timetable should incorporate.

Development History

In 1987, my research group was approached by Kent County Council, which wanted to investigate the feasibility of applying AI to its timetable problems. Council members believed that better use could be made of the county's teaching staff by, for example, sharing some teachers between adjacent schools. It was estimated that a ½percent saving could be made in the annual education budget of $680,000,000.

Such a solution would only be acceptable if it did not compromise the educational quality of the current timetables. The first prototype was developed in 15 days at a 1,600-pupil school, using Intellicorp's KEE on a Symbolics Lisp machine. Although adequate, its solutions were not favored by the school doing the evaluation because staff members did not have sufficient control over the process. The first prototype was completely discarded, and in the interests of efficiency, a new version was implemented in Lisp. The user was provided with a graphic interface through which s/he could select a lesson that needed to be scheduled in a timetable, place it on a free period, and select the resources needed by the lesson. The machine would advise him(her) (graphically) in the choice of lesson, time slot, and resources. The user could also ask the machine to explain its advice, so s/he could make a more informed choice when choosing to override the machine's suggestions.

This solution proved satisfactory, but the machine was not solving the problem: It was merely acting as a decision support tool for the user, who was the final arbiter in the choice of lesson allocation. It was clear that one could add an automatic timetable facility to the program by making it follow the advice that it was offering the user. The user could freely switch between automatic and advisory mode, reallocating choices made by the machine that s/he did not like. Together with its use of AI techniques, this design feature was what set SYLLABUS apart from earlier systems.

The prototype's performance was acceptable, taking roughly 3 hours to produce a timetable for a medium-sized school. However, the hardware was far too expensive (about $85,000). From published Lisp benchmarks, it was estimated that porting the Lisp implementation to 386-based personal computers and 68030-based Macintoshes would degrade the performance of syllabus by a factor of 5 to 7. This performance would have been unacceptable, so it was necessary to redesign the scheduling algorithm.

To maximize portability between the two platforms, the scheduling kernel was completely separated from the user interface by adopting an object-oriented design. The interface is in control of the overall program and treats the kernel as a black box to be interrogated. It communicates with it by sending messages, such as "Timetable another lesson;" "Add a new teacher, called Mr. Peters, who teaches French as a primary subject and German and games as secondary subjects;" or "Why can't I place this lesson here?" The kernel never calls interface functions, it merely obeys commands and occasionally complains about what it has been asked to do (for example, if the teacher Mr. Peters were already defined, then it would signal an error to the interface, which would then decide what to do about it).

The use of object-oriented techniques provided a clean division between interface and kernel, speeded development, improved portability, and facilitated maintenance. The kernel was defined as an object that handles a certain message-passing protocol. This narrow bandwidth communication channel enabled the implementation of a dummy version of the kernel in three days, which meant that the user interface on each platform could be developed independently of the kernel.

With its newly designed scheduling kernel, syllabus is 100 times faster than its predecessor on a Lisp machine. On a 68030-based Macintosh, it is 15 times faster than the earlier Lisp machine version, producing a timetable for a medium-sized school in about 12 minutes. Considering the complexity of the task, this performance is acceptable. The size of the Macintosh application is 3 megabytes (MB); thus, it runs comfortably on a 4-MB machine.

The Macintosh and IBM PC–compatible implementations were developed by a team of 3, one working on the kernel, and the other 2 each working on one of the interfaces. The kernel was developed in 2 person-months, and each interface took about 3 person-months. Another 4 person-months were devoted to optimizing the kernel in an effort to obtain acceptable performance on the IBM PC; the latter goal was not achieved. Despite the fact that they were running the same scheduling kernel, the IBM PC version ran about 5 times more slowly than the Macintosh version and required a minimum of 6 MB. From a hardware perspective, one would not expect code generated by a Lisp compiler on a 386 to be any slower than that for a 68030. The problem was that the only Microsoft Windows-based Lisp compiler available for the IBM PC–generated 286 code; this code is inherently more verbose than 386 code based on a flat memory model.

The researchers in my group believe that the decision to use Lisp, rather than a conventional language such as C, led to the relatively short development time. When delivering on low-specification hardware, it is common practice to recode an AI application in a more conventional language. However, experience has shown that through good design, it is possible to produce Lisp applications that are efficient in both space and time on standard hardware.

Once developed, SYLLABUS was beta tested in 10 separate schools. This period spanned 4 months, during which bugs were removed, and new functions were added. It was relatively easy to incorporate the requests of the beta test sites for two reasons: (1) the features of Lisp that foreshorten development time (object orientation; automatic memory management; wide choice of data structures) also make extensions easier to incorporate and (2) the constraint-based architecture means that new constraints can be added without having to fundamentally alter the kernel's architecture.

The beta test cycle was complete in June 1990, at which point the Macintosh product was fully released in the United Kingdom. In the 6 months since June, it sold about 50 copies; this number is high, given that the United Kingdom Macintosh market is only 10 percent of the size of the personal computer market.

An Outline of the SYLLABUS Functions

The user enters details about the school through a set of data-input windows. The school parameters window is used to define the format of the school week (number of days, periods in each day, break and lunch times, and periods not available for teaching).

The user can then enter details of the subjects to be taught and any pedagogic constraints (for example, avoid setting the subject physics next to chemistry). Teaching profiles are entered through the teachers window (figure 1). In this example, the teacher Thomas Boots is defined as primarily a chemistry teacher; however, he can also teach mathematics and physics. He does not teach on the last 3 periods of Monday; this condition is shown in the grid that represents the week as 5 days (rows) of 6 periods (columns), with breaks after the second and fourth periods. Thomas Boots also requires 10 free periods each week. Further data-input windows are used to define the characteristics of the

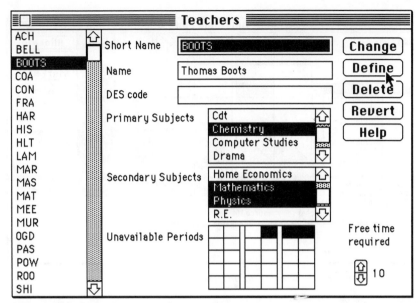

Figure 1. The Definition of a Chemistry Teacher.

classrooms and the structure of the curriculum. The user can then invoke an automatic set of feasibility checks on the data. This module analyzes the data and prints a report of why, if at all, it is impossible to generate a timetable. This facility is invaluable because it is easy for an inexperienced person to enter a curriculum requirement that is impossible to satisfy. Common errors include (1) assigning insufficient teachers for the quantity of subjects being taught, (2) giving a group of pupils more lessons than can fit in a week, and (3) grouping the options within the option groups so that the dependencies between all option groups preclude the production of a valid timetable. Error 3 entails examining the connectivity between option groups, as defined by their possible resource profiles, and is equivalent to the graph-colorability problem. It highlights groups of lessons that must be placed back to back; a timetable cannot be produced if the total length of a lesson sequence is greater than the number of periods in the week.

Once any problems discovered by the feasibility checks are rectified, the user can start producing the timetable. The task is performed through the timetable pane (figure 2). SYLLABUS sorts the classes (shown by the leftmost list) in terms of how constrained they are. The user should select the uppermost class in the list because it has the most constrained lesson in the whole school. The lessons for the selected class are then displayed in the adjacent list, again sorted by how constrained

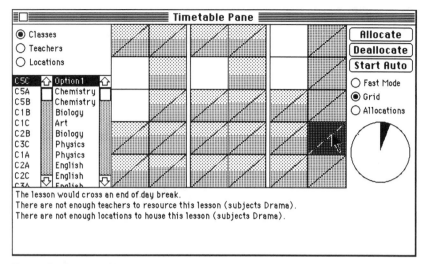

Figure 2. Creating Timetable Option1 Interactively.

they are. The user then selects the uppermost lesson in this list and is presented with a shaded timetable grid. The lesson cannot be assigned to those time slots that are shaded with a diagonal line; those that are shaded but have no diagonal line are inadvisable but valid (for example, cell (2,2) is inadvisable because option 1 is a double lesson and, thus, would straddle the midmorning break). The unshaded cells are those that SYLLABUS recommends for the selected lesson.

The figure shows the user clicking on the last period on Thursday to find out why the lesson cannot be placed there. The reasons appear in the pane below the shaded grid. Note that each barred period has a different level of grey; this level signifies how impossible the period is. Those with a higher level of grey have more reasons why they cannot be used than those with a lower level. In the limit, where there are no periods available for allocation, the different levels of grey enable the user to identify those periods with the fewest problems. For example, a period with only a room missing is fairly easy to satisfy; the user only needs to shift the lesson currently in the room to a different period. However, a period that is short of several teachers and rooms and for which several of the classes are unavailable would be hard to free up.

In interactive mode, the user is not forced to follow the system's advice. In fact, interactive mode is generally used when the user wants to override the SYLLABUS choices, for example, when allocating lessons that are fixed points in the timetable (for example, the lessons are the same every year). The user can pass control to SYLLABUS by clicking on the start auto button. SYLLABUS then starts producing the timetable by selecting the most constrained lesson, shading the grid, choosing the best cell for the lesson, and then allocating it together with an appropriate set of resources. The user can monitor this process and interrupt at any time to override a system choice (for example, edit the resources chosen by SYLLABUS, or move an allocated lesson to another cell).

An Overview of the Implementation

In automatic mode, the SYLLABUS control structure consists of three operations: First is *choose-event*. This operation selects the most critical lesson. Informally, this lesson has the least flexibility at a given point in time; in other words, it has the fewest time slots and resources available to it.

Second is *choose-time*. Given a most critical lesson, this operation chooses the best time slot for this lesson and combines the following factors: (1) a good spread of similar subjects (for example, English lessons are evenly spread throughout the week, and French lessons are kept apart from German ones); (2) multiple-period lessons evenly spread throughout the week; (3) a smooth distribution of teaching load; (4) a given group of pupils always taught a given subject by the same teacher; (5) multiple-period lessons not crossing an intraday break unless absolutely necessary; and (6) a time that maximizes the use of primary, rather than secondary, resources.

Third is *choose-resources*. Given a lesson and a selected time slot, this operation selects the best set of resources for the lesson on the basis of factors 3, 4, and 5 for the choose-time operation.

The SYLLABUS approach is based on the view that producing a timetable is a constraint-satisfaction problem. A constraint-satisfaction problem consists of a set of variables, $V = \{v_1, \ldots, v_n\}$; a set of related domains $\{D_1, \ldots, D_n\}$; and a set of constraint relations between these variables, $\{C_1, \ldots, C_m\}$. Each variable, v_i, takes its values from the finite domain, D_i. Each constraint, C_j, is expressed with respect to some subset of the variables in V and defines the consistent tuples of domain values that this subset can take (that is, $C_j \subseteq D_1 \times \ldots \times D_n$).

Each lesson is associated with a set of constraint variables: time, teachers, and locations. In the simple case, a lesson has only one teacher and one location; however, with option groups, the lesson typically involves a number of teachers teaching in different locations. Given a set of variables in a lesson, the actual legal subset of values that these variables can take is defined by the set of constraints.

Although time can be viewed as a resource, SYLLABUS treats this variable in a special manner for two reasons: (1) Users are familiar with the notion of allocating a lesson with a set of resources to a given time period; therefore, it makes sense to schedule from this perspective because the advice and explanations will more easily be understood. (2) Time is a particularly constraining resource: A lesson (option group) can have a set of teachers and a set of locations, but it can only be assigned one time period.

Each time period for a lesson is associated with a number denoting the *resource overflow-underflow* (RVF). These values are incrementally updated as resources are allocated to, and deallocated from, other lessons. For example, if a lesson requires eight teachers, but only three of the appropriate kind are available during the first period, then RVF would be −5. SYLLABUS sums the positive values in this time vector to obtain a measure of the *survivability* of the lesson. The lesson with the lowest survivability is the most critical and is chosen by choose-event. When a resource is allocated to a lesson, the survivability of all lessons that could have used this resource is updated. Here, the key to efficiency lies in making incremental updates rather than recomputing the survivability from scratch on each cycle. When a set of resources, R_i, is assigned to a lesson, l_i, at time, t_i, then for each lesson that might have used one or more of R_i, SYLLABUS decreases RVF for t_i. If this value is already negative, then the survivability remains unchanged. However, if this value is positive, then the incremental change is applied to the survivability measure. The inverse procedure is applied when freeing resources.

SYLLABUS makes extensive use of bit vectors to rapidly compute the effects of assignments. For example, each resource is associated with a bit vector that represents those lessons that it is allowed to use in the timetable (regardless of time period). When a given set of resources is assigned to, or removed from, a lesson, the set of lessons whose survivability is affected can rapidly be computed from the inclusive Or of these bit vectors (that is, the union of these sets). The set of resources available at a given time period is represented as a bit vector (the *resource-availability-bv*). To compute the set of resources available to a particular lesson at a given time period, SYLLABUS takes the bit vector that represents those resources that can supply the subject taught in the lesson and computes its logical And and the resource-availability-bv.

As the timetable process progresses, the variable domains are gradually reduced by forward checking (Haralick and Elliot 1980; Van Hentenryck and Dincbas 1986). In this scheme, when the domain of a variable is reduced by some action, the invalidated domain elements of other variables are immediately removed, saving a number of the consistency checks that must be performed. For example, if a group of pupils has five science lessons during the week, and the first of these lessons is assigned a teacher, r_i, the other four pupils have their teacher domains reduced to $\{r_i\}$. This number, in turn, usually restricts the time periods available to the other four lessons (because r_i might be busy at these times).

SYLLABUS is both space efficient and fast. Much of this speed and compactness results from the use of bit vectors to represent the domains of variables and perform set union, intersection, and complement operations.

Discussion

SYLLABUS provides its users with a number of benefits. The most obvious of these benefits is the time saved by the senior staff member who normally has to spend weeks producing the timetable. A customer survey shows that new users take between one and five days to produce a final timetable. This total time includes the time taken to enter all the raw data (note that entering the raw data goes quickly after the first year because much of them remain constant from year to year). The upper bound of five days is surprisingly quick because it relates to users who are computer naive and have no experience producing a timetable. Those who are experienced producing a timetable manually complete the task in under two days and are delighted with the time saved and the quality of the results.

Because of the time saved, it is now possible to experiment with different timetable scenarios; thus, SYLLABUS becomes a planning tool. Schools can now obtain answers to questions such as "Can we add environmental studies to the curriculum without hiring another teacher?" This ability not only increases the educational choice of the pupils but gives the school a competitive advantage over others. This bonus is important for private schools that are competing with others for a limited supply of paying pupils. Because SYLLABUS can dynamically reschedule those parts of the timetable that are affected by an unexpected external event (for example, absent teacher or storm or fire damage to one of the school buildings), it can be used as a crisis-management tool.

SYLLABUS gives schools the opportunity for substantial cost savings. Sharing teachers between adjacent schools has already been mentioned; in a private school, cutting the staffing needs by one teacher can save about $42,000 each year (which favorably compares with the cost of SYLLABUS: $1,700). One private school has used SYLLABUS to remove the need for Saturday morning teaching from their timetable, representing the first time that it has been able to generate a full timetable that fits in less than 5½ days. Furthermore, this five-day timetable was judged to be of better quality than any of the 5½–day schedules manually produced in previous years. Some schools can use SYLLABUS to generate income by releasing resources such as sports halls and language laboratories. This task is achieved by making the rooms in question unavailable for, say, a complete afternoon and then running SYLLABUS to see whether it is still possible to produce a satisfactory timetable. A similar approach can be used to save on winter fuel bills by switching off the heating in some blocks of the school building.

To date, these potential savings remain an unexploited benefit of SYL-LABUS. Schools prefer to use SYLLABUS to improve the educational quality of the timetable (after all, education, rather than cost savings, should be the primary goal). It would be a shame if SYLLABUS were used to ruthlessly cut costs at the expense of educational quality. Schools in the United Kingdom are currently going through a transition period from a state in which cash savings are returned to the education authority to one in which the school is allocated a budget and can use the funds as it sees fit. Only when this transition is complete will it be worth using SYLLABUS to make cash savings that can be redeployed within the school.

Those who have been responsible in the past for producing a timetable by hand are particularly taken with the feasibility checks because they can now make a watertight case that a given curriculum cannot fit in a timetable. In the past, they have had to waste weeks struggling to produce a timetable before the head of the school finally relented and allowed changes to the curriculum.

In delivering SYLLABUS, it was important to the research staff that it look like any other application. In this market, the use of AI has a negligible effect on users' perception of the product. This situation meant that SYLLABUS had to be compact and responsive; users would not be satisfied with excuses such as "Well yes, it is slow, but it is doing some very clever things." SYLLABUS is sold as a school timetable program, not a Lisp-based AI application. The researchers in my group believe that it is unique in being a mass-market, off-the-shelf AI application implemented in Lisp. Having successfully delivered the final product, they believe that the time is ripe for using Lisp to deliver mass-market, microcomputer-based AI applications.

Acknowledgments

Apart from myself, many people have been involved in the development of SYLLABUS. Geoff Forster has been involved with the project from the start. Mark Dalgarno and Stuart Watt worked on the design and implementation of the first product. Ian Assersohn, Diana Billigheimer, and Jane Pusey have been involved with augmenting the SYL-

LABUS functions. Pauline Wilson has been advising schools with timetable problems for 20 years; her input to SYLLABUS has and continues to be invaluable.

References

Dincbas, M.; Simonis, H.; and Van Hentenryck, P. 1988. Solving the Car-Sequencing Problem in Constraint Logic Programming. In Proceedings of the Eighth European Conference on Artificial Intelligence, 290–295. London: Pitman.

Fox, M. S., and Smith, S. F. 1984. ISIS: A Knowledge-Based System for Factory Scheduling. *Expert Systems* 1(1): 25–49.

Haralick, R. M., and Elliot, G. L. 1980. Increasing Tree Search Efficiency for Constraint-Satisfaction Problems. *Artificial Intelligence* 14: 263–313.

Keng, N. P., and Yun, D. Y. Y. 1989. A Planning/Scheduling Methodology for the Constrained Resource Problem. In Proceedings of the Eleventh International Joint Conference on Artificial Intelligence, 998–1003. Menlo Park, Calif.: International Joint Conferences on Artificial Intelligence.

Keng, N. P.; Yun, D. Y. Y.; and Rossi, M. 1988. Interaction-Sensitive Planning System for Job-Shop Scheduling. In *Expert Systems and Intelligent Manufacturing*, ed. M. D. Oliff, 57–69. Amsterdam: North-Holland.

Van Hentenryck, P., and Dincbas, M. 1986. Domains in Logic Programming. In Proceedings of the Fifth National Conference on Artificial Intelligence, 759–765. Menlo Park, Calif.: American Association for Artificial Intelligence.

Chemical Regulation

Lubrizol MSDS System
The Lubrizol Corporation & Andersen Consulting

The Application of Artificial Intelligence in the Field of Chemical Regulation

Giorgio Sorani and Robert A. Lauer

The Lubrizol Corporation is a specialty chemical company with headquarters near Cleveland, Ohio. Lubrizol was founded over 60 years ago and has enjoyed a reputation for being a leader in the innovative development of specialty chemicals for use in industry and agriculture. A small manufacturing facility is located on the corporate headquarters site. Two large manufacturing facilities complete the domestic operations, one located in Painesville, Ohio, and the other spanning two sites in Deer Park, Texas, and Bayport, Texas. The corporation maintains additional research and manufacturing facilities around the world.

Because it is a worldwide manufacturer and supplier, Lubrizol has an obligation to provide information about the content, hazards, and handling of its specialty chemicals to various organizations, including customers, carriers, communities, and plant personnel. This information is contained in a document known as a *Material Safety Data Sheet* (MSDS). A portion of one MSDS is shown in figure 1.

As a company selling products containing chemicals that can be haz-

The Lubrizol Corporation
29400 Lakeland Boulevard
Wickliffe, Ohio 44092
216/943-4200

MATERIAL SAFETY DATA SHEET

PRODUCT TRADE NAME: FINISHED PRODUCT

CAS NO: Mixture.
SYNONYMS: None.
GENERIC/CHEMICAL NAME: Mixture.
PRODUCT TYPE: Automotive gear oil additive.
PREPARATION/REVISION DATE: 11/19/1990
TRANSPORTATION EMERGENCY PH NO (CHEMTREC): 1-800-424-9300.
NFPA CODE: Health: 2   Fire: 2   Reactivity: 0
HMIS CODE: Health: 2   Fire: 2   Reactivity: 0
PRINCIPAL HAZARDS:

                    WARNING
                    – HARMFUL IF INHALED.
                    – COMBUSTIBLE LIQUID.
                    – MAY CAUSE ALLERGIC SKIN REACTION.

SECTION 1 - HAZARDOUS INGREDIENTS

– This material is not known to contain greater than 0.1% of any carcinogen required to be listed under
the OSHA Hazard Communication Standard (29CFR 1910.1200).
– From 1 to 5 percent Oleylamine;
– From 0.5 to 1.5 percent Isopropyl alcohol, CAS no: 67-63-0; OSHAPEL: 400.00 ppm; OSHA STEL:
500.00 ppm ACGIG TLV: 980.00 mg/ cuM., 400.00 ppm; ACGIH TLF STEL: 1225.00 mg/ cu M., 500.00
ppm;
– From 0.1 to 1 percent 1,2,4-Trimethylbenzene, CAS no: 95-63-6;
– Please note that the chemical identity of some or all of the above hazardous ingredients is confidential
business information and is being withheld as permitted by 29CFR 1910.1200 and various State Right to
Know Laws.

SECTION 2 - FIRE AND EXPLOSION HAZARDS

FLASH POINT: 63 Deg C 145.4 Deg F (PMCC)
UPPER FLAMMABLE LIMIT: Not determined.
LOWER FLAMMABLE LIMIT: Unknown
EXTINGUISHING MEDIA: CO2, dry chemical, alcohol foam. Water can be used
          to cool and protect exposed material.
SPECIAL FIREFIGHTING PROCEDURES: Recommend wearing self-contained breathing apparatus.
UNUSUAL FIRE & EXPLOSION HAZARDS: Toxic fumes, gases or vapors may evolve on burning.
          Vapors may be heavier than air and may travel along the ground to a distant ignition
          source and flash back. Container may rupture on heating.

Figure 1. Example of an MSDS.

ardous if not handled properly, Lubrizol is required by federal and
state regulations to have MSDSs for all products on site. It must also
supply MSDS to customers with the shipment of a product they are
purchasing for the first time and with the shipment of a product whose
MSDS changed since the customer's last order. At a minimum, all customers must receive MSDSs for their products once a year. The generation of this document is a complex process because the chemical make-
up of each ingredient of a product must be analyzed to determine
potential health and safety effects.

Prior to 1989, the writing of these documents was a manual function partially automated by the use of a word processing package. Because of the volume of MSDSs required for Lubrizol's 10,000 products, intermediates, raw materials, and research materials, several full-time employees were needed to create and maintain these documents. Because the complex government regulations applicable to the content of MSDSs are subject to interpretation, a sheet written by one individual could contain different wording than a sheet written by another individual for the same product. Although both MSDSs would be in compliance and within the limitations imposed by the government, they might send different messages to the reader. Because of the amount of time and resources necessary to keep Lubrizol's MSDSs current and accurate, it was determined that automating the MSDS process would reduce the associated cost and bring consistency and standardization to the content of the documents.

A project was initiated in January 1987 to develop a system that would be able to store data about all Lubrizol chemicals, utilize these data to determine the content of MSDS for any material, and determine when MSDS had to be sent to a customer. The system would provide for a series of online transactions to be used by the people who formerly wrote MSDSs to capture raw data about each chemical in a relational database. These data would be used to generate the MSDS document. Additional system functions would allow online viewing of the document and printing for shipment to customers. The result would be the complete automation of all MSDS business functions, including the complex process of generating MSDS itself.

Decision to Use AI

As the requirements of the system were defined, several functional aspects presented complex challenges. The major issue was the feasibility of capturing, within the system, the process used by the experts to create MSDS. This highly intricate process involves hundreds of rules and data elements, which are constantly changing to adapt to new types of chemicals and better chemical hazard information. In addition, federal and state government regulations concerning chemicals and MSDS requirements change constantly, causing the process to become even more dynamic. Finally, the sheer volume of chemicals handled by Lubrizol raised issues regarding the performance implications of completely automating the process. The system would need to automatically revise MSDS information for all chemicals containing a particular ingredient if the hazard information on this ingredient changed. These requirements for complexity, ease of maintenance, and the ability to manipulate large volumes of data indicated that a solution involving AI technology might apply.

At the time, Lubrizol had little experience with AI technology and vendors. An evaluation of five of the more popular expert system packages was undertaken by members of the management information system team. The evaluation included a review of each package's technical architecture, ease of use, cost, and other features. The evaluation took three months and consisted of reviewing literature and visual demonstrations for each product.

The results of the evaluation indicated that none of the packages perfectly addressed Lubrizol's needs. However, it was recognized that the technology was still maturing and that improvements were anticipated in the AI market. Recognizing the risk of pursuing an alternative method to traditional system development approaches, Lubrizol purchased ADS from Aion Corporation. This product appeared strongest in the evaluation and met the majority of Lubrizol's requirements. The intent was to use ADS to develop a workstation prototype of the logic needed to generate MSDS that would be ported to Lubrizol's IBM 3090 mainframe for volume testing and eventual implementation.

Knowledge Acquisition

The first step in automating the MSDS function was to work with the experts (Lubrizol's toxicologists) to define and understand the process of determining the MSDS content. This process proved to be time consuming primarily because of the great complexity of the process as well as the need to standardize the approach for all types of Lubrizol chemicals. The ideal result was a common set of rules to manipulate the hundreds of data elements and parameters used to determine MSDS content for the more than 10,000 Lubrizol products, intermediates, raw materials, developmental products, research blends, research concentrates, and waste materials.

The complexity of the process as a whole is a result of the nature of MSDS itself. MSDS for each chemical consists of 11 separate sections, each with multiple information items. This arrangement results in nearly 80 separate sets of logic to determine all items. The logic for most of these items is complex in itself, usually involving many data elements, parameters, and rules and having many possible results. For example, the logic to determine the value of the fire codes (figure 1) involves evaluating 13 different pieces of data about each chemical by 25 related rules. The complexity of the entire process is increased by many dependencies between sections. The result of one item (if it exists) can be used in determining a different item, and multiple items can all be dependent on each other.

Given the complexity of the business rules for writing MSDS, it was necessary to document the experts' knowledge in a format that could easily be converted into expert system rules. A variation of a decision table was used to capture this information. (An example of a simple MSDS decision table is shown in figure 2.) Over 100 decision tables were documented by the experts. These tables were turned into states, objects, and rules in the expert system.

This approach to documenting the logic had a number of advantages. Not only did it help the management information system staff turn business rules into computer logic, it also helped the experts organize their thoughts to better communicate their needs to the management information system staff. It also facilitated the documentation of test conditions and expected results when testing of the knowledge base began. The result was the increased quality of the knowledge-acquisition process and increased speed of prototyping and testing.

Building the System

Concurrent with documenting the experts' knowledge, the surrounding functions of the system were constructed using more traditional development methods. All online conversations and batch functions, except for the MSDS generation knowledge base, were built using the COBOL application generator TELON from Pansophic Systems, Inc. Although they did not directly communicate with it, these system components had to be integrated with the knowledge base to the extent that they shared and processed the same information on Lubrizol's chemicals.

In addition to internally integrating multiple technologies, the system also had to be integrated with other Lubrizol business systems. Formulation information from the manufacturing system was passed to the knowledge base for use in creating new MSDSs or revising existing MSDSs. Information was obtained from the order-handling system to synchronize the printing of MSDS documents with customer orders. The degree of integration with other business systems was highly innovative for an AI application.

On completion of knowledge acquisition, a prototype of the MSDS knowledge base was developed using ADS on an IBM PS/2 workstation. An iterative approach to prototyping was used to confirm the accuracy of the logic documented in the decision tables and the feasibility of deploying the logic as an expert system. The prototyping process was also used to evaluate various approaches to the architecture of the knowl-

Is The Value For Percent Volatile Null?	Is Any Component Prevalence > = 100%?	Is The Component Value For Percent Volatile Null?	Percent Volatile Field Result
No	–	–	Value of material percent volatile
Yes	No	–	"Unknown"
	Yes	No	Value of component percent volatile
		Yes	"Unknown"

Figure 2. Example of a Decision Table.

edge base, considering issues such as size, efficiency, and ease of maintenance.

The architecture that was chosen for the knowledge base allowed the organization of the logic by MSDS section. The rules for each section were combined in a distinct state, and a controlling state was used to initiate the others, as needed. In addition to the rules related to generating MSDS, the knowledge base also contains components for addressing the complex task of formatting the text into a high-quality document and storing the information in the database for future access. The knowledge base uses integrated forward and backward chaining, as well as heuristic search techniques, to generate MSDS. A portion of the data access needed to support the process is always performed at the start of execution, but various other input-output functions are executed when dictated by inferencing.

At the completion of prototyping, the knowledge base was ported to the mainframe, enhanced, and tuned to operate in its target environment (figure 3). This process of redeployment on the mainframe involved using the ADS *high-performance option*. This facility converts the knowledge base to Pascal and assembler code, allowing normal compiling and linking in the mainframe environment. By using this option, the knowledge base was executed in a fashion similar to traditional mainframe programs.

All data for the system are stored in the DB2 relational database. Although this database management system represented a strategic direction and many benefits for Lubrizol, it posed some important challenges for the system. At the time, few AI products had been integrated with DB2 in production systems. This installation was one of the first of such systems using the ADS product. In addition, the architecture of

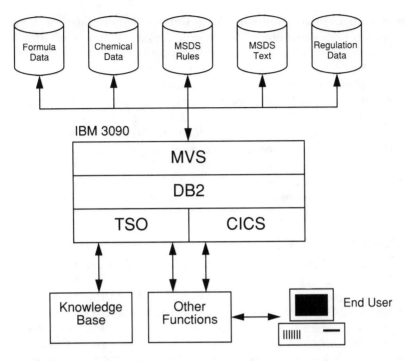

Figure 3. Technical Environment.

ADS-DB2 communications used dynamic SQL for processing DB2 data, which required additional analysis and design of the database structure to avoid possible performance degradation.

Extensive testing of the knowledge base was critical in resolving these issues as well as ensuring the accuracy of MSDS generated by the system. To achieve the greatest degree of accuracy possible, the system was used to generate MSDSs for all Lubrizol chemicals. Seventy percent of these MSDSs were reviewed by the experts. This subset of all MSDSs included chemicals of all types, complexities, and exceptions to assure that the logic was correct. All errors were identified and traced to their source, which was either erroneous logic or incomplete and inaccurate data. The experts corrected the data and worked with management information system personnel to modify the decision tables, as needed, to correct or enhance the logic. This iterative process continued until Lubrizol was satisfied with the accuracy of the information being produced by the system.

The major difficulty encountered during the testing process was the lack of a basis of comparison for the results of the new system. Because the logic used in the knowledge base included many approaches that were new to Lubrizol, and the current manually generated MSDSs were known to be inaccurate, the experts' review was based on assessing the accuracy of each piece of information in each new MSDS. In addition, MSDSs on materials within a chemical family were compared to ensure the consistency of information across similar chemicals.

The completion of system development and testing occurred close to 2½ years after the project was initiated. During this time, a diverse team of experts, users of MSDS information, and management information system personnel participated in all project phases. The total effort expended on the system was approximately 2,400 workdays, or nearly 11 person-years. Additional cost was incurred to purchase the ADS software for both the workstation and mainframe platforms.

Production

Because of its volume and complexity, at implementation, the system was impressive for an application using AI technology. The knowledge base used to generate MSDS information and format the documents contains several hundred parameters and rules. The data supporting the generation of all Lubrizol MSDSs are stored in 17 DB2 tables containing nearly 3,000,000 rows of data. The system maintains MSDSs on nearly 10,000 Lubrizol raw materials, intermediates, finished products, and research materials.

The Lubrizol MSDS system has been in full production since October 1989. Lubrizol employees at all domestic locations have the capability to view MSDS documents online and request printed copies. The system generates the proper MSDS documents for shipment to customers with orders of Lubrizol products and on special request. MSDS data are transmitted daily from corporate headquarters to Lubrizol's facility in Bromborough, England, for translation into several languages and to ensure standardization across the corporation. A cooperative processing system that creates Canadian-English MSDSs by running a clone of the knowledge base on a workstation platform was implemented in October 1990. With many other enhancements planned, the system is positioned as a strategic tool for Lubrizol.

Since implementation, the knowledge base has frequently been revised and improved. The major catalysts are changing government regulations, new approaches to the logic arising from better information about the chemicals, and periodic identification by the experts of errors in MSDSs. In addition, various performance issues, such as the overhead of using dynamic SQL, are being addressed through a series of enhancements.

Changes to the logic in the knowledge base originate from the experts. Management information system personnel then work together with the experts to modify the decision tables to reflect the desired changes in the logic. Management information system personnel physically implement the change and generate a variety of example MSDSs, which are reviewed for accuracy by the experts prior to production implementation of the change.

Currently, there are no plans to allow the experts to directly maintain the knowledge base because of the technically complex nature of the process. However, recent developments in the evolution of the ADS software indicate that ease of use might increase in the future to the point where maintenance by the experts is feasible.

Benefits

The system has provided significant benefits to the corporation in a number of areas. Most importantly, Lubrizol is ensured of accurate and timely MSDS information in compliance with government regulations. This ability increases the safety of Lubrizol employees and customers who work with Lubrizol chemicals. Second, the system has given Lubrizol the ability to adapt to constantly changing regulations governing the content and distribution of MSDSs. Third, the cost required to create and maintain MSDSs is drastically reduced. The system is able to handle hundreds of MSDS generations each day, many times the manual capabilities of the experts. Finally, the system standardizes the appearance and content of MSDSs, allowing simplified interpretation by users of the information.

To quantify the value provided by the system, these benefits must first be categorized as tangible and intangible. Tangible benefits include compliance (potential savings are in the hundreds of thousands of dollars in government fines), flexibility (cost of maintaining MSDSs is reduced by hundreds of workdays each year), and speed (in mass revision situations, the system outperforms a manual approach by a tremendous margin, which adds to the labor savings). Intangible benefits include greater accuracy (increasing the level of safety of Lubrizol employees and customers) and standardized MSDS appearance and content (leading to increased customer satisfaction). It should be noted that an exact quantification of the savings provided by the system would be difficult to calculate because of major differences in MSDS format and content between the system and its manual predecessor. The system has allowed Lubrizol to provide significantly greater functions in MSDSs at a much lower cost.

Summary

AI technology proved to be an excellent solution to the unique requirements and constraints of the MSDS application. The use of an expert system provided the flexibility and ease of maintenance necessary for such a complex application and delivered adequate performance in processing large volumes of data in a dynamic environment. In addition, the use of the AI technology in this manner facilitated the process of knowledge acquisition and prototyping, which improved communication between the experts and management information system personnel. These features contributed to the delivery of a system with higher quality and adherence to user requirements. It is believed that the cost of building and maintaining the system was lower than would have been required for developing the system using purely traditional methods.

The Lubrizol MSDS system is considered innovative for the following major reasons: First, the system is on the leading edge of a new wave of AI applications addressing chemical regulation and is one of the first to automate the MSDS function so completely. Second, at implementation, the system was one of the first large mainframe applications to integrate AI technology with a DB2 relational database. Third, the application of AI technology is highly integrated with existing business systems of more traditional architectures.

For the success of the system and the reasons previously indicated, Lubrizol was granted the 1990 Computerworld Smithsonian Award for technologically advanced applications contributing to the benefit of society. This achievement confirms the applicability of AI technology to the field of chemical regulation and business systems in general.

Customer Service

Automatic Letter Composition
Cognitive Systems, Inc..

Automatic Letter Composition for Customer Service

Stephen Springer, Paul Buta, and Thomas C. Wolf

Corporations worldwide have seen a sharply increasing need for customized client correspondence in recent years. Financial institutions, mail-order companies, legal firms—any corporation that maintains a Customer Service Department—must generate written correspondence that clearly communicates specific, individualized information to clients. Indeed, in a slumping economy, much has been made of the need to differentiate one's business from the competition by providing higher-quality customer service (Agins et al. 1990). However, the industry continues to express this commitment through a combination of awkward form letters and expensive original letters composed by hand. This chapter describes an application of Cognitive Systems' Intelligent Correspondence Generator (ICG), which has increased the quality, reduced the complexity, and drastically cut the turnaround time associated with the production of personalized letters at its installation site. Users with little or no training in business correspondence can invoke the system to automatically compose complete, high-quality letters specifically tailored to the addressee's situation.

The Correspondence Problem

The application has been deployed at a major credit card organization for approximately 1 year. The needs of this organization are both complex and representative of most customer service organizations. At heart is a familiar trade-off between quality and cost. An automated form-letter system originally formed the core of this organization's correspondence facility. Because its letters must specifically discuss different kinds of financial transactions, the system has grown to include close to 1,000 different form letters to address the simplest divisions of common problems. However, in practice, most of these letters are never used: Customer service representatives, working under pressure to handle as many cases as quickly as possible, tend to use 10 to 20 letters that they are familiar with and that are close enough to describing the client's situation rather than take the time to discriminate between slight variations within the form library. When a client's situation even slightly varies from these forms or encompasses a combination of topics addressed in separate form letters, a new letter must be composed by hand if the client is to be convinced that s/he has received individual attention. Form-letter systems might come cheap, but they don't always stay that way, and the quality of output for any particular situation can never be very high.

High-quality correspondence, in fact, is difficult to guarantee even when left to human beings. Figure 1 is an example of the desired standard for writing quality, in this case, a typical request by the credit card organization for more information from the card holder. Being both professional and polite, the writer must manage to clearly discuss the nature of the problem, the amount in dispute, prior communications, the exact information required, how to contact the company, and several other transactions and events related to the central problem.

Customized letters such as the one shown in figure 1 are pleasing to the card holder: They are clear, concise, and polite and convey a sense that a particular representative has handled one's situation individually. However, it has proven extremely difficult for our credit card organization and other corporations we spoke with to consistently produce this level of quality. We noted numerous examples of customer service representatives slipping into an inappropriate tone, for example, when they couldn't bring themselves to be as polite as expected to a truly unreasonable card holder or when they became inadvisably familiar with a more deserving client. Customer service representatives also often operate under a quota system, having to handle a minimum number of cases each day, thus increasing the pressure to finish a letter and move on. In short, corporate letters written by hand might be as good as the

January 4, 1991

Reid Scott
554 Menlo Drive
Burgess Park, CA 93496

Account # 7151-719-910-368

Dear Professor Scott,

Thank you for your letter regarding the ski equipment you purchased from Herman's Sporting Goods for $213.39. I recently tried phoning, but was unable to reach you.

Before I recontact the store, I need you to tell me what brand of equipment you returned, if you were issued a credit slip at the time, and on what date you returned the merchandise. Please send me this information and a copy of your credit slip in the enclosed pre-addressed envelope, or call me. You can reach me at 1 (800) 444-4400, extension 1002.

While waiting to hear from you, I have issued a temporary credit for $213.39 to your account. This credit will appear on your February 1991 statement. If I do not receive a response from you by January 31, I will have to cancel the temporary credit and close this investigation. I appreciate this opportunity to be of service.

Very truly yours,

Fiona Markov
Senior Representative
Customer Service
FM/csi

Figure 1. Typical Correspondence Example.

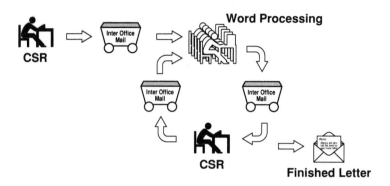

Figure 2. Standard Correspondence Work Flow.

example in figure 1, but they can just as easily contain anything from typographic errors to significant omissions to rude treatment. They can also appear formulaic if the customer service representative reverts to "corporate-speak" rather than carefully writes each new letter.

Customized letters have also been expensive to produce. Customer service representatives must be trained in corporate writing style, which can involve a combination of a few days in a training class and many hours of on-the-job review at our credit card organization. The customer service representatives must take the time (on the average, 45 minutes) to compose each letter from scratch—even though the letters almost always address relatively slight variations on familiar problems. A separate word processing staff must be maintained to type in, edit, and print the letters. The *turnaround time*—the time between receiving the client's request and mailing a reply—was never less than three days and could be as long as two weeks if there were errors or miscommunication with the word processing staff. The general confusion of the standard correspondence work flow is detailed in figure 2.

As figure 2 shows, each letter is drafted and written in longhand by a customer service representative; forwarded to word processing; printed; returned to the customer service representative; reviewed; sent back to word processing if errors are discovered (or if circumstances have changed since the letter was first drafted!); and, eventually, printed and mailed.

Our task was twofold. First, we had to design a text-generation system capable of generating a wide variety of quality output in a specific corporate style in a few seconds. Second, we had to ensure that such a system could be integrated into the credit card organization's work environment, could effectively be used by designated users with limited

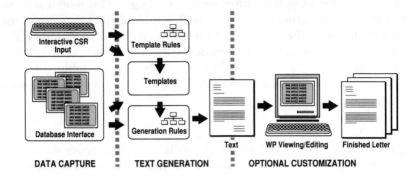

Figure 3. ICG Functional Breakdown.

writing skills, and could improve the existing production routines required by the high-volume individualization of letters.

In fact, the entire letter shown in figure 1 was composed, printed, and mailed by a customer service representative using the ICG system. (The only changes made to the letter involve the account number and some direct word substitutions to protect the anonymity of the card holder and the organization.) For a limited group of customer service representatives, ICG has already replaced the entire form-letter system and the write-from-scratch method. It is currently producing letters daily that exceed the organization's standards for handwritten letters and reduced or eliminated the need for separate word processing and quality control staffs.

The Text-Generation Technology

The functional breakdown of the ICG technology is shown in figure 3.

ICG's functional architecture is similar to the Penman system (Mann 1983). Internally, it is organized around a blackboard-based expert system, supplemented by a text-generation controller and utilities. All data and inferences involved in generating a document are placed on the blackboard, which provides a common place to organize information from all the modules.

When composing a document, ICG executes the following steps: First, the information that is needed to generate the document is collected from the credit card organization's existing client database and the customer service representative. This information is placed on the blackboard. Second, inference rules operate on the blackboard to organize the information, building a frame-based model of the situation to be discussed as well as other related concepts. This model is independent of the output language. Third, template rules determine the basic structure of the document to be generated. Fourth, based on the set of templates selected, generation rules perform lower-level text planning and realization, building a complete letter. Fifth, the final document is formatted and presented to the user in a Microsoft Word document.

Data Capture

The system's input is collected through both an interactive user interface and a transparent interface to the organization's IMS database. When the user invokes the system, ICG first scans the database fields for the account most recently displayed and makes inferences from what is available, retrieving baseline information such as name and address, identifying relevant financial transactions and recorded prior communications, and performing a rough problem categorization based on the pattern of transactions identified. That is, before the first question is asked, ICG can already have modeled much of the situation to be discussed. Then, the user interface only needs to request a basic confirmation and a few data items not available online. This information is collected by asking the user to supply multiple-choice answers to a series of questions presented in an on-screen, color-coded form. Because the form modifies itself based on each multiple-choice answer as it is supplied by the customer service representative, interactive dialogs are usually no longer than 15 queries.

The Blackboard

We chose a blackboard-based design (Engelmore and Morgan 1988) to facilitate communication between the different ICG modules. The blackboard serves as a repository for information retrieved by the database and dialogs as well as a place to organize inferences about the information and the generation process. The information is stored on the blackboard as object-based frames that can be retrieved by unification patterns similar to those found in OPS5 (Brownston et al. 1985).

The objects described in frames are organized in a knowledge hierarchy that allows the inheritance of information such as lexical reference methods, origin of information, and relationships to other objects. The installed ICG application includes definitions for well over 600 objects, including the associated methods for generating text to describe many of them. These concepts include people (card holders, customer service representatives, store employees, and so on), institutions (the credit card organization itself, stores and other types of service providers, branches of the federal government, and so on), various kinds of merchandise and services that can be purchased with a credit card, events associated with using a credit card (purchase, signing of receipt, third-party shipments, merchandise return, and so on), account transactions (credits, debits, payments, and charges that can be temporary, permanent, and periodic), policies and contracts (of both the organization and the service providers), dispute classifications and problem resolutions, documents (account statements, sales receipts, shipping receipts), dates (specific and month-long time periods), and money amounts.

The system also includes representations of generation-specific concepts, including tone (both of the card holder and the reply being generated), stylistic connectives in text, and the structure of the letter being generated (objects for sentences, paragraphs, and the letter).

Text Generation

Text generation has traditionally been considered a three-part process: content determination, text planning, and realization (Grosz, Sparck Jones, and Webber 1986). *Content determination* in ICG roughly corresponds to the rule system's task of organizing the information collected into the appropriate frames on the blackboard. *Text planning* in ICG occurs at two levels: First, *template-selection rules* are checked to determine the outline of the letter to be generated. These rules can combine several predefined groupings of topics to assemble a basic ordering of topics to be discussed. Based on this ordering, *generation rules* then organize the paragraphs and sentences. Unlike most systems (McKeown 1985; Nirenburg, Lesser, and Nyberg 1989), ICG does not have a formal planning mechanism to control text organization. Forward- and backward-chaining rules simply determine the relevant content and its general organization.

In the *realization* process, ICG traverses a large library of generation rules. Generation rules are indexed off particular topics, as described in the letter outlines. Their associated actions modify the letter object being built on the blackboard, adding a date line or sentence or starting a new paragraph. Unlike the vast majority of generation systems, ICG deliberately does not require that text be generated from an internal knowledge representation. All text to be generated is expressed in generation rules as strings (figure 4). Although ICG prescans these strings to recognize references to blackboard objects, variable text, and limited syntactic structure, it does so only to identify sufficient information to make the addition of these nuggets of text flow smoothly in the

```
defgenrule   deposit-as-additional-charge
  :template  additional-charge-template
  :section   bill-explanation
  :test      (and (deposit-on-separate-receipt   :deposit ?deposit
                                                  :total-charge ?amt)
             (?sp = service-provider)
             (?service = service)
             (case   :disputed-charges (? :charge ?charge)
                     :account ?account))
  :action    START-NEW-PARAGRAPH
             ADD-SENTENCE
             "the ?sp's itemization shows a total charge of ?amt"
             ADD-SENTENCE
             "as you know, you initially left a ?deposit with ?sp"
             ADD-SENTENCE
             "~because the total amount of the ?service was
             more than the deposit, ?sp has submitted an
             additional ?charge to your ?account"
```

Figure 4. Sample Generation Rule.

final letter. In this way, we avoided the pitfall of having to implement a complete grammar for text generation, which is dangerous both because of its inherent difficulty and because we are not aware of any other current generation research that is flexible enough to be precisely adapted to the writing style of a given corporation.

Our philosophy resembles that of a phrasal lexicon, which was first proposed by Becker (1975) for language understanding. The use of a phrasal lexicon was more recently adapted to the problem of text generation in Hovy's (1988) PAULINE system (see also Kukich [1988]). We have essentially taken the notion of generating text from a phrasal lexicon to the extreme: The *phrases* are unusually long (generally sentence-length) snippets of the corporation's specific wording preferences regarding familiar aspects of its business. The phrasal lexicon's keys are complex unification patterns that describe the situations the phrases apply to; these patterns are organized by the system's generation templates. We do not mean to say, however, that we are simply stringing together canned sentences. A combination of shallow parsing by the system and judicious analysis by the application's knowledge engineer allows us to abstract out the conceptual aspects of each phrasal unit. The ICG system then supplies the utilities for reconstructing cohesive text from these processed phrases. For example, the most significant system utility is ICG's noun phrase generator. With each new reference to an object in the letter, the noun phrase generator consults the system's discourse model to see how it previously referred to it as well as to other similar objects. Based on the model, it either chooses to use a pronominal reference or selects the minimum set of attributes necessary to uniquely and naturally identify the object. Cognitive Systems' ICG technology is described in further detail in Buta and Springer (1990).

Implementation and Deployment

In this section, we discuss the project schedule, the platform and environment, and the knowledge engineering process.

Project Schedule

Our contract with the credit card organization allowed six calendar months of development followed by rigorous acceptance testing and a limited production rollout to three representatives in a designated customer service unit. This development and deployment stage was to be followed by a two-month period of postrelease bug fixing and support by Cognitive Systems. The development period included three phases with interim deliverables at three months, five months, and six months from project start. Cognitive Systems had already developed and tested a working ICG engine at the start of the project, although it had done no modeling of credit card situations in general or of the credit card organization's specific environment, problems, or policies. Thus, each delivery consisted mainly of a new library of objects, rules, and templates to cover a new domain area. (The first interim deliverable also included the system integration necessary for initial installation.) This approach ensured that with each deliverable, the customer service representatives could use the entire system, from dialog to printed letter, and would know in advance of the extent of the system's knowledge. In our planning, we took care both that knowledge engineering was equally divided among the deliverables and that users would intuitively grasp what types of letters they could expect the system to generate at any given time.

Platform and Environment

The original working environment for the customer service representatives was a mainframe computer, with a separate word processing system and typing staff. In the new environment provided with ICG, the customer service representatives have full control over the entire dispute-resolution process. The credit card organization had already begun to upgrade the customer service representatives' platform before the ICG project. The customer service representatives involved in the ICG project work on IBM PS/2s (Model 70) running MS-DOS (with an extended memory manager) that are linked to the mainframe. With ICG, each customer service representative has conventional terminal emulation with full mainframe database access to continue standard problem-resolution tasks; the ICG user interface; Microsoft Word for viewing the generated document; Grammatik, the grammar and spelling checker (not needed for ICG text—the letter generated by ICG includes control characters to actually block Grammatik from spell checking proper names—but used for any changes made by the customer service representative); direct hookup to an easily accessible laser printer; and function-key support to facilitate movement among these elements.

The dispute-resolution process is generally the same as before ICG. The customer service representative studies the case and takes whatever actions s/he thinks are appropriate. These actions can include issuing a temporary credit, contacting a service provider, or ordering a copy of a document. As before, the specific actions taken are stored in a mainframe database entry that describes the case. When correspondence is required, the writer invokes ICG. As previously outlined, ICG reads the database information about the current case and infers as much as possible from the prior actions recorded in the case database. In the example letter in figure 1, ICG noted the logging of an attempted telephone call prior to its invocation and the issuing of a temporary credit. Next, ICG runs through its interactive dialog with the customer service representative, verifying unclear database references and asking for any new actions the customer service representative intends to take as well as for composition details such as the appropriate tone for the outgoing letter. ICG then switches the customer service representative into Microsoft Word with the letter displayed. If any changes are made, they are automatically passed through Grammatik. Additionally, the user has the option of returning to the dialog screen to change any of his(her) earlier responses. When finished, the letter is printed on a local laser printer. The customer service representative simply folds the letter and places it in a windowed envelope along with any relevant enclosures.

In addition to generating the letter, the ICG system also generates a cover sheet that is printed along with the letter. The cover sheet records background information relevant to the credit card organization, including the card holder, the customer service representative, and the general dispute information; the amount of time spent in different ICG tasks, such as interactive dialog and database retrieval and generation time; important internal inferences used in producing the letter; and other related information. These tracking data are produced, formatted, and printed by the same utilities that generate the card holder's letter.

In short, the customer service representatives had to learn a total of two new screen environments: the ICG dialog screen (which always displays relevant choices and provides context-sensitive help for each query) and Microsoft Word.

The maintenance interface to the system is a standard programmer's interface (file editing and compiling, and so on). Maintenance does not require knowledge of any programming language other than the syntax of ICG's dozen or so restricted forms. Significant changes to the system currently require a person at the level of an expert system engineer. Cognitive Systems is developing a graphic user interface for the maintenance and development of ICG applications to simplify these tasks.

Knowledge Engineering

Knowledge engineering for ICG—the principal task across the six months of development—presented a challenge to us for two different reasons:

First, substantial effort was required to simply model the situations that would be discussed in letters. A credit card domain requires representations for all possible relationships between at least three actors: the credit card organization, the card holder, and the provider of the service or merchandise. When it was necessary to distinguish between the credit card organization and the customer service representative or a department store and a store employee, the situation grew even more complex. Although we had experience building a much narrower and deeper application (which discussed billing misunderstandings for a mail-order company), we found the credit card domain to be considerably broader and somewhat shallower. The first two full months of the project were spent in designing the overall structure of the knowledge to be represented.

Second, knowledge engineering for text generation in particular requires the consideration of additional factors, involving the communication of information. Some of these factors include the overall content and organization of the letter, the importance of the writing-style components and the manner in which they are modeled, the organization and presentation of the events, the handling of a combination of topics, the referencing of the parties, contributions to the card holder's satisfaction on reading the letter, and the company's efforts to guarantee this satisfaction.

Conveniently, for the credit card organization's writing experts, even a knowledge engineer with limited writing skills can appreciate what an expert correspondent includes in a letter. In addition, most corporations have a vast supply of reference material for such a system in the form of existing form letters and recent original letters. The Cognitive Systems knowledge engineers took a large collection of the credit card organization's recent correspondence and reduced the letters to their component topics and wordings (introduction, account actions, and so on), deducing the appropriate text rules in many cases. However, as we expected, many inconsistencies and questions arose. Resolving these writing issues formed a substantial part of the knowledge engineering process throughout development. We had little research to fall back on in this case. To our knowledge, although many text-generation investigations have considered questions of *linguistic competency*—the ability to generate various constructions and communicate various intents—few have attempted to build a system within the extremely tight *stylistic constraints* imposed by the correspondence standards of a corporation. (See, however, Hovy [1987] for a discussion of pragmatic criteria in text generation.)

The final ICG application contains over 100 composition templates, which can be nested in different ways to produce an overall letter outline. It contains almost 900 rules, about half of which are generation rules, whose actions construct the final document.

Results

In this section, we discuss project results in terms of system acceptance, speed enhancements, and quality enhancements.

Acceptance

We evaluate acceptance of the system by how the ICG users responded to it as well as by formal software acceptance procedures.

As it turned out, the customer service representatives liked the system so well that they started sending letters out to card holders after the first deliverable. That is, the system was put into production far ahead of schedule, after only two months of design work and one month of knowledge engineering. A number of factors contributed to the rapid deployment:

First, because ICG output directly appears on the customer service representative's screen in a word processor, the customer service representative could review and modify all generated text. Second, considerable general knowledge was included in the initial deliverable that was applicable across all problem classifications. For example, if the customer was receiving a credit, ICG could generate a general description of the account action regardless of missing knowledge about the problem classification. Third, when the system failed to fully understand part of a situation, it left this section of the letter blank. The writer could simply fill in the missing details.

Now that the project is complete, the ICG users almost never modify text generated by the system. Changes to letters only occur when the customer service representative wants to add some piece of information beyond the system's stated capabilities.

Formal acceptance required that the system generate a set of test cases with 100 percent accuracy, that is, with no errors. Each letter was judged using the following categories within a quality matrix: opening and closing paragraphs, grammar, spelling and punctuation, tense, length of clauses (clarity of individual sentences), succinctness of entire letter, clarity, the addressing of each of the card holder's issues, and correct information extracted from the database.

In addition to receiving a perfect score from the set of test cases, the system had to achieve an 80 percent hit rate on a random sample of 100 cases. That is, it was expected to generate 80 percent of the letters without a single error.

ICG successfully passed both acceptance tests by the end of the 8-month contract. At the time of this writing, the system has been deployed for over 1 year. No changes in system behavior have been requested since the project was completed over 6 months ago. Currently, 3 customer service representatives use ICG exclusively to generate their correspondence, averaging a total of 20 letters a day.

Training

ICG required little training. The system was designed by implementing a user model to index the various system templates and specific textual-content decisions. Therefore, if the customer service representative understood enough to resolve the card holder's dispute, s/he should know enough to go through ICG's dialog without referencing a manual. The only training necessary was syntactic—which button to press to invoke the system, how to perform various edit operations in the word processor, and how to use the grammar checker. The representatives received a cheat sheet of about 10 operations that are needed to use the system.

The customer service representatives who initially used the system received 4 hours of introduction and training before they started sending letters out live on their own. They received no additional training from us after this first training session. In fact, these representatives then trained other users to use the system. The credit card organization informed us that customer service representatives can now be productive with only 30 minutes of training. This situation can be com-

CSR   **Printer**   **Finished Letter**

Figure 5. Correspondence Work Flow with ICG.

pared with a several-day course needed for certification in the use of the credit card organization's form-letter system.

Another major saving in training came from the system's ability to replace many of the previously handwritten letters and to frame letters that it can't produce in detail. As mentioned previously, one of the unit's biggest problems involved training its representatives to become quality letter writers. Writing high-quality letters is a skill that the credit card organization taught in the production environment by making supervisors randomly review the outgoing letters of the customer service representatives. This process was time consuming for the supervisor and complicated the education of the representative because s/he did not have samples of high-quality letters with which s/he could compare his(her) writing. However, because ICG continually illustrates good letter-writing style by example, a customer service representative can more quickly become proficient at writing in the same style. Thus, customer service representatives can produce better-quality letters with less training when they need to add text to an ICG letter or write a letter from scratch if it is outside ICG's target domain.

Production Turnaround

We mentioned previously that customer service representatives began using the system after our first three-month deliverable. In fact, acceptance went beyond just occasional use of ICG. The supervisor of our customer service representatives instructed them to stop using both the form-letter system and the word processing staff within a few weeks of the initial ICG installation. Even during development, using ICG to help write a letter was preferable to drafting one from scratch and relying on the word processing department. The high-level architecture of the system allowed the standard work flow to be drastically simplified. Compare figure 5 with the old work-flow pattern shown in figure 2.

The turnaround for a handwritten letter before ICG averaged three days, possibly taking as long as two weeks. Generating a letter with ICG now takes a representative—from the time s/he invokes the system to the time s/he stuffs the envelope—an average of five minutes.

Employees' Time

The actual time the customer service representative spent writing a letter before ICG was installed varied considerably, depending on how proficient s/he was at writing. Most representatives would spend a minimum of 45 minutes writing a letter by hand. A typist in word processing would then take a few minutes to enter the letter and would frequently need to contact the representative because of illegible handwriting or unclear instructions. ICG cut the customer service representative's involvement to the same 5-minute average previously mentioned (once all queries are answered, the finished letter is generated in under 30 seconds) and eliminated the need for word processing and interoffice mail personnel to even know that a letter was sent.

Unfortunately, at this time, we cannot estimate the cost savings to the credit card organization based on these reductions. There has been an increase in productivity, but computing a dollar amount would require, among other things, statistics such as the percentage of the word processing staff's time spent preparing these letters. The credit card organization is currently preparing such estimates. Meanwhile, we caution that such savings are only one part of ICG's contribution to profit. There is, perhaps more importantly, the harder-to-quantify goal of increasing client satisfaction and loyalty through higher-quality customer service.

Quality

In the first random sample by the credit card company's Quality Control Department (at the beginning of acceptance testing), 90 percent of ICG's letters were rated errorless. This percentage compared to about an 80 percent errorless score for handwritten letters sent without ICG. Many of these original errors dealt with capitalization or expansion of abbreviations of fields from the client database. Because ICG converts all name and address fields to mixed-case text and expands abbreviations, mistakes in either of these routines were considered an error. It is important to note that the form-letter system did not need to worry about converting to mixed case. The system always left all database fields in capitals. The quality control group did not consider this problem an error! These and other errors are now fixed, and over 95 percent of the letters produced with ICG are error free.

Conclusion

This installation of ICG bodes well for future applications. The system is well liked by both its end users and the credit card organization's management. It has made the customer service representatives' job more enjoyable, improved letter quality, and slashed turnaround time. Most importantly, we found the credit card organization site to be highly representative of other customer service organizations, both in form and in the types of correspondence issues it must address.

Much of what we learned building this application was general. We have now developed a substantial knowledge base associated with general customer service, mail-order, and credit card business. Building the next application in any of these fields will be substantially easier than our first effort. In fact, long-term plans include the development of several market-specific knowledge base modules.

We also found that ICG's design philosophy agrees extremely well with the way people actually think about and undertake the task of producing institutional correspondence. At the same time, its functional behavior dovetails nicely with the way many customer service operations go about their business. Future work will also include designing an advanced developers' interface to the system to allow design and enhancement by analysts with less formal training and in less time as well as run-time modifications to support ICG's deployment in different customer service environments.

Finally, we continue to investigate the somewhat delicate trade-off between providing a generation system that adheres to any level of stylistic constraint and providing a system that demonstrates the most power to create original compositions. We are convinced that any institutional use of text-generation technology requires both capabilities.

Acknowledgments

The authors want to gratefully acknowledge all who contributed to the success of this project, especially Mark Kriegsman, Vic Lanzillotti, Mark Wachsler, Park Walker, and Philip Werner.

References

Agins, T.; Bennet, A.; Deveny, K.; Milbank, D.; Fuchsberg, G.; Solomon, J.; and Rigdon, J. E. 1990. Customer Service: Challenge for the '90s. *The Wall Street Journal*, November 12–20 (multiple-issue series).

Becker, J. 1975. The Phrasal Lexicon. In *Theoretical Issues in Natural Language Processing*, 70–73. Cambridge, Mass.: Association of Computational Linguistics.

Brownston, L.; Farrell, R.; Kant, E.; and Martin, N. 1985. *Programming Expert Systems in OPS5*. Reading, Mass.: Addison-Wesley.

Buta, P., and Springer, S. 1990. OMBUDSMAN: The Correspondence Generation System. In Proceedings of the Tenth International Workshop on Expert Systems and Their Applications: Natural Language Processing, 195–204. Avignon, France: EC2.

Engelmore, R., and Morgan, A., eds. 1988. *Blackboard Systems.* Reading, Mass.: Addison-Wesley.

Grosz, B.; Sparck Jones, K.; and Webber, B., eds. 1986. *Readings in Natural Language Processing.* San Mateo, Calif.: Morgan Kaufmann.

Hovy, E. 1988. Generating Language with a Phrasal Lexicon. In *Natural Language Generation Systems,* eds. D. McDonald and L. Bloc, 353–383. New York: Springer-Verlag.

Hovy, E. 1987. Some Pragmatic Decision Criteria in Generation. In *Natural Language Generation,* ed. G. Kempen, 3–17. Dordrecht, The Netherlands: Martinus Nijhoff.

Kukich, K. 1988. Fluency in Natural Language Reports. In *Natural Language Generation Systems,* eds. D. McDonald and L. Bloc, 280–309. New York: Springer-Verlag.

McKeown, K. 1985. *Text Generation.* Cambridge: Cambridge University Press.

Mann, W. 1983. An Overview of the PENMAN Text-Generation System. In Proceedings of the Third National Conference on Artificial Intelligence, 261–265. Menlo Park, Calif.: American Association for Artificial Intelligence.

Nirenburg, S.; Lesser, V.; and Nyberg, E. 1989. Controlling a Language Generation Planner. In Proceedings of the Eleventh International Joint Conference on Artificial Intelligence, 1524–1530. Menlo Park, Calif.: International Joint Conferences on Artificial Intelligence.

Diagnosis

AGATHA
Hewlett-Packard

The Thallium Diagnostic Workstation
Analytics

AGATHA: An Integrated Expert System to Test and Diagnose Complex Personal Computer Boards

Daryl Allred, Yossi Lichtenstein, Chris Preist, Mike Bennett, and Ajay Gupta

PA-RISC is Hewlett-Packard's (HP) reduced instruction set computer (RISC) architecture that is used in its high-performance computer systems (Mahon et al. 1986). Implementations of this architecture have produced some of the most complex processor boards that HP makes (Robinson et al. 1987; Gassman et al. 1987): They can contain as many as 8 very large scale integrated (VLSI) chips—most of them custom, from central processing units to bus controllers to floating-point processors—several high-speed random-access memory arrays, one or more high-speed buses with over 100 lines, and many other components. In large part because of this complexity, the testing of PA-RISC processor boards became a bottleneck, resulting in an undesirable backlog of undiagnosed boards, growing at a rate of 10 percent each month.

Testing PA-RISC Processor Boards: The Process

Part of a typical production flow for a PA-RISC processor board is dia-grammed in figure 1, emphasizing the board test. After the board is fabricated, it is run through an in-circuit, or *bed of nails test*. This pro-cess consists of individually testing the components and connections on the board and catches misloaded or missing parts and most of the open circuits and shorts between circuits.

Next, the board is tested on a PRISM tester, a Hewlett-Packard propri-etary test system that integrates scan-based testing with functional test-ing (Schuchard and Weiss 1987; Weiss 1987). *Functional testing* involves testing the behavior of various subsystems on the board, verifying that they behave properly in a system environment. *Scan-based testing* takes advantage of HP's proprietary scan methodology, which is implement-ed on its VLSI chips to poke around their internal registers and test in-dividual blocks of the chips or buses between them. All these tests can be run at various voltages and frequencies on the PRISM tester.

At any point in the production line or even in the field, a faulty board can be returned for diagnosis and repair. Diagnosis is normally done at a PRISM test station, where the technician has access to a battery of diagnostic tests that can help in localizing the problem.

The Problems with Testing

Because of the board's complexity, technicians found it difficult to di-agnose failed boards. Consequently, manufacturing began to en-counter several problems that became severe:

First, the PRISM test station became a bottleneck in the production pro-cess. The difficulties in diagnosing failing boards, along with long test times, began to interfere with the flow of boards on the production line.

Second, an unacceptable backlog of undiagnosed boards accumulat-ed, growing at a rate of 10 percent each month. This backlog resulted from the time and difficulty in diagnosing certain failure modes.

Third, the thorough diagnosis of boards was a time consuming and tedious process. Thus, the technicians would take shortcuts to save time. However, these shortcuts sometimes led to an incorrect part being replaced, resulting in further repair cycles being needed.

Fourth, it was difficult to effectively train new technicians to diagnose PRISM failures. The learning curve was large. Furthermore, new manufac-turing sites were being opened worldwide, exacerbating the problem.

The difficulties of diagnosing faulty processor boards in manufactur-ing were attributable to the following conditions:

First, because the processor board is complex, it has many subsys-

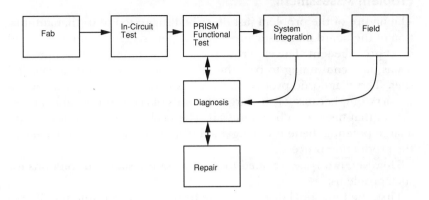

Figure 1. PA-RISC Board-Test Process.

tems with different functions. PRISM addresses these various subsystems with different tests, yielding a diversity of test output. A few tests try to suggest a failing component or subsystem; others just report a failure mode or code that only indirectly identifies a fault. Still others dump a lot of internal processor-state information that can only be interpreted in light of the processor architecture and the test strategy. The technician has to become familiar with the output of these diverse tests to effectively diagnose boards.

Second, it is difficult for the technician to remember lots of special-case failure modes. Some of these failure modes are identified by unique patterns in the data, often across several test results. Because these special cases are less frequent than the normal failure modes, they are easily forgotten.

Third, some diagnostics produce reams of data. It is difficult and time consuming for the technician to deal with such diagnostics, and important information can be overlooked in the large volume of data.

Fourth, some test results are low level—hex numbers and bit patterns—that must manually be manipulated, indexed into tables, and cross-referenced to map to a component. This work is tedious and error prone.

Fifth, there is some uncertainty in some of the test results. For example, a test might suggest replacing a certain chip, but in fact, this chip is the actual fault only part of the time. Additionally, some faults exhibit intermittent behavior, such that a discriminating test might not always detect it.

Problem Assessment

The nature of the problem just described suggested to us that automation of the board diagnostic process by expert system technology would be of great benefit. The expertise was available but in short supply, and it was time consuming to pass the information to new individuals and sites. The diagnostic process was understandable, although laborious to carry out, because of the large amounts of data and possible failure modes that needed to be addressed. The problem was significant, with a large potential benefit to be gained from removing the bottleneck in the production process.

However, two issues seemed to go beyond the standard solutions for such problems:

First, the functional diversity of the board and, as a result, the diversity of the testing and diagnosing techniques demanded several different inference strategies and knowledge bases. It appeared to be impractical to expect a single expert system to diagnose all the different tests.

Second, the difficulties that technicians and operators suffered in interacting with the tester suggested that the expert system should replace the current front end of PRISM and become not only a diagnostic inference machine but also a high-level human interface.

The different tests were analyzed along several dimensions to start designing and implementing a diagnostic expert system. These dimensions were the following:

First was the quality of output. Some tests produce internal information that can be used in diagnosis. Others output only pass-fail data.

Second was the amount of data, from a single line to hundreds of lines of hexadecimal data.

Third was the degree of interaction necessary with the user. Some tests require no interaction, whereas others require complex manual tests to perform diagnosis.

Fourth was the sophistication and depth of the knowledge used by the expert, from simple heuristic matching to a deep understanding of causality within a subsystem.

System Design

To solve these design issues, we decided to implement a suite of mini expert systems, called *slices*. Each slice diagnoses the results of a single test. The inference process for each slice was tailored to how the test measured according to the previous four dimensions. Where large amounts of data and causal rules are available to a slice, it uses a generation-elimination process with many data abstraction predicates and no user interaction. Other slices need to interact with the user to gather more data before recommending further tests, so they use a table lookup process.

All slices cooperate with each other and communicate through a *diagnose manager*, a further slice that is responsible for coordinating the overall diagnostic process and interfacing with the tester. The entire system, named AGATHA, is fully integrated with the PRISM tester; furthermore, with a user interface, it forms the new front end of the tester.

The Slice Architecture

The overall architecture of AGATHA (figure 2) consists of 9 different slices, with 27 associated knowledge bases and databases. The 9 slices need only 6 different inference engines between them; sharing of inference machinery is allowed between slices with similar inference strategies. The diagnose manager slice is responsible for passing control among the other slices, depending on previous test results and diagnostic hypotheses. It is also responsible for feeding results from the slices to the user and information from the user to the relevant slice.

To show the different inference methods involved in the slices, we focus on three slices: the diagnose manager, the cache bus, and the diagnostic interface port (DIP). We chose the latter two because they are different from each other in terms of the dimensions described in Problem Assessment. The cache bus slice illustrates a slice with large amounts of data but little user interaction. It analyzes the data using causal rules derived from the expert. The DIP slice, however, has sparse data and uses heuristics and close interaction with the user in performing further tests to yield the final diagnosis.

The Diagnose Manager. The diagnose manager has overall responsibility for coordinating the test runs, invoking slices to interpret them, reporting suspected faulty components, and servicing requests to repair them. It delegates these tasks to three separate submanagers: The *slice manager* invokes the proper slice for a failed test; coordinates the display of suspects; and directs other requests by the slice, such as to run a test, to the diagnose manager. The *repair manager* services requests to perform repairs, usually after the slices finish analyzing the test data. After repair, it reruns the original test to confirm the problem on the board was fixed. The *test manager* services all requests for tests to be run on the tester, providing a common interface to PRISM.

The most interesting of these submanagers is the test manager. For each test request, it must perform the following five tasks: (1) select a test point at which to run the test (the *test point* is the power supply voltage and clock frequency to be supplied to the board under test by

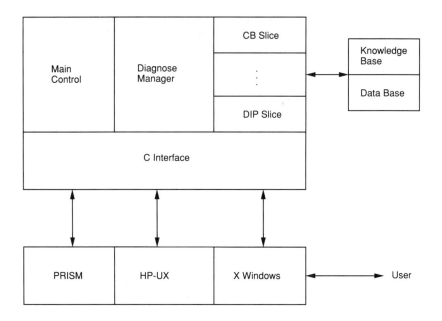

Figure 2. AGATHA *Architecture.*

the PRISM tester), (2) run the test, (3) determine the failure mode of the test (for example, is this test intermittent?), (4) retry the test if necessary, and (5) recommend to the diagnose manager what to do next.

First, the test manager selects a test point at which to run the test. It can select one of a set of predefined test points or an entirely new one in an attempt to get a test to fail more reliably. The test manager then runs the test at the computed test point, parses the test output, and makes a summary decision about whether it passed or failed. No attempt is made to otherwise interpret the test results at this point.

Next, based on the pass-fail results of the test, a new failure mode is computed. The test manager supports the following failure modes:

First is *hard*: Failing tests fail at all test points with little or no variation in their output (that is, they don't differ dramatically from test point to test point).

Second is *dependent-repeatable*: Dependencies on voltage or frequency were determined (that is, it only fails at certain voltages or frequencies), and it's repeatable.

Third is *dependent-nonrepeatable*: Dependencies on voltage or frequency were determined, but it's not repeatable (it only fails sometimes at these voltages or frequencies).

Fourth is *intermittent*: It's not failing hard, but no dependency can be determined (for example, random failures).

The failure mode is a symbolic representation of uncertainty in the test results, accounting for possible intermittent test failures. Heuristic knowledge about tests, along with data about test results, is used to infer the failure mode; for example:

IF   this board is a field return AND
              the board test passed
THEN   the failure condition is intermittent
BECAUSE   this board has failed before (in the field)
              but won't fail now

With a new failure mode computed, the test manager next determines whether the test should be rerun using heuristic rules. A test might need to be run because of suspected uncertainties in the test results. An example of a heuristic follows:

IF   the test passed AND
        the failure mode is either dependent-nonrepeatable or intermittent
THEN   the test should be rerun up to 3 times until it fails

Finally, the test manager is ready to recommend to the diagnose manager what to do next. If the test failed, the associated slice is determined, and it is recommended for invocation. If the test passed, then the previous slice is reinvoked with this new information; as a result, the slice can recommend further tests. Thus, the test manager uses heuristic knowledge embedded in procedural control to run tests and manage uncertainty in their results, removing this burden from the slices.

The Cache Bus Slice. The cache bus subsystem on the assembled circuit board consists of several large VLSI chips that communicate through a bus of about 150 lines. Each chip is connected to a subset of these lines and is able to transmit onto the bus by driving values onto the lines. These lines can, in turn, be read by the other chips.

Failures that can occur in this system include shorts between lines, opens on lines, and chips failing to properly transmit or receive. A fault can be intermittent; that is, sometimes a test will miss it, but at other times, it will show up. Also, multiple faults can occur. For example, several shorts can be caused by solder being splashed across the board.

The PRISM tester tests the cache bus by getting each chip to drive a series of binary values onto the bus and getting all chips to read each value back. This process is done automatically and produces a large amount of data. Discrepancies between the expected values and the observed values in these data are used by the cache bus slice to diagnose the fault.

The cache bus slice is responsible for diagnosing failures in the

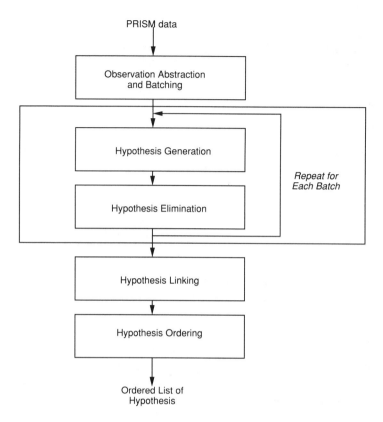

Figure 3. Cache Bus Slice Architecture.

cache bus test. The design of this slice (figure 3) allows it to handle both intermittent faults and the majority of multiple faults. Rather than dealing with the bus system as a whole, it divides it into semi-independent subsystems, namely, each line.

The data from the test is divided into *batches*, one associated with each line that is exhibiting bad behavior. Each batch contains only those data that were received incorrectly off its associated line. These data are then used to deduce the fault on this particular line. Hence, rather than assuming that the cache bus as a whole has only a single fault, the system can treat each line independently and assume that there is at most one fault for each line. The single fault assumption is replaced with the single fault to a line assumption.

A template generates a list of hypotheses for each line. Where a multiple fault on a single line is to be considered, this information is explicitly entered in the template. Elimination rules are then used to remove as many of these faults as possible. The knowledge in these rules is derived from the causal rules of the expert by taking its contrapositive—if a hypothesis makes a prediction, and this prediction is found to be false, the hypothesis can be eliminated. Elimination rules take the following form:

IF   a '1' is observed on the line when a '0' was expected
ELIMINATE   short to ground and short to another cache bus line
BECAUSE   these faults can only pull a line to '0'

After elimination, each line has a small number of hypotheses associated with it. However, a line is only semi-independent. Many hypotheses, such as "short between lines" and "bad VLSI," manifest their behavior on several lines. Hence, *linking rules* are used. These rules take hypotheses associated with different lines and combine them, where appropriate, into single hypotheses that explain the bad behavior of several lines. They have the following form:

LINK: Short to cache bus on line 1
WITH: Short to cache bus on line 2
IF: Line 1 and line 2 are adjacent somewhere on the board
TO GIVE HYPOTHESIS: Short between line 1 and line 2

Finally, the remaining hypotheses are ordered, using heuristic knowledge, according to their likelihood. This list is returned to the diagnose manager for presentation to the user.

Thus, the cache bus slice combines causal-based rules with heuristic knowledge. The causal rules are used to deduce which hypotheses are possible and which are impossible. The heuristic knowledge is then used to determine the relative likelihood of the hypotheses that remain. Full details of the cache bus slice are available in Preist, Allred, and Gupta (1991).

The Diagnostic Interface Port Slice. Before scan-based tests can be performed on a VLSI chip, the DIP on the chip, which is the serial scan port, must be tested to verify that the tester is able to properly communicate with the chip and that other electronic subsystems are working reasonably well (that is, the power, clocking, and reset subsystems). The DIP test tests the DIP port on all VLSI chips, and the DIP slice diagnoses any failures.

Unlike the cache bus slice, the DIP slice works with simple pass-fail and test-point information from the DIP test and interacts with the user to give the final diagnosis. Because of the sparsity of data, it is unable, alone, to deal with intermittent and multiple faults, relying instead on the user to explore these possibilities.

The DIP slice performs its diagnosis in two stages: First, it proposes which subsystems it considers are the main and secondary suspects. Second, it aids the user in performing further manual tests on a particular subsystem to determine if it is indeed faulty and, if so, exactly where.

The first stage, generating suspects, uses a heuristic mapping from the symptoms to the possible causes. The symptoms are the pass-fail data of the DIP test. The possible causes, divided into main and secondary suspects, are the candidate subsystems and connections, at least one (possibly more) of which is faulty. There are 20 such mapping rules; the following is an example:

IF   all chips failed the DIP-test
AND   the System-Test passed
THEN   suspect the MDA as a main suspect
AND   the Reset, Clock, Power, and System-bus-connector
            as secondary suspects.

The main-secondary distinction is a simple form of probability handling. More complex schemes were rejected because the expert couldn't substantiate a finer separation of fault likelihood.

The second stage of reasoning—guiding the user in manual tests—is an iterative process. The user chooses to concentrate on a particular subsystem and tries to find out which of its components (if any) are faulty. The decision of which subsystem to focus on is left to the user.

Each subsystem is composed of a set of components and a list of tests to test them, both automatic and manual. A table (figure 4) then represents the knowledge that tests would give about the components, as follows: If a test fails, at least one of the components with an F entry in the table will be faulty; if a test passes, all the components with a P entry in the table will be functional (not faulty).

With this knowledge, together with an approximate cost of performing each test, the DIP slice presents the user with an ordered list of tests that are worth carrying out. The user then chooses which test to perform, receives instructions on how to do it, performs the test, and enters the result (pass or fail) into the system. This process continues until the DIP slice is able to diagnose a component as faulty, or the user chooses to explore another subsystem.

Hence, the user, working with AGATHA, is able to explore the different candidates and diagnose exactly which of them is indeed failing. The user is always in control but can rely on an ordered set of tests, arranged to isolate the fault as fast as possible.

Tester Integration

As previously indicated, to solve crucial testing issues, Agatha would not only act as an automated diagnostic system but would also provide a user interface and become the new front end to PRISM.

The challenge here was to integrate AGATHA into an old PRISM system

Components:

1	Tester
2	System-bus (signals PON/NPFW)
3	Reset-buffer
4	SIU
5	Cache-Bus (signals NRS0 and NRS1)
6	VLSI chips (other than SIU)

Tests:

1	Probe NRS0/1 on Cache Bus
2	Scope NRS0/1 on Cache Bus
3	Ohm out NRS0/1 on Cache Bus
4	Probe PON/NPFW on System Bus
5	Scope PON/NPFW on System Bus
6	Ohm out PON/NPFW on System Bus
7	Probe and scope PON/NPFW on both sides of buffer
8	Inspect System Bus connector
9	Test rest path through tester subsystem

F/P Table:

1 Tester	2 Sysbus	3 Buffer	4 SIU	5 Cache Bus	6 VLSI	Tests to perform
F	F	F	F	F		1
			F/P	F/P		2
				F/P		3
F	F	F				4
F/P	F/P	F/P				5
	F/P					6
			F/P			7
	F/P					8
F/P						9

Figure 4. Diagnostic Interface Port Slice Knowledge for the Reset Subsystem.

whose code had not been touched for a long time. We opted to layer AGATHA on top of PRISM, as diagramed in figure 5. Communication is through the HP-UX interprocess communication facilities. With this layering, the PRISM code remains virtually untouched except for minor modifications of the stream files or scripts.

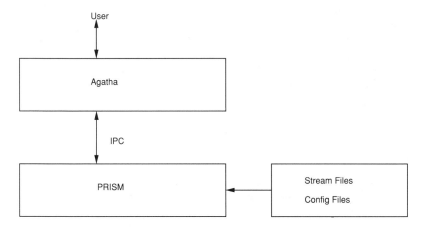

Figure 5. AGATHA-PRISM *Interface.*

The layering of AGATHA on top of PRISM had several advantages:

First, the PRISM code remained unmodified, minimizing its maintenance requirements.

Second, a new, friendlier front end was now provided for PRISM.

Third, AGATHA now detects some failures that PRISM could not detect before. For example, some messages are printed by system tests that PRISM never recognized, possibly passing faulty boards. AGATHA now detects these failures and reports them accordingly, improving the reliability of the testing process.

Fourth, some tests that required a long, tedious sequence of commands to execute are now automated by AGATHA. This process saves time and is more thorough because the technician would otherwise shy away from running the test to completion or even running it at all.

How AGATHA Is Used

In manufacturing, operators test the boards on the PRISM testers, separately binning the good and bad boards. Later, technicians put the failed boards back on the tester and diagnose them. This procedure was modeled in AGATHA, supporting three levels of users. These users are, in order of increasing capability, (1) the operator (the user can only test boards and bin them), (2) the technician (the user can also diagnose boards, including running manual tests, as well as access other utilities, such as review or print results), (3) the maintainer (the user can also edit the knowledge bases and databases and drop down into Prolog).

This approach made a simpler interface for the operator to learn, greatly reducing the learning curve. At the same time, additional flexi-

bility was available for technicians, making their task simpler. This flexibility proved to be a significant contribution of AGATHA—a major
benefit to our users.

With this model, AGATHA could run several additional diagnostic tests
while in operator mode, which would save time for the technician who
would otherwise have to run them later. Thus, a mode is provided,
called *automatic test*, where AGATHA automatically runs all tests it believes
necessary, provided no intervention is required from the user. This approach provides a significant time savings to the technician and effectively reduces the skill level required for this task. This feature can be
turned off during times of heavy workload, where higher throughput is
needed from the operators.

One major decision was whether to provide a diagnostic system or a
diagnostic adviser. Specifically, would it dictate to the user what to repair or only advise? During knowledge acquisition, we found that
which component to repair would vary depending on certain circumstances, including variations in the production process that could
cause one failure mode to start appearing more frequently. Hence,
AGATHA only advises the user on repairs, presenting an ordered list of
candidates to the technician, who chooses the most suitable. The technician would usually pick the first item from the list, unless s/he was
aware of extenuating circumstances that might suggest another.

Development

AGATHA was a joint development effort between the Knowledge-Based
Programming Department (KBPD) of HP Labs, Bristol, England, and the
Integrated Circuit Business Division (ICBD) in Fort Collins, Colorado.
The development process was broken down into the following phases:

The alpha phase produced a prototype version that was deployed
first in ICBD. It consisted of only three slices. The goal was to gain experience with it and get user feedback.

The beta phase reviewed this feedback, producing major refinements to the slices and a new diagnose manager. More slices were
added. This phase produced the first production version of AGATHA,
which was installed at a user's site.

The refinement phase continued to add slices and make refinements
to the knowledge. More users were added, leading to the manufacturing release of AGATHA.

The maintenance phase followed, where minor enhancements and
refinements are ongoing.

Implementation Language

Prolog was chosen as the principal implementation language for AGATHA. (In the figure 2 diagram, everything above the C interface box was written in Prolog, including the knowledge bases and databases.) The main reason for choosing a language, rather than an AI shell or tool kit, was the need to be able to code different inference strategies for the different slices. These strategies do not always fit into the classical forward-backward chaining regimes provided by shells and, thus, would have been awkward and inelegant to code in this way. The disadvantage with this decision is that we lose the support that the shell provides, namely, a good user interface and ready-written inference strategies. These elements had to be coded and maintained, imposing some additional burden on the project, yet could completely be tailored to the task, not restricted by what a shell or tool kit provides.

Verification

Prior to AGATHA, all tests run on PRISM were directly sent to the printer. We had lots of printouts to use in the design of AGATHA but no machine-readable tests to verify the implementation. Therefore, scaffolding was built to capture the test results on disk to be used for verification. With this scaffolding, a large suite of verification cases was gathered from the following sources: (1) poisoned boards (faults were caused on an otherwise good board, including shorts, opens, and missing parts), (2) bad VLSI (bad VLSI—acquired from field returns, and so on—were inserted into a socketed board), and (3) actual cases (later on, the verification cases were augmented with actual cases that AGATHA encountered while in use on the production line).

These verification cases helped to verify the knowledge and functions of AGATHA and refine it while in use. They helped assure the delivery of a reliable, confident system to our users.

Maintainability

Maintainability was a foremost consideration throughout the design and implementation of AGATHA for two reasons: First, it was decided from the outset that the original designers of significant parts of the system, HP Labs, would not be responsible for their maintenance. Instead, it would be the work of ICBD. Second, the system had to be able to deal with new board types, which were structurally different from the original board but were tested using the same tester.

This approach led to the clear separation in each slice of the knowledge specific to a certain board type and the knowledge specific to the tester. Hence, the tester rules had to deal with an abstract board and call the structural knowledge base to gather information specific to a certain board type.

Where the knowledge consisted of simple relations (such as which faults resulted in the failure of which further tests), it was directly represented as relational tables. Rules then access these tables as necessary. This approach reduces the number of rules needed and allows easy and rapid maintenance.

This policy has paid off. The system is now entirely maintained by ICBD. It has successfully updated the system to support three different board families, with a fourth nearly completed. (Some families have multiple board types distinguished by varying cache random-access memory sizes, and so on, all of which AGATHA has to know about.) This update process was partly automated. C routines access design data files that are used by the PRISM tester and extract structural information that is relevant to AGATHA, constructing files of Prolog clauses. The update process takes only a short amount of time to deal with a new board family.

Other than supporting new tests and board families, most of the maintenance since the production release of AGATHA has been in adding new features and enhancements rather than refining the slices or their knowledge. In addition, most of these enhancements were outside the slice architecture proper.

Deployment

AGATHA has been in routine use since January 1990. It was successfully deployed at 3 sites within HP—2 are manufacturing facilities; the third is a field repair center. One manufacturing site, for example, uses it 24 hours a day: Operators test boards on the production line, often letting AGATHA diagnose them to the extent that manual testing isn't required. Technicians then examine failure reports and let AGATHA work on boards that might need further diagnosis.

The field repair center receives failed boards from the field and diagnoses them on AGATHA. Although the center doesn't see the volume of boards that the production sites do, AGATHA is perhaps even more critical to its operation for this reason: It preserves diagnosis and repair knowledge that it might otherwise lose with low volumes. Furthermore, it has a great need for some of the features of AGATHA that support uncertainty. Because a board returned from the field is suspected to be faulty, one can't simply return it if the board test passes when run just once; it must be thoroughly exercised and checked out. AGATHA addresses such intermittences by running a test many times to try to get it to fail.

Results

AGATHA has been favorably received by its users and has proved to have many benefits for them. It has addressed many of the production problems that were being experienced prior to AGATHA:

First, the PRISM test station is much less a bottleneck in production. Although the long, raw test times (which AGATHA has no control over) are at times cause for congestion in production, the savings in diagnostic time have greatly alleviated this problem.

Second, AGATHA, in combination with other efforts on the production line, has helped to virtually eliminate the backlog of undiagnosed boards.

Third, AGATHA saves time by automatically running tests, especially when run by an operator. AGATHA also automates some tests that used to be painstaking, manual tests, saving additional time. Time savings is one of the principal benefits hailed by all AGATHA users.

Fourth, costs are saved when AGATHA automatically runs tests. By effectively lowering the skill level required, the test runs can be done by operators rather than technicians.

Fifth, AGATHA makes a more thorough diagnosis, eliminating many common human errors. It also improves test reliability by detecting failures not formerly caught by PRISM.

Sixth, AGATHA has provided an easier-to use-interface to the PRISM tester. In a recent survey, users gave a top score to AGATHA's friendly user interface. Coupled with automation, this interface has significantly reduced technician and operator training time and greatly improved user satisfaction.

It's difficult to quantify the full impact of AGATHA within HP, but we list some benefits here:

First, during AGATHA's development, test time was reduced by 80 percent on one board, yielding tremendous cost savings. Although there were several factors at work here, AGATHA was a principal contributor in this effort.

Second, the field repair center indicates AGATHA reduced scrap rate, average repair time, training costs, and material costs. These savings add up over the life of a product and could especially be valuable toward the end of its life when expert knowledge on an aging board could otherwise be scarce.

Third, one production site related a one-fourth reduction in technician training time, with the ramp-up time for a new technician dramatically improved. It also reported a 40-percent reduction in diagnostic time and a significant increase in user satisfaction with the friendlier interface.

In addition to the gratifying manufacturing results, the joint development effort between HP Labs and ICBD proved to be of mutual benefit: ICBD gained expertise in the design, development, and deployment of expert system technology. HP Labs gained knowledge of realistic problems in electronic circuit diagnosis. This knowledge has been used to drive a longer-term research program in model-based diagnosis.

Acknowledgments

We want to recognize the valuable contribution of many others: Rick Butler was the domain expert who consulted on the project. Caroline Knight of HP Labs invested a lot of time in training ICBD in knowledge-acquisition techniques. Jason Brown was a summer student who helped code part of AGATHA. In addition, we want to express our gratitude to the many operators and technicians who gave invaluable time and assistance on, and feedback to, the AGATHA project.

References

Gassman, G. R.; Schrempp, M. W.; Goundan, A.; Chin, R.; Odinea, R. D.; and Jones, M. 1987. VLSI-Based High-Performance HP Precision Architecture Computers. *HP Journal* 38(9): 38–48.

Mahon, M. J.; Lee, R. B.; Miller, T. C.; Huck, J. C.; and Bryg, W. R. 1986. Hewlett-Packard Precision Architecture: The Processor. *HP Journal* 37(8): 4–21.

Preist, C.; Allred, D.; and Gupta, A. 1991. An Expert System to Perform Functional Diagnosis of a Bus Subsystem, Technical Paper HPL-91-16, HP Labs, Bristol, England.

Robinson, C. S.; Johnson, L.; Horning, R. J.; Mason, R. W.; Ludwig, M. A.; Felsenthal, H. R.; Meyer, T. O.; and Spencer, T. V. 1987. A Midrange VLSI Hewlett-Packard Precision Architecture Computer. *HP Journal* 38(9): 26–34.

Schuchard, R. A., and Weiss, D. 1987. Scan Path Testing of a Multichip Computer. In *1987 IEEE International Solid State Circuits Conference Digest*, 230–231. Gables, Fla.: Lewis Winner.

Weiss, D. 1987. VLSI Test Methodology. *HP Journal* 38(9): 24–25

The Thallium Diagnostic Workstation: Learning to Diagnose Heart Imagery from Examples

Rin Saunders.

The thallium diagnostic workstation (TDW) is an integrated workstation for the learning and application of diagnostic rules for thallium heart imagery. TDW learns diagnostic rules from training sets of images, using a symbolic induction algorithm developed specifically for this application. TDW uses machine vision to identify image features of diagnostic significance (findings), which are described to the physician in a write-up. The physician can perform automated diagnosis by applying a rule set to the findings, selected from TDW's catalog of learned rules. The physician can also view imagery, record his(her) own findings, and enter a diagnosis. TDW informs the physician of its concurrence or non-concurrence with the physician's diagnosis.

TDW is deployed at the United States Air Force School of Aerospace Medicine (USAFSAM). Physicians at USAFSAM qualify fliers for aeromedical fitness. Significant coronary artery disease, causing narrowing of the arteries supplying blood to the heart muscle, is grounds for disqualification. Because Air Force standards are strict, fliers can be disqualified even if there are no overt symptoms of coronary artery disease (such as angina pectoris). The Air Force can disqualify a flier for the loss of 30 percent of the diameter of a coronary artery. However, coronary artery disease often produces no severe symptoms until close to 90 percent of the diameter is lost, making the diagnosis of aeromedically significant coronary artery disease a harder proposition than diagnosing coronary artery disease in a conventional clinical setting.

USAFSAM uses thallium imagery to screen fliers suspected of having coronary artery disease. A thallium scan is graded normal, borderline, or abnormal. Patients with borderline or abnormal scans are subject to angiography, the definitive technique for diagnosing the disease. In *angiography*, puffs of radiopaque dye are released from a catheter that is passed through the femoral artery to just above the coronary circulation. A moving X-ray image is taken that shows the course of blood through the coronary arteries. Angiography is invasive, requiring cardiac catheterization and the use of a dye sometimes associated with allergic reactions. Using thallium imagery lowers patient risk by reducing unnecessary angiography.

Diagnosing asymptomatic coronary artery disease from thallium imagery is difficult and subjective. Physicians at USAFSAM show considerable variation in their thallium-reading skills (evaluated as the percentage of thallium-based diagnoses confirmed by angiography). The physicians' skill level correlates well with time on the job at USAFSAM (Kay 1989). Physicians become skilled in the technique through on-the-job experience, then leave after a three- to four-year rotation.

Benefits

TDW provides the following benefits to USAFSAM physicians: First, TDW leverages expertise. It enables physicians to perform as well as the best available diagnostician. TDW can also be trained on angiographic diagnoses; in which case, it performs comparably with USAFSAM's best diagnosticians. Second, TDW conserves expertise. USAFSAM physicians become experts in thallium interpretation and then leave. TDW preserves the expertise of physicians for use by their successors. Third, TDW objectifies expertise. TDW's learned rule sets enable experts to compare and evaluate objective criteria for classifying thallium images. Fourth, TDW provides consistent and reproducible diagnoses. Although thallium interpretation is somewhat subjective, precise numbers underlie the image. TDW provides a diagnostic standard that is consistent and reproducible across both doctors and patients. This approach benefits longitudinal studies that involve multiple doctors and patients.

These benefits are provided by traditional expert systems. TDW's machine vision capability provides an additional benefit: It can train incoming physicians. TDW is not primarily intended as a tutoring system. In general, expert systems do not perform well as tutors. However, TDW is useful in honing incoming physicians' *expert vision*, the ability to detect features of diagnostic significance. Because TDW's findings can be displayed on a screen with imagery, the novice thallium reader can use the findings as a guide.

TDW's machine-learning capability provides the following benefits: First, it reconstructs expertise. A longitudinal study of coronary artery disease might include patients diagnosed by physicians who left the study years ago. TDW can reconstruct the physicians' diagnostic criteria from examples. The reconstructed criteria can be used to evaluate puzzling diagnostic calls. The call can be consistent with TDW's learned criteria for this physician, justifying the call. If the call is inconsistent with the learned criteria, the call can be treated as an anomaly. Second, TDW supports studies. USAFSAM physicians are concerned with diagnosing low-grade coronary artery disease. What is the least degree of this disease that can reliably be distinguished from normality? Training TDW on specially selected image sets can help answer this question. Third, TDW is a self-maintaining knowledge base in the sense that users can update the diagnostic rules by training TDW on new cases.

Innovative Application of Machine Vision & Machine Learning

Medical imagery is potentially a high-payoff domain for expert systems. For chest films, Garland (1950) showed that radiologists routinely miss about 30 percent of all abnormalities. However, building an expert system to classify images poses challenges beyond those normally associated with expert systems.

An expert system for medical imagery must incorporate machine vision. Human diagnostic reasoning proceeds from high-level image features rather than pixel intensities. A nuclear medicine specialist learns to see features of diagnostic significance in an image—an expert vision based on pattern recognition rather than deductive reasoning.

TDW emulates the physician's expert vision. Previous automated thallium diagnostic systems used statistical profiles to classify images (Burow et al. 1979; Garcia et al. 1981; Watson et al. 1981). TDW's AI approach is an improvement because it reasons from features that physicians can see in the imagery and presents its findings in terms used by physicians. This approach helps build physicians' confidence in the correctness of TDW's conclusions.

Knowledge acquisition for image classification presents another challenge. Knowledge acquisition is difficult enough when the expert reasons from facts and assumptions that are objectively true or false. However, physicians classify thallium imagery using subjectively defined image features that are construed differently by different physicians or even by the same physician over time. Further, in becoming an expert, the physician fuses feature extraction and diagnostic reasoning into a single process called judgment that the physician cannot explain. Knowledge elicitation produces textbook explanations that bear little relationship to how the physician actually interprets images.

TDW uses machine-learning techniques to automate knowledge acquisition. It deals with the problem of inconsistency by seeking rules that replicate the physician's judgments in as many cases as possible. Because TDW learns from examples rather than explanations, it is not confused by a physician's misunderstanding of his(her) own decision processes.

System Architecture and Function

TDW is implemented on a Science Applications International Corporation SIGMA-1 microcomputer incorporating a 25-megahertz 80386 processor, an 80387 numeric coprocessor, a floating-point coprocessor rated at 22 MFlops, and a VGA monitor. Microsoft WINDOWS provides a windowed user interface. Much work went into the interface design. As a result, TDW has only two menu bars (one for viewing images and one for all other functions) and no submenus. Although TDW has separate programs for learning and diagnosis, this separation is transparent to the user because WINDOWS provides a seamless interface. The Nexpert Object expert system shell maintains information about cases, image features, diagnoses, and diagnostic rules. Nexpert Object was selected because it offers a class-object–oriented frame system and flexible agenda control during inferencing, and it can be embedded under WINDOWS.

TDW performs two main functions: learning diagnostic rules from sets of diagnosed images and applying rules to produce diagnoses. TDW has a subsystem for each function. The subsystems are constellated around a central knowledge base. The learning subsystem inserts rule sets into the knowledge base and the application subsystem runs them.

Processing begins when TDW receives an image file from USAFSAM's medical imaging system over an ethernet. The image file contains the patient's name, the physician's name, and other identifying information as well as raw pixel intensities. TDW enters the patient information into the knowledge base and performs image processing to improve the quality of the raw data. TDW's feature extractor identifies features of diagnostic significance in the image. These features are entered into the knowledge base and associated with the patient data.

The physician can view imagery using the TDW image viewer. The viewer can display six images belonging to a case (three anatomical views taken at two intervals after thallium injection) either simultaneously or separately for higher resolution. Grey-scale, full-color, and a quantized color-scale views are available. Both raw and processed images can be displayed. A mouse-driven pixel meter enables the physician to evaluate individual pixel intensities. The physician can view TDW's findings by opening a window that displays the feature descriptions in narrative English.

TDW presents the physician with a list of current cases. The patient's name and number, the physician's name, the image date, angiographic results (if available) and diagnoses from thallium reading by physicians, angiography data, and TDW's rules are displayed for each case. The physician can view imagery, record findings and diagnoses, view TDW's findings, and apply rule sets to perform automated diagnosis. TDW lists the available rule sets and displays English translations of the rules. When system capacity is reached, cases are automatically archived to disk.

TDW learns diagnostic rules from training sets of diagnosed images. It enables physicians to construct training sets by grouping cases that meet user-specified screening criteria. The criteria enable the physician to include diagnoses based on the source—specific physicians or angiography. Cases can also be selected based on image data range, concurrence or nonconcurrence of the angiographic result with the thallium scan, or the presence or absence of key words that physicians can associate with cases. A physician can edit the training set to enter or remove individual cases.

The learning subsystem uses a symbolic induction technique called METARULE, which was developed specifically for TDW. As learning proceeds, the current best rule is displayed in English translation on the screen. TDW requires approximately 10 minutes to learn rules covering a training set of 100 cases. When learning is complete, the rule set is translated into Nexpert syntax and compiled into the knowledge base. The English translation is also stored for review by the physician.

How the Thallium Diagnostic Workstation Works

I now take a closer look at how thallium imagery is produced and interpreted by physicians, how TDW extracts features of diagnostic significance from digitized imagery, and how learning is done.

Thallium Image Interpretation

In the thallium technique, patients are run on a treadmill until the electrocardiogram shows physiologic stress. At this point, the heart muscle is low in potassium ions. Depletion occurs most prominently in the left ventricle, which is the main pumping engine of the heart. The patient is injected with thallous-201 chloride as a bolus through an intravenous line. The thallium ion chemically resembles potassium, so it is absorbed by the heart muscle where the muscle is perfused with blood. If perfusion is normal, thallium is rapidly absorbed, then gradually washes out, typically attaining the halfway point in 84 minutes (Gerson 1987).

The patient is imaged under a gamma camera, providing an array of 128 x 128 pixels, within 6 minutes of injection. Three views are taken: the anterior, the 45-degree left anterior oblique, and the 70-degree left anterior oblique. The images are repeated after 4 hours of rest. The two sets of images are called the *stress images* and the *rest images*, respectively.

I studied how physicians grade images by asking the clinical staff members to describe their interpretation techniques. I also obtained talking protocols in which physicians described how they evaluate images while the evaluations are being performed.

The physicians stated that thallium imagery indirectly reveals the presence of coronary artery disease by depicting the perfusion of blood into the left ventricular myocardium. *Arterial narrowing* (stenosis) can delay the uptake and the washout of thallium. An image region that washes out too slowly is a *washout abnormality*. More severe stenosis can delay uptake so that the rest images show thallium is washing in rather than out. An image region showing washin is called a *reperfusion defect*. A reperfusion defect, combined with a washout abnormality, is called a *matched defect*. A still greater degree of stenosis can produce a region with little uptake on either set of images, which is called a *perfusion defect*. A perfusion defect can indicate scar tissue in the myocardium from a prior infarct. According to the clinical staff members, washout abnormalities have the weakest evidentiary strength for coronary artery disease, followed by reperfusion defects, matched defects, and perfusion defects.

The talking protocols revealed additional feature types. When large regions of an image show washin, but the intensity is never sufficient to warrant being called a reperfusion defect, physicians call the defect *low-grade pervasive reperfusion*. A *reversing horseshoe* is a pattern in which the valve plane is hotter than the apex on the stress image but colder on the rest image. This pattern, more formally known as *reversing apical hypoperfusion*, is viewed as highly diagnostic for coronary artery disease.

In general, physicians grade an image with sufficiently intense perfusion defects, horseshoes, or matched defects as abnormal. Reperfusion defects can result in a grade of abnormal or borderline. Washout abnormalities or low-grade pervasive reperfusion warrant a grade of borderline. An image without defects or with low-intensity defects is graded normal.

Feature Extraction

Thallium image features have their visual basis in regions that appear hot or cold relative to the rest of the image and their evolution over time. To automatically extract features, we must quantify the terms by which physicians describe features, for example, hotness, coldness, size, intensity, and location. We must decide how hot, big, intense, and so on, an image region must be to qualify as a feature. We must also decide how to quantify the time evolution of a feature. The beating of the heart makes it impossible to subtract the rest image from the stress image by superposition. The two sets of images do not coincide in shape.

Image Preprocessing. Thallium imagery based on raw pixel intensities is coarse and noisy. Automated and human interpretation alike are greatly facilitated by preprocessing to smooth the image and reduce noise.

TDW applies Watson's (1981) method of bilinear subtraction and Laplacian filtering to reduce noise from background radiation, tissue cross-talk, and absorption of thallium by organs other than the heart. Then, TDW identifies the boundaries of the myocardium. Because the edges are not sharp, I use thresholding rather than gradients or related methods. Pixels that make up the myocardial image are normalized to lie in the range from 0 to 55. The image is smoothed with a Gaussian convolution. The image centroid and cardiac apex are located, and the image is partitioned among the heart muscle walls.

Feature Extraction. The feature extractor uses template-based methods to identify image features. The image is divided into 12 radial segments about the centroid. Because the image was normalized, regions that are hot or cold relative to the image as a whole can be identified through thresholding. The appropriate values were found through experimentation. I also found that a region must occupy at least 10 percent of the area of the myocardium to be considered a candidate feature.

When physicians assess the magnitude of a defect, they consider its size and intensity and the change in size and intensity over time. A candidate feature is confirmed if the magnitude is sufficiently large. About two dozen measures of magnitude were explored, derived from the defect's maximum pixel intensity, the average intensity and size, and the absolute and percentage changes in these values. For reperfusion defects, I found that two measures of magnitude predicted the physicians' assessments: (1) the average pixel intensity of the region on the stress image times the absolute change in area and (2) the difference in the region's average intensity between the stress and rest images times the difference in area divided by the area of the region on the stress image. Other measures proved useful for the other feature types.

Learning

Learning rules from examples is not part of expert system technology but machine learning. Machine learning is still a research area. Several commercial expert system shells claim to learn rules from examples, but none perform adequately on any but simple problems (Thompson and Thompson 1986). This situation is in part because learning is a difficult problem and in part because different types of learning are appropriate to different domains, making it hard to build a general-purpose program. In addition, efficient learning often requires some domain knowledge beyond the examples themselves. I now turn to the requirements imposed by the thallium image domain.

Requirements for Learning Diagnostic Rules for Thallium Imagery. A machine-learning system for thallium imagery must deal with both categorical and numeric data. The type and anatomical location of a defect is categorical; the intensity is numeric. The learning system must be able to generalize about ranges of values. For example, a defect might warrant a grading of abnormal if it is sufficiently large in area or magnitude.

The learning system must tolerate counterexamples in the data. Many learning algorithms will learn a rule only if the rule is never contradicted. Medicine is not an exact science. Expert judgment will not be 100 percent consistent. A few anomalous cases should not always invalidate a rule.

The learning system should assess the quality of its rules. Because rules might not be valid for all the cases from which the system learns, the user must know how often a rule can be expected to be correct.

All other things being equal, preference should be given to rules that are simple and readable and make sense to human experts. The learning system should be biased toward simple rules.

How TDW Learns. A machine-learning algorithm named METARULE was developed to meet the requirements of the thallium domain. METARULE learns diagnostic rule sets in three phases. First, it learns rules for diagnosing normal cases. Then, it learns rules for diagnosing abnormal cases. The five best rules are retained for normal and abnormal cases. Finally, METARULE selects combinations of these rules to produce a complete rule set.

When learning about normal or abnormal cases, METARULE begins by making simple assertions about what makes a case positive (that is, makes an abnormal case abnormal or a normal case normal). These assertions make up the inductive kernel. Rules in the kernel reference aspects of the image, such as which feature types are present, how many features there are, what numeric values exist for feature attributes, and so on. Rules involving ranges of numeric attributes are formulated by seeking cut points with the greatest discriminatory power.

If the case is positive, METARULE postulates that the presence of its feature types and attributes makes it positive. For example, a positive case with a reperfusion defect having a magnitude of 100 might lead METARULE to postulate that (1) a reperfusion defect makes a case positive, (2) a reperfusion defect with a magnitude of at least 100 makes a case positive, or (3) having at least one feature makes a case positive. For negative cases, METARULE postulates that the feature, attribute value, and number of features prevent the case from being positive.

METARULE builds more complex rules by combining existing rules. Promising combinations are identified using a beam search. The search space is the space of all first-order formulas that can be built from the kernel using the Boolean predicates And, Or, and Not.

A rule can be regarded as a characterizer or a discriminator (Michalski 1983). A *characterizer* lists things that positive cases have in common; a *discriminator* tells what separates positive cases from negative cases. Discriminators are the object of the search. If a rule is not a good discriminator, it might be useful as a characterizer. A characterizer covers the positive cases well but includes too many negative ones. In a sense, a characteristic description is half a solution (few false negatives) in search of its other half (a description that reduces the number of false positives).

For each promising characterizer, METARULE seeks discriminators that preserve the coverage of positive cases but reject any false positives. Promising characterizers are combined with discriminators to form conjunctive rules. Disjunctive rules are formed by combining complementary characterizers to extend their coverage. Rules do not need to be conjunctive or disjunctive exclusively and can grow to an arbitrary level of complexity.

METARULE maintains lists of the best performing characterizers and discriminators. The search begins with the strongest characteristic description. For each characterizer in order of strength, METARULE generates a list of promising disjunctive rules, ranked from strongest to weakest. METARULE forms new rules by joining the most promising discriminators with the current characterizer. For each promising characterizer, METARULE finds other descriptions that extend the coverage but include few or no false positives. These descriptions are separated to form new rules. As new rules emerge, the lists of characterizers and discriminators are continually updated.

Several elaborations on this basic strategy are intended to speed the search or provide a bias toward simpler rules. If METARULE discovers that two candidate rules are logically equivalent (that is, can be reduced to the same expression by symbolic manipulation), the simpler of the two rules is retained. This approach speeds the search and promotes the use of simple rules. Similarly, if two rules are empirically equivalent (that is, classify each case the same way for the same reasons), only the simpler rule is retained. Finally, a rule's simplicity can partially make up for a small lack of accuracy when selecting a rule to elaborate. The simplest rule is selected for elaboration from rules that rate within three percentage points of the best-scoring rule.

The METARULE algorithm most resembles the AQ family of inductive-learning programs (Michalski 1990). The algorithm evolved during development. The first version could generalize about classes of features—a hierarchical learning capability similar to that of OTIS (Kerber 1988). This capability was dropped from the final version when it became clear that features are best considered individually rather than as members of classes.

METARULE's method of incorporating domain knowledge underwent a fundamental change during development. The core of METARULE is a general learning program and is not tailored to a specific domain. Originally, domain knowledge was incorporated as commonsense rules to guide the search and derived features. The commonsense rules were propositions such as "Defects are associated with abnormal cases." These propositions were used to prevent the search from exploring primrose paths. Derived features included LAD-DISTRIBUTION, which was added to feature descriptions of cases showing a pattern of defects consistent with stenosis of the left anterior descending (LAD) coronary artery. I found that the search spent far too much time elaborating portions of the kernel that were not productive for thallium. The kernel contained many rules that were useful in general learning problems but not specifically for thallium. Tailoring the inductive kernel for the domain proved a much more effective way of creating an efficient search than imposing knowledge-based constraints on the use of a general-purpose kernel.

Development, Deployment, and Evaluation

The development strategy for TDW was a modified version of rapid prototyping. The rapid prototyping strategy is useful when users' requirements are not well understood (perhaps even by the users themselves) and must be discovered along the way. I believed, correctly, that I understood the functional requirements well at the outset. However, I needed to manage the technical risk imposed by incorporating machine learning and vision in an expert system.

The machine-learning component involved the greatest technical risk; so, I began by prototyping METARULE. METARULE was prototyped in INTERLISP-D on a Xerox 1186 Lisp machine, then ported to C for delivery. The use of Lisp greatly speeded development because of the power and flexibility of the language and the INTERLISP environment for programming, debugging, evaluating, and changing code. The salutary effect of Lisp on development time can be gauged by the fact that porting METARULE to C took as long as the initial prototyping effort—six months.

I demonstrated TDW to USAFSAM sponsors and clinicians about every four months. This process allowed the future users to evaluate the user interface and function and request changes or additional features. Each new capability was added in two steps: First, the user interface was built and demonstrated to the users to show the concept of operation. I modified the concept and the interface, based on users' comments, then built the capability. Once a capability was built, I never had to modify it. Except for the METARULE prototype, I rarely had to discard code during development. This point is significant because many expert system projects that plan to use rapid prototyping find that there is never enough time or money to throw code away and start over.

This strategy can be called *incremental prototyping* because it falls between rapid prototyping and incremental development. Like rapid prototyping, the users could specify their requirements as changes to a prototype rather than having to write them down cold. As in incremental development, I developed the riskiest parts first and could have aborted the project should TDW have proved infeasible. This strategy worked well for TDW. I recommend it for systems in which the user requirements are largely (but not completely) understood at the beginning, and considerable technical risk needs to be managed.

TDW was researched, developed, and tested during a 2.5-year effort involving about 3.75 person-years of effort at a cost of about $500,000 (including equipment and labor). It was deployed at USAFSAM in December 1990.

I evaluated TDW's ability to learn to read thallium imagery like a USAFSAM physician—that is, learn rules that predict physicians' grading of a thallium image—and learn to predict coronary artery disease from thallium imagery independent of the methods used by physicians—that is, learn rules that predict the outcome of angiography.

TDW was tested on training sets varying from 50 to 115 cases in size.

(Below 50 cases, METARULE began to tailor its rules to the quirks of individual cases rather than generalize.) A rule set's performance on cases not included in the training set always closely mirrored its ability to classify the training set itself.

TDW's best rule for grading images like a physician correctly predicts 82 percent of the gradings. This figure is comparable to the level of consistency among physicians: A study of intercoder reliability in thallium interpretation showed that physicians agree about 87 percent of the time (Trobaugh et al. 1978). TDW successfully learns diagnostic rules that replicate the judgment of expert physicians.

It is noteworthy that TDW's rules are much simpler than the physicians' own explanations of how they diagnose. In the talking protocols, physicians consider many subtleties. For example, the positioning of the heart within the chest could present an extra thickness of muscle wall to the camera, accentuating a hot region. However, the learned rules show that the presence of horseshoes and the characteristics of the largest single reperfusion defect adequately predict the physicians' diagnostic calls.

The best rule for predicting angiographic results correctly predicts 76 percent of the outcomes (62 percent of abnormal cases and 83 percent of normal cases). For comparison, USAFSAM's most skilled physicians correctly predict 74 percent of angiographic outcomes (60 percent for abnormal cases and 82 percent for normal cases). Learning by example as physicians learn on the job, TDW performs comparably with USAFSAM's best diagnosticians.

TDW will improve patient care and reduce cost by reducing the number of cardiac catheterizations. A study of diagnoses by less experienced physicians shows that TDW would have prevented as many as half of the catheterizations. There is no satisfactory method for measuring the number of catheterizations that TDW saves because it is difficult to tell how a physician would have diagnosed a case without TDW's assistance. Based on retrospective data from the 1989 case load, TDW should save 15 catheterizations this year. The cost reduction is difficult to calculate because USAFSAM physicians do not charge their patients for the procedure.

Discussion

There is a growing concern among practitioners of AI in medicine about the paucity of deployed applications. Discussion has centered on four issues: (1) some problems in this field are too hard to solve well; (2) the lack of computerized patient records in most hospitals gives AI medical systems little to work on unless someone takes the time to enter patient information; (3) medical AI applications might automate the most enjoyable part of the physician's job; and (4) AI medical applications, like most new medical technology, improve patient care but increase costs. If AI medical applications reduced costs, wouldn't we see an explosion of deployed applications?

TDW owes much of its success to the selection of a diagnostic problem that is significant, requiring the use of emerging technologies, but not overwhelming. Feature extraction from thallium imagery can be performed using well-established pattern-matching techniques. If feature extraction had required extensive object reconstruction and scene analysis, TDW would still be where those technologies are—in the lab. The problem posed by learning diagnostic rules was harder than the vision problem, and the technological solution was correspondingly more mature. Machine learning is ready to start migrating from the lab into applications, and TDW is one of the first applied learning systems in medicine.

The patient data required by TDW, digitized imagery, already existed in computerized form. The typing required of the physician is no more than physicians already do in writing up their findings and diagnosis.

Because TDW encourages the physician to make judgments and compare them with TDW's, the workstation appears to be more of a colleague than a replacement. I hope that physicians will find it enjoyable to use.

TDW's development cost was substantial because it included research, development, and production—the system had to be robust and friendly enough for clinical use. Like other AI medical applications, it improves patient care at a cost.

I hope that TDW will encourage other researchers to deploy applications that apply emerging technologies such as machine learning to significant, manageable problems in medicine.

Acknowledgments

The development of TDW was sponsored Drs. Bryce Hartman and William Clardy at the United States Air Force School of Aerospace Medicine (USAFSAM), Human Systems Division (ASFC), USAF, Brooks AFB, TX 78235-5301. Drs. Londe Richardson and Michael Blick of the USAFSAM clinical staff provided thallium expertise. Lalitha Sekar programmed most of the TDW system.

References

Burow, R.; Pond, M.; Schafer, A.; and Becker, L. 1979. Circumferential Profiles: A New Method for Computer Analysis of Thallium-201 Myocardial Perfusion Images. *Journal of Nuclear Medicine* 20(7): 771–777.

Garcia, E.; Maddahi, J.; Berman, D.; and Waxman, A. 1981. Space/Time Quantitation of Thallium-201 Myocardial Scintigraphy. *Journal of Nuclear Medicine* 20(771): 309–319.

Garland, L. 1950. On the Reliability of Roentgen Survey Procedures. *American Journal of Roentgenology* 64(2): 32–41.

Gerson, M. 1987. *Cardiac Nuclear Medicine*. Englewood Cliffs N.J.: Prentice Hall.

Kay, T. 1989. Personal communication at USAFSAM.

Kerber, R. 1988. Using a Generalization Hierarchy to Learn from Examples. In *Proceedings of the Fifth International Conference on Machine Learning*, 1–7. San Mateo, Calif.: Morgan Kaufmann.

Michalski, R. 1990. Learning Flexible Concepts: Fundamental Ideas and a Method Based on Two-Tiered Representation. In *Machine Learning: An Artificial Intelligence Approach*, volume 3, eds. Y. Kodratoff and R. Michalski, 63–111. San Mateo, Calif.: Morgan Kaufmann.

Michalski, R. 1983. A Theory and Methodology of Inductive Learning. In *Machine Learning: An Artificial Intelligence Approach*, volume 1, eds. R. Michalski, J. Carbonell, and T. Mitchell, 83–134. San Mateo, Calif.: Morgan Kaufmann.

Thompson, B., and Thompson, W. 1986. Finding Rules in Data. *Byte* 11:12.

Trobaugh, G.; Wackers, F.; Sokole, E.; DeRouen, T.; Ritchie, J.; and Hamilton, G. 1978. Thallium-201 Myocardial Imaging: An Interinstitutional Study of Observer Variability. *Journal of Nuclear Medicine* 19(4): 359–369.

Watson, D.; Campbell, N.; Read, E.; Gibson, R.; Teates, C.; and Beller, G. 1981. Spatial and Temporal Quantitation of Plane Thallium Myocardial Images. *Journal of Nuclear Medicine* 22(7): 577–584.

Engineering & Manufacturing

Redundant Resolutions of Nonconformances
General Dynamics Electric Boat Division

Assembly System Design
The Charles Stark Draper Laboratory, Inc.

CAMES
Lamb Group of Companies

QDES
Nippon Steel Corporation

A Case-Based Reasoning Solution to the Problem of Redundant Resolutions of Nonconformances in Large-Scale Manufacturing

Stuart J. Brown and Lundy M. Lewis

By *large-scale manufacturing*, we refer to the manufacture of a few large, complex items over a long period of time as opposed to the manufacture of many smaller items during a shorter period of time. For example, more than five years are required to build one ship, whereas thousands of automobiles are built at a single plant during one year. Further, thousands of person-years go into the making of a single ship. As a result of the complexity of large items and the effort and time required to build them, it is inevitable that episodes of atypical problem solving are unknowingly duplicated. This situation results in lost opportunities and less than optimal production costs.

The Problem

We illustrate this situation with a common engineering problem in ship building. A particular type of valve is used in some thousand fluid systems on a specific class of ships, and often, it is used in many places on a single fluid system. The operations performed on each valve are "receive," "inspect," "install," "test," and "accept." Each of these operations is controlled by different cognizant engineers, and a different set of cognizant engineers is responsible for each fluid system. When an operation fails, a well-defined investigatory procedure follows. If the investigatory procedure is sufficiently robust, a repair method for the failure is invoked. However, if a repair method is not evident, the investigatory procedure becomes unstructured. Usually, the cognizant engineer confers with colleagues or superiors. When a repair method is found, it is documented but is not made public. An engineer with a similar problem in the future is lucky if someone in his(her) group remembers the old repair method and retrieves the applicable document. More often than not, engineers confront atypical problems afresh, without opportunities to exploit similar past solutions.

In the ship-building industry, these sorts of problems are called nonconformances. Specifically, a *nonconformance* is the failure of a system or subsystem whose repair method is not dictated by standard resolution procedures. Nonconformances occur with all components of mechanical, electric, and structural systems. In our facility, some 35,000 noncomformances occur annually. The problem of redundant resolutions of a nonconformance (RRN) occurs when a nonconformance is researched and resolved in relative isolation. The RRN problem arises because useful expertise that can be applied to nonconformance problems is transient and distributed over both time and space. For example, (1) a particular nonconformance is addressed by different people as a result of personnel turnover, (2) similar nonconformances recur at different times during the construction cycle of systems or subsystems, (3) similar subproblems of large complex nonconformances are addressed on different occasions by different personnel, and (4) a particular nonconformance is addressed by different departments or different people within the same department.

The RRN problem is compounded in large-scale manufacturing because communication among the experts is sparse. The obvious solution to the problem is to identify and categorize nonconformances and their respective problem-solving strategies and resolutions and make this knowledge readily available to all engineers for application to current nonconformances. However, this solution is difficult because knowledge must be extracted from multiple experts, the knowledge must uniformly be represented, and relevant knowledge must be accessible to any one expert.

The Solution

In January 1986, a manufacturing and production engineering project was initiated to demonstrate the feasibility of a paperless nonconformance system using AI technology. The initial approach was to express the requisite knowledge as rules in a production system. A prototype system was developed in KEE on an AI workstation and then later reimplemented in Goldworks on a personal computer. The initial results were promising. However, as the system became increasingly complex, it began to suffer the problems of brittleness and knowledge-acquisition bottleneck. The system could not resolve nonconformances that were not already explicit in the knowledge base, and the experts found it increasingly difficult to express their knowledge as a collection of rules.

The results of an internal research and development project during 1988–1989 demonstrated that case-based knowledge representation is a close match to the properties of the RRN problem (Lewis 1989). By 1990, a case-based reasoning application to the RRN problem was constructed, and by the second quarter of 1990, it was deployed with a sufficiently large, albeit incomplete, knowledge base.

The basic idea of case-based reasoning is to recall, adapt, and execute traces of former experiences in an attempt to deal with a current experience. Former experiences are represented as a library of cases that reside in memory, where individual cases are related through various link types, including abstraction, exemplar, index, and failure links. When confronted with a new problem, a case-based reasoning system retrieves a maximally similar case, and information from the case is adapted to the new problem in an attempt to solve it. If the solution is successful, the new case is embedded in memory for future problem solving. If the solution is unsuccessful, the case is tagged and embedded in memory with the reasons why it did not work.

The characteristics of case-based reasoning that render it suitable for the RRN problem are (1) *case structure*, through which previous paper reports of nonconformances and their solution strategies and resolutions are representable; (2) *similarity metrics*, by which relevant representations of nonconformance reports and solutions are retrieved; (3) *adaptation techniques*, by which the resolution of a current nonconformance problem is derived from a retrieved report; and (4) the *organization of the case library*, through which experience with a current disposition is embedded in memory for future use.

The primary advantages of case-based over rule-based knowledge representation are that the problems of brittleness and knowledge-acquisition bottleneck are less severe. Case-based reasoning systems are designed to adapt an old solution to a new, similar problem. Further, the expert is more comfortable relating his(her) expertise constrained by case-oriented knowledge representation as opposed to rule-oriented knowledge representation, and the knowledge base is refined and updated during use.

In the following discussion, we provide the groundwork for the development of the system and then describe the system and its benefits. Other problem areas to which case-based reasoning techniques have been applied and from which we borrowed some fundamental ideas include legal domains (Ashley and Rissland 1988; Bain 1986; Rissland and Skalak 1989b), medical domains (Koton 1988), engineering design (Daube and Hayes-Roth 1989; Huhns and Acosta 1988), and software diagnostics (Simoudis and Miller 1990). Overviews of case-based reasoning are provided in Riesbeck and Schank (1989) and Slade (1991). Experimental case-based reasoning systems are discussed in Hammond (1986) and Kolodner, Simpson, and Sycara-Cyranski (1985). A hybrid system consisting of a case-based reasoning component and a qualitative reasoning component is discussed in Koton (1988). A hybrid system consisting of a case-based reasoning component and a rule-based component is discussed in Rissland and Skalak (1989a, 1989b). The production of a generic case-based reasoning tool (CABARET) is in progress at the University of Massachusetts for the purpose of studying issues concerning case-based reasoning (Rissland and Skalak 1989a), and a case-based reasoning shell sponsored by the Defense Advanced Research Projects Agency is discussed in Stottler, Henke, and King (1989).

Groundwork 1:
Similarity Metrics for Case-Based Reasoning Systems

Assume that an object can be represented as a list of n attribute-value pairs, where each value is numeric. An object is represented as a point in n-dimensional space, where the dimensions represent the attributes, and the object is the point whose coordinates are determined by the attribute values. The geometric definition of distance quantifies the similarity between two objects. Smaller distances indicate increasing similarity. A library of objects is represented as points plotted in n-dimensions, where clusters of similar objects and unique objects are identifiable (Stottler et al. 1989). To illustrate, suppose the object is a part, and the dimensions of the part are height and weight. The two parts

[height(6),weight(100)], [height(5),weight(110)]

are more similar than

[height(5),weight(100)], [height(2),weight(30)] ,

with the closeness measure of each pair calculated as approximately 10 and 70, respectively.

Assume now that attribute values are symbolic. A first-order definition of similarity is prescribed by the larger number of exact matches of attribute-value pairs of any two objects; that is, a larger number of matches indicates increasing similarity. Although this definition appears to be reasonable, numerous counterexamples can be construed for which high similarity does not warrant the extension of a known attribute of an object to a target object. For example, if two nonconforming parts are determined highly similar based on irrelevant attributes, the fact that the one nonconformance is resolved by method M does not warrant the inference that the other one can be resolved by M. If it is known, however, the extent to which certain attributes are relevant to a nonconformance, and the values of the relevant attributes match in each case, then the inference of M to the other part is more reasonable. Thus, similarity is defined as the larger number of matches of attribute-value pairs relevant to a particular nonconformance. This idea is worked out conceptually in the *theory of determinations* (Davies and Russell 1987). The theory suggests that a library of prior nonconformances and their solutions be augmented with a set of determination rules that record relevance information among sets of attributes and possible nonconformance solutions.

A related approach argues that similarity is a function of the purpose of object comparisons (Kedar-Cabelli 1986). Knowledge about the purpose of the comparison of two objects focuses attention on the relevant attributes of the objects. In this approach, similarity is defined as the number of matches of attribute-value pairs constrained by the purpose of comparison. The approach suggests that a library of nonconformances be examined with an explicit purpose, where determination rules record relevance information between purposes and sets of attributes. To expand the previous example, suppose the purpose of reviewing a library of nonconformances is to collect those nonconformances that involve a certain vendor. A determination rule will have associated the vendor with a range of attributes and values, and thus, a cluster of nonconformance reports are retrieved accordingly.

We note that determination rules preserve semantic information about the relations among sets of attributes. A subsidiary problem is, of course, how determination rules come to exist. In our domain, determination rules are articulated by expert engineers in ship building and are not always accurate. An alternative domain-independent approach, the *structure-mapping theory* (SMT), avoids this problem by couching similarity as a function of syntax only (Gentner 1983). First, we distinguish between attributes, relations, and higher-order predicates, for example, $a(X)$, $a(X,Y)$, and $a(b(X,Y),c(Y,Z))$, respectively. The *systematicity principle* states that "a predicate that belongs to a mappable system of mutually interconnecting relationships is more likely to be imported into the target than is an isolated predicate" (Gentner 1983, p. 163). *Similarity*, then, is defined as the degree of match between higher-order predicates whose arguments denote increasingly interconnected relationships. For example, the predicate

[material(diaphragm,X), temp(X,Degree,Beginning,End)] —>
[fail(diaphragm, End + N)] ,

where $N = f(X,\text{Degree,Beginning,End})$ and —> denotes causation, states that the failure of a diaphragm is caused by, and is a function of, the material that the diaphragm is made of, the extent to which it is heated, and the interval during which it is heated. SMT suggests that a predicate of this form affords more similarity import than, say, material(diaphragm, X). Further examples and empirical support of SMT are provided in Gentner (1983). Although we have not used this technique in our application, we consider it a promising approach to a domain-independent formalization of similarity.

Groundwork 2:
Adaptation Techniques for Case-Based Reasoning Systems

A simple adaptation technique of a retrieved case is *structural adaptation*, in which adaptation rules apply directly to a solution stored in a case. Here, we describe four kinds of structural adaptation (Riesbeck and Schank 1989).

First is *null adaptation*. The simplest technique, it directly transfers an old solution to a new problem. Note that this technique can be achieved with methods simpler than case-based reasoning, including lookup tables and associative connectionist systems.

Second is *parameterized adaptation*, which adjusts the solution variables of a target case relative to the solution variables of a source case. For example, a problem variable X in a source case can be related to a solution variable Y according to the rule "As X increases, Y decreases." The value of X in a target case is compared to the value of X in the source case, and the value of Y in the target case is instantiated relative to the value of Y in the source case. Refer to Bain (1986) and Rissland and Ashley (1986) for further discussion and application of this technique.

Third is the *abstraction-respecialization* technique, which presupposes the organization of attributes of a case library into an is-a hierarchy and considers constraints on possible solutions to a problem in a target case. The idea is that if a solution of a source case does not satisfy the constraints of the target case, then one should abstract and respecialize over the source attribute and check the new value against the constraints. For example, suppose repair(pump(diaphragm)) is proposed as a solution to faulty(pump) through a source case, and a constraint imposed on the solution of the target case is not(repair(pump(diaphragm))). Abstraction and respecialization over the attribute *faulty(pump)* in the source case might issue replace(pump(diaphragm)), which is consistent with the constraint. The idea of tweaking a solution involves higher abstractions and respecializations over several parts of the source case and working each part back to satisfy multiple constraints of the target case. Refer to Alterman (1986) for further discussion and application of this technique.

Fourth is *critic-based adaptation*, which occurs when a critic repairs a retrieved solution to fit the target case. The repair method is then attached to the solution and embedded in memory for future use. An example of this technique is to reorder the steps in the retrieved solution. For example, suppose a solution to paint(chair) and paint(ceiling) is paint(chair), climb(ladder), paint(ceiling), and descend(ladder). A similar problem, paint(ladder) and paint(ceiling), might propose paint(ladder), climb(ladder), paint(ceiling), and descend(ladder), which the critic will note is unacceptable. One way to repair the solution is to reorder the steps into climb(ladder), paint(ceiling), descend(ladder), paint(ladder). Refer to Hammond (1986) for further discussion and application of this technique.

A more complex adaptation technique is *derivational adaptation*, in which a known method for solving an old problem is tried on a similar new problem (Riesbeck and Schank 1989). For example, suppose a case represents a problem space, including initial and goal states and a method for solving the problem. Let the relevant attributes for measuring similarity between two cases be the initial states and goal states. Suppose the source case is a solution to a particular sliding block puzzle that was solved by representing the problem as A^* search. The case will contain an initial state, a goal state, a set of operators for traversing the problem space, a heuristic function $f^* = g^* + h^*$ that estimates the merit of each state generated, and a sequence of moves representing the solution. One way to adapt the case for solving a similar problem is to rerun the A^* algorithm against the new problem parameters of a similar case. A more complex version of this technique is discussed in Carbonell (1983), in which the relevant dimensions for measuring similarity are the initial state, the goal state, path constraints, and operators. A retrieved case is adapted by reducing the differences between it and a new similar case along each dimension, in concert.

Description and Operation of the System

The current system consists of five modules: (1) an *input module* for the acquisition of resolved nonconformance reports and known information about current unresolved nonconformances, (2) a *reasoning module* that retrieves a select group of (possibly adapted) nonconformance reports, (3) a *display module* that reports potential solutions found by the reasoning module, (4) an *edit module* that allows the user to manually adapt the retrieved solution, and (5) an *accept module* that prints the solution and updates the case library (Brown 1990). Figure 1 shows the system architecture. We discuss the operation of the system in the following subsections. The system was developed on an IBM personal computer using Borland TURBO C and C++.

Input

The input module consists of a *case-acquisiton submodule* that is used to build and edit the case library and a *problem-acquisition submodule* that is used to submit known problem parameters of a current nonconformance. The structure of a case is the same in both submodules. A primary concern in determining case structure is the following: If case structure is overly specific, the case library becomes overly large, and the retrieval and adaptation of a case is similar to a lookup table. However, if case structure is underspecified, the case library is smaller, but complex adaptation techniques are required, and the system approaches analogical reasoning. The structure of a case in our system naturally models previous paper reports of nonconformances and their resolutions. Case attributes include both numeric and symbolic values, and the attributes are mapped directly from existing nonconformance documents. Although the earlier rule-based systems were inadequate, much of the domain knowledge collected for these systems was transferable to the case-based reasoning system. This approach expedited the construction of the case library and resulted in a fair trade-off between adjustment complexity and the number of cases.

Reason

The reasoning module consists of the *retrieve* and *adapt* submodules. The retrieval of previous similar nonconformances is guided by a set of determination rules that represent relevance information between particular nonconformance problems and sets of attributes. The purpose of the determination rules is to focus attention on previous nonconformances and resolutions that are most similar to the current problem. The determination rules are initially provided by experts. For example, an engineer often associates the problem "leaky valve of type X" with

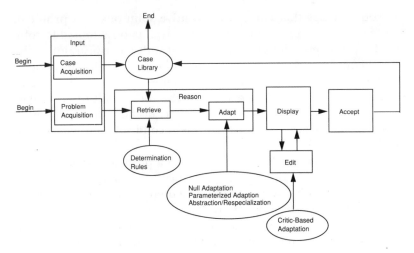

Figure 1. The System Architecture.

the manufacturer of the valve, and this additional piece of knowledge serves to narrow the selection of possibly applicable nonconformances.

Standard nonconformance solutions are stored in a secondary knowledge base, and determination rules can point to this knowledge rather than retrieve a similar, adaptable solution from the case library. This knowledge is the same as the usual investigatory procedures invoked for typical nonconformances.

Structural adaptation techniques are used to adapt the solution of a retrieved case to a target case. Three of the four adaptation techniques are automatically performed by the reasoning module: null adaptation, parameterized adaptation, and abstraction-respecialization.

Null adaptation occurs when determination rules point to a standard nonconformance solution in the secondary knowledge base.

Parameterized adaptation occurs when the system notices that a nonconformance is similar to a prior case in the case library whose solution variables vary proportionally with the variables in its problem definition. A new solution is proposed by adjusting the parameters of the old solution to comply with the requirements of the new problem. For example, some cases contain a variable X in the problem definition that represents the difference between the actual and desired amounts of pressure released through a valve, a variable Y in the solution that represents the number of quarter turns of an adjustment screw, and an equation relating X and Y. A similar valve with a similar problem, for which such an equation is unavailable, will use the equation in the source case to propose a solution to the new problem.

The abstraction-respecialization adaptation technique occurs over those source cases that contain alternative solutions to a problem. Some features of a problem impose constraints on admissible solutions. If a proposed solution is inconsistent with any constraint of the new problem, an alternative solution is proposed. A typical example is the failure of a valve for which the preferable solutions are to repair the valve (most preferred), replace the valve, or consult the manufacturer (least preferred). If during problem acquisition, the user indicated that the valve cannot be repaired, the second solution is proposed instead of the first.

Derivational adaptation techniques, in which a problem-solving strategy is applied to problem parameters of a current nonconformance, are under investigation but were not implemented in the system. Whereas structural adaptation techniques are simple and easy to understand by users, derivational techniques are relatively complex. It is suspected that the derivational technique will discourage users. For similar reasons, we did not use SMT as a similarity metric for retrieving cases.

Display

The display module redisplays the problem and offers possible solutions found by the reasoning module. The user examines the solutions and chooses to either edit a solution or accept one of the solutions offered.

Edit

Critic-based adaptation is used in the edit module when the user knows that the proposed solution is unacceptable and can modify the solution to make it fit the target case. For example, a particular manufacturer's valve cannot be repaired but must be replaced. In the source case, the manufacturer's name was not included in the description of the problem. Everything else being equal, the proposed solution was to repair the valve, which the user knew would not work. Thus, s/he changed the solution to "replace valve" and entered the manufacturer's name in the appropriate slot of the problem description. When the knowledge base is updated with this new information, the reasons why the original solution did not work become implicit in the new case.

Accept

Continuing the previous example, the accept module prints a nonconformance document and updates the case library with the new knowledge. The current method of knowledge update is to add the newly adapted case to the library. Ideally, the original case and the adapted case would be fused into a more general case that covers both problems. This subject is one for future research and development.

Deployment and Discussion of Benefits

In total, 10 person-years went into the development of the current system, some 5 of which were spent on the manufacturing and production engineering project developing the earlier rule-based systems, and 2 person-years were spent on the AI internal research and development project. At roughly $75,000 for each person-year, the application cost $750,000. The system was deployed by the second quarter of 1990. Currently, it is used in 3 of 6 engineering departments that are involved with some phase of fluid system construction. The number of users makes up approximately 2.5 percent of the total engineering force. To date, the system has been used on more than 200 atypical nonconformances. The return during the first year of use is estimated to be $240,000, based on the following calculations: Some 20,000 nonconformances were processed. The manual resolution of nonconformances takes 3 hours for each nonconformance, on the average. At an hourly rate of $40, this figure calculates to $2,400,000. Overall, the system reduced the average time to process a nonconformance by about 10 percent, as estimated by current users and management. Thus, the estimated return for the first year of deployment is $240,000. This figure does not reflect additional savings realized from reduced scheduling delays, nor does it reflect other benefits derived from the internal research and development and manufacturing and production engineering projects. For example, the internal research and development project resulted in proposals of AI solutions for other problems in ship manufacturing and command and control systems (in progress or under evaluation), and the early trial development work of the manufacturing and production engineering project was used as a resource for applications suited for rule-based systems.

Generally, the case-based reasoning system demonstrated an increasing robustness and flexibility that was missing in the earlier rule-based systems. Engineers appear to be more comfortable with case-based reasoning techniques than with rule-based techniques. A general lesson learned from our efforts is that an engineer is more likely to use X if s/he understands X. In contrast with the rule-based systems, the knowledge base for the case-based reasoning system is compiled and maintained by users, and the knowledge base is automatically updated during use. The current task of the manufacturing and production engineering project is to deploy similar systems for electric and structural systems and investigate coupling the systems with existing databases. As the systems become more widely deployed and as the case libraries expand with use, we hope to see our return increase exponentially.

References

Alterman, R. 1986. An Adaptive Planner. In Proceedings of the Fifth National Conference on Artificial Intelligence, 65–69. Menlo Park, Calif.: American Association for Artificial Intelligence.

Ashley, K., and Rissland, E. 1988. A Case-Based Approach to Modeling Legal Expertise. *IEEE Expert* 3(3): 70–76.

Bain, W. 1986. A Case-Based Reasoning System for Subjective Assessment. In Proceedings of the Fifth National Conference on Artificial Intelligence, 523–527. Menlo Park, Calif.: American Association for Artificial Intelligence.

Brown, S. 1990. Nonconformance Resolution Using Case-Based Reasoning, MRR-EB90-046, General Dynamics Electric Boat Division, Groton, Connecticut.

Carbonell, J. 1983. Learning by Analogy: Formulating and Generalizing Plans from Past Experience. In *Machine Learning: An Artificial Intelligence Approach*, eds. R. Michalski, J. Carbonell, and T. Mitchell, 137–161. San Mateo, Calif.: Morgan Kaufmann.

Daube, F., and Hayes-Roth, B. 1989. A Case-Based Mechanical Redesign System. In Proceedings of the Eleventh International Joint Conference on Artificial Intelligence, 1402–1407. Menlo Park, Calif.: International Joint Conferences on Artificial Intelligence.

Davies, T., and Russell, S. 1987. A Logical Approach to Reasoning by Analogy. In Proceedings of the Tenth International Joint Conference on Artificial Intelligence, 264–270. Menlo Park, Calif.: International Joint Conferences on Artificial Intelligence.

Gentner, D. 1983. Structure-Mapping: A Theoretical Framework for Analogy. *Cognitive Science* 7: 155–170.

Hammond, K. 1986. CHEF: A Model of Case-Based Planning. In Proceedings of the Fifth National Conference on Artificial Intelligence, 267–271. Menlo Park, Calif.: American Association for Artificial Intelligence.

Huhns, M., and Acosta, R. 1988. ARGO: A System for Design by Analogy. *IEEE Expert* 3(3): 53–68.

Kedar-Cabelli, S. 1986. Purpose-Directed Analogy: A Summary of Current Research. In *Machine Learning: A Guide to Current Research*, eds. T. Mitchell, J. Carbonell, and R. Michalski, 81–85. Boston: Kluwer.

Kolodner, J.; Simpson, R. L.; and Sycara-Cyranski, K. 1985. A Process Model of Case-Based Reasoning in Problem Solving. In Proceedings of the Ninth International Joint Conference on Artificial Intelligence,

284–290. Menlo Park, Calif.: International Joint Conferences on Artificial Intelligence.

Koton, P. 1988. Reasoning about Evidence in Causal Explanations. In Proceedings of the Eighth National Conference on Artificial Intelligence, 256–261. Menlo Park, Calif.: American Association for Artificial Intelligence.

Lewis, L. 1989. AI Technology Development Year-End Report, GDEB-ERR-EB89-024, General Dynamics Electric Boat Division, Groton, Connecticut.

Riesbeck, C., and Schank, R. 1989. *Inside Case-Based Reasoning*. Hillsdale, N.J.: Lawrence Erlbaum.

Rissland, E., and Ashley, K. 1986. Hypotheticals as Heuristic Device. In Proceedings of the Fifth National Conference on Artificial Intelligence, 289–297. Menlo Park, Calif.: American Association for Artificial Intelligence.

Rissland, E., and Skalak, D. 1989a. Case-Based Reasoning in a Rule-Governed Domain. In Proceedings of the Fifth IEEE Conference on AI Applications, 46–53. Washington, D.C.: IEEE Computer Society.

Rissland, E., and Skalak, D. 1989b. Combining Case-Based and Rule-Based Reasoning: A Heuristic Approach. In Proceedings of the Eleventh International Joint Conference on Artificial Intelligence, 524–530. Menlo Park, Calif.: International Joint Conferences on Artificial Intelligence.

Simoudis, E., and Miller, J. 1990. Validated Retrieval in Case-Based Reasoning. In Proceedings of the Eighth National Conference on Artificial Intelligence, 310–317. Menlo Park, Calif.: American Association for Artificial Intelligence.

Slade, S. 1991. Case-Based Reasoning: A Research Paradigm. *AI Magazine* 12(1): 42–55.

Stottler, R.; Henke, A.; and King, J. 1989. Rapid Retrieval Algorithms for Case-Based Reasoning. In Proceedings of the Eleventh International Joint Conference on Artificial Intelligence, 233–237. Menlo Park, Calif.: International Joint Conferences on Artificial Intelligence.

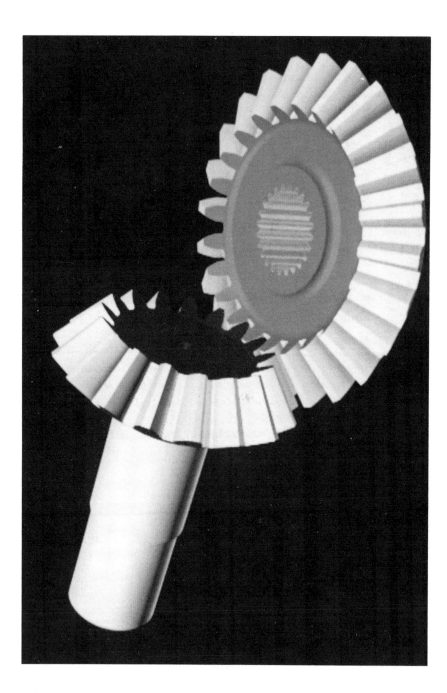

Intelligent Decision Support for Assembly System Design

J. A. Hernandez, T. J. Peters, D. E. Whitney, S. C. Luby,
R. E. Gustavson, H. W. Leung, P. M. Hutchins, T. L. De Fazio,
J. L. Nevins, A. C. Edsall, R. W. Metzinger, and K. K. Tung

The design of an assembly system is a complex problem, often requiring large teams of engineers with significant experience and expertise. Based on studies of the product design, these teams must select an assembly sequence, generate a corresponding process plan, identify the resources capable of completing the tasks in the process plan, and group these resources into a system of workstations to accomplish the required assembly operations. The resulting system must be economically viable but have sufficient capacity to meet production requirements.

The successful, timely design of such an assembly system depends on the team's ability to effectively share and communicate large volumes of information and have rapid feedback concerning cost, producibility, quality, and other important engineering criteria. Unfortunately, few available tools focus on fabrication or assembly: Those tools that do are often unable to share data. As a result, design teams are forced to do much of the work manually and are unable to effectively share information. Even large manufacturers find their teams spending considerable efforts just to enter the same data into multiple computer systems.

Much work has been done to address various aspects of the assembly system design problem. For example, systems have been developed for modeling (Dixon 1988; Pratt and Wilson 1985; Luby, Dixon, and Simmons 1986), assembly design (Boothroyd and Dewhurst 1987), sequence selection (Lui 1988; Homem de Mello 1989), process planning (Delchambre, Coupez, and Gaspart 1989), and assembly line design (Gustavson 1988; Graves and Holmes 1988; Cooprider 1989). As a result, much has been learned about these particular areas. However, little work has been done to integrate these systems. Work on integrating these systems has required limiting assumptions, such as the use of embedded domain-specific knowledge (Sriram et al. 1989), or application to parametric products only (Phillips and Aase 1990).

The goal of this work is to provide assembly system design teams with an integrated environment that is capable of intelligent decision support for work on complex assemblies. The system was developed through the combined efforts of a group of software developers and a team of electric, industrial, and mechanical engineers. The engineers have worked on design and assembly for 20 years, doing both basic research and consulting work with several large manufacturers. The choice of functions for the system was driven by the engineers' need for a set of tools to handle recurring problems in their consulting work. The tools address issues that occur over a wide range of industries and that are critical to the design of technically sound, yet economical assembly systems.

Cognitive Model

In addition to the basic functions, we felt it important for the system to incorporate basic principles of cognitive modeling. We identified five principles that have a strong impact on the flexibility and usability of the system. According to these principles, the system should perform five functions: First, the system should use the designer's customary vocabulary, thus raising discourse to the conceptual level and making design more natural. The result is an increase in user productivity and a decrease in the probability of errors because complex calculations are automatically done by the computer. Second, the system should provide incentives for the user, for example, permitting the creation of designs that will stand scrutiny on design for manufacturing and assembly and cost criteria. This approach will assist users in learning appropriate methodologies and motivate them by providing rapid, positive feedback. Third, the system should maintain a record of the user's intent in making design decisions. This information can be used at a later time to understand the varied and complicated interactions among different aspects of the design. In addition, we are investigating knowledge representation schemes that can make the designer's intent accessible to application modules for analysis and recommendations. Fourth, the system should allow the user a choice of techniques and methodologies to follow. This function lets the user explore various approaches to a problem, which could lead to alternate problem formulations and better solutions. Fifth, the system should support modules that are themselves stand-alone systems, providing users with flexibility on how to use the system.

These five principles, together with the functional requirements, led us to the development of the architecture shown in figure 1. The system consists of six major modules: a feature-based modeler, a constraint-identification module, an assembly sequence selection module, a process planner, an assembly system synthesis module, and an economic analysis module.

The *feature-based modeler* allows the user to construct a product design that includes assembly information that indicates the mating relations between the parts. The *constraint-identification module* then uses this information, together with the results of a guided question-answer session with the designer, to determine constraints on the assembly process. Once all the constraints are known, the designer can invoke the *assembly sequence generator*, which generates the search space of all the feasible assembly sequences. The designer can then prune the sequences through the use of various automated techniques or manual editing. An *assembly process plan* can then be generated for each selected sequence. Each task in the plan includes information on part and subassembly orientation, size, weight, and relative task difficulty. This information can be used by the *assembly system design module* (Gustavson 1988) to select assembly resources and create a least cost system to meet required production rates and investment targets.

The user can begin with any module or can bypass the use of any module and let the system act as an expert to generate solutions to the modules being bypassed. Moreover, the user can investigate alternatives by studying the effects of making revisions to the original design, selecting a different assembly sequence, or changing cost and production requirements.

In the rest of this chapter, we discuss each of these modules using a moderately complex design to demonstrate the capabilities of the system. Then, we place the work in perspective and discuss related research.

The system combines a variety of technologies; is implemented in I-DEAS, Lisp, and C; and runs on Sun 3 workstations. I-DEAS provides a strong computer-aided design (CAD) environment over which we were able to build a feature-based modeler. C is used for modules requiring many computations but no symbolic processing. The major portion of

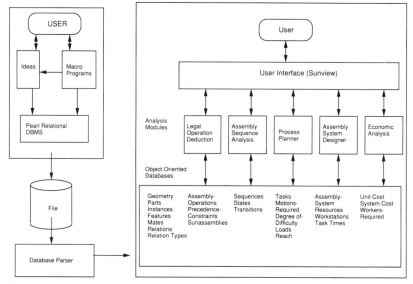

Figure 1. System Architecture.

the system is written in Lisp to support an object-oriented database representation of both product and economic information and support symbolic reasoning. We chose to use only one platform to avoid networking issues.

Building the Product Model

Our approach to product modeling begins with *feature-based design*, a technique that permits designers to express design intent while they create the product geometry (Dixon 1988; Pratt and Wilson 1985). This approach both requires and permits the designer to think beyond mere shape and explicitly state what portions of a part are important and why. In addition, feature-based design brings modeling closer to the user's conceptual level, making design more natural. It also results in a format that is well suited to object-oriented technologies, making it simple for the program to reason about the design to generate and evaluate assembly plans.

Feature-Based Design

We developed a feature-level parts and assembly modeler on top of the I-DEAS package using SDRC, Inc.'s, IDEAL programming language and PEARL relational database facility. This feature-based modeling layer al-

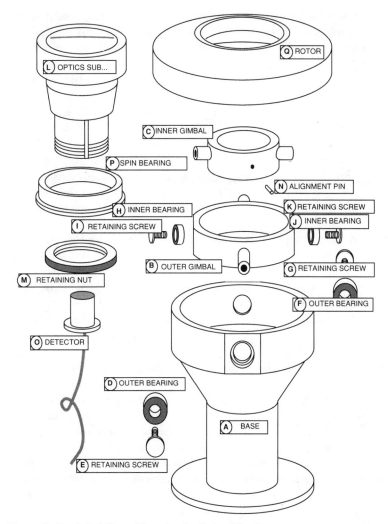

Figure 2. Exploded Parts View for the Seeker Head.

lows a user to create geometry using higher-level commands and builds a database of feature-level information as the user works on a design. The downstream analysis applications (assembly process analysis and economic evaluations) can then access this database and reason about the designer's intent.

The feature-level modeler is divided into two main modes: part modeling and assembly modeling. In *part modeling*, the designer can create product components as generic pieces of geometry that are augmented and modified by subsequent feature modeling. Each component can have multiple instances. For example, a ⅜-inch bearing part can have a left and right instance with unique names and positioning. The designer can also build components out of features that are represented by existing geometry. This capability handles cases where it is simpler to create some geometry using primitive solids (for example, by revolving a profile) or allow for feature types (for example, Flats) not easily created from primitive solids. Once the basic part data are entered, the modeler computes further information required for the application modules, for example, assembly weight, assembly center of gravity, assembly bounding box, and feature reference directions.

Figure 2 shows an exploded parts view of an 17-part product we used as a test case. It is the mechanical structure of a generic seeker head, a complex component of tactical air-to-air missiles.

After creating the parts, the user switches to the *assembly modeler* and defines the assembly as a set of mated part instances. In this way, the assembly topology is explicitly described by simply specifying the mates between component part instances. The system uses the database information about reference directions and locations of the features to align parts in their proper relative location and orientation for the final assembly state of the product. Figure 3 shows a cross-sectional view of the final assembled product.

The designer is also able to provide information about interface features. For example, is a mate composed of a spline in a through hole or a peg in a blind hole? Typical assembly information provided by the user includes feature-mate type, presence of lubricants or adhesives, and permission to grip on the feature or attach a fixture on the feature.

During modeling, the program layer builds a database of the higher-level part and assembly information using the I-DEAS PEARL relational database facility. After modeling, this database is downloaded to the rest of the system and converted into an object database. The system then uses this information to find clearances and degrees of freedom for mates, relative extraction directions for mating features, and total weight and bounding-box size for the product and all subassemblies and distances between features on different parts.

Assembly Information

Based on the information contained in the database downloaded from the feature-based modeler, the system generates a graph of all mates that connect parts in the assembly. Because mating features are linked by mating relations, and features have links to corresponding assembly parts, the system can traverse these links to identify all mates between

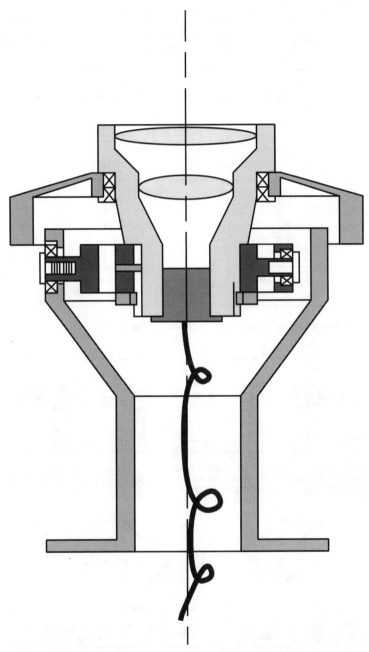

Figure 3. Cross-Sectional View of the Assembled Seeker Head.

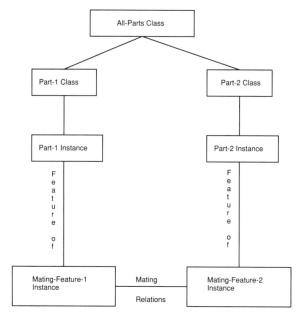

Figure 4. Representation of Relations between Components.

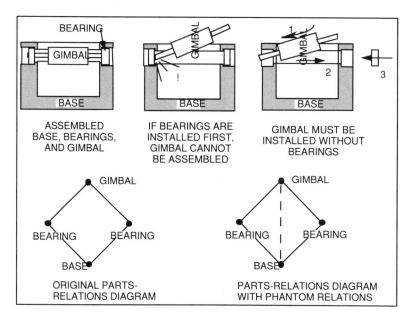

Figure 5. Assembly of Parts That Do Not Directly Mate.

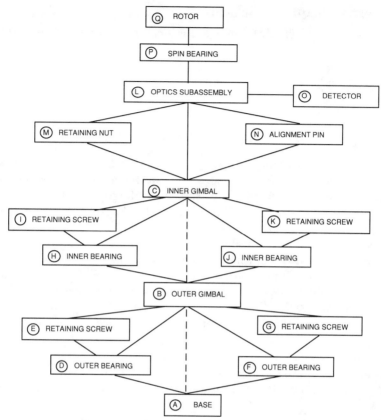

Figure 6. Parts Relation Graph for the Seeker Head.

components. Figure 4 demonstrates the representation of mates between assembly parts as relations on the corresponding part features.

In addition, it can happen that the relation between parts that do
not mate with each other must also be added to the graph. This situation occurs when temporary fixtures are necessary to align one of the
parts with an existing subassembly that contains a second part. This approach is sometimes necessary for full product assembly to be possible.
Figure 5 demonstrates this situation for the gimbal and base components of the seeker head.

The graph showing all mating and nonmating relations between
seeker head assembly components is shown in figure 6. Note that the
graph consists of 24 mating relations and 2 nonmating relations. There
is 1 nonmating relation between the inner gimbal and the outer gimbal and 1 between the outer gimbal and the base.

Assembly Sequence Selection

The choice of assembly sequence is critical to the proper design of an assembly system. The system provides the user with a choice of modes to use for sequence selection: The *assistant mode* gives the user full flexibility in exploring alternate sequences, and the *expert mode* uses heuristics to automatically select a sequence for the user. Alternatively, the user can directly enter a sequence.

Representation

Figure 7 shows a graphic display of some partial feasible assembly sequences for the seeker head. Each node in the graph represents an assembly state. The node in row 0 (starting at the top of the figure) represents the null assembly, and the node in the last row (not shown, but this terminal node would have all its cells blackened) represents the completed assembly. Consecutive assembly states are represented as nodes linked by accomplished relations. Each path from row 0 to the bottom row identifies a unique assembly sequence. Figure 7 depicts only a small percentage of all the assembly sequences. The full diagram for the seeker header contained 15 rows, the widest row contained 34 columns, and the total number of possible sequences exceeded 20,000.

Assembly Constraints

Three major constraint categories were identified for assemblies (Homem de Mello 1988). *Geometric-feasibility* constraints require collision-free paths joining subassemblies. *Mechanical-feasibility* constraints require the establishment of attachments acting on contacts of the subassembly decompositions. Finally, *stability constraints* require that subassemblies maintain their relative position and do not spontaneously break contact.

Many of the geometric and mechanical constraints can be determined from the relations among parts and the mating directions, but the automatic generation of all the constraints inevitably requires a general solution to three-dimensional path planning.

Because the designer can usually solve such problems almost instantly if shown a sufficiently realistic drawing of the product parts, we chose to involve the user to obtain assembly constraint information that cannot logically be deduced from the features (Baldwin et al. 1991). This task is accomplished by guiding the user through an illustrated question-answer dialogue. The number of questions asked of the designer varies considerably from product to product; for the seeker, 58 questions were asked. The computer answered 20,3754 other questions itself using feature information.

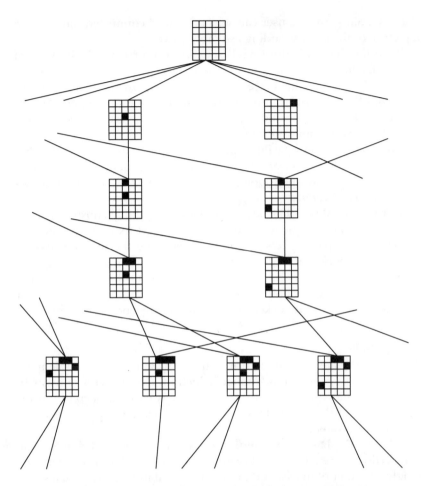

Figure 7. Some Partial Assembly Sequences for the Seeker.

Assistant Mode

The assistant mode first generates the search space of all physically possible assembly sequences (Lui 1988). This set consists of all sequences meeting the geometric and mechanical feasibility constraints. The search space can contain tens of thousands of sequences even for products of only moderate complexity and part count. Therefore, it is crucial to provide the user with utilities to navigate through this search space and tools for pruning it to a manageable size. The user can become acquainted with the possible assembly sequences by scanning and zooming options for the display. In addition, by selecting a state on the graph, the user can see a picture of the assembly represented by the state. Similarly, the user can select a pair of connected states to see a picture of the corresponding assembly move.

Once familiar with the search space, the user can edit it. Manual editing facilities allow the user to delete states, transitions, or entire sequences from the state space. The user can also prune the space by specifying logical constraints on the system, for example, constraints that require that a specified group of mates not be established simultaneously or require an ordering on mates.

Automated pruning facilities permit pruning at a coarser scale. Possibilities include the automatic elimination of sequences representing equivalent assembly line topologies (that is, have the same part groupings) (Amblard 1989).

A program (Abell 1989) also addresses the stability constraint problem and finds the sequences requiring the fewest fixtures and reorientations. This capability lets the designer evaluate the inherent cost of fixture and reorientation operations required by the given design. By using these tools, the designer can thoroughly consider the possibilities and arrive at a reasonable set of sequences in less than an hour for products similar to the seeker head in complexity and part count.

Expert Mode

As part of a related research effort, one of the authors also implemented an expert system for sequence selection. The process consists of three main steps: First, a base component is chosen. Second, an exploded view of the assembly is established. Finally, a sequence is incrementally generated.

To select the base component, the system goes beyond simple mate count (Ko and Lee 1987) and reasons about the trade-off between size, weight, number of mates, and difficulty of establishing these mates.

The exploded view of the assembly is then generated using the information obtained from the feature-based modeler. This step generalizes the approach used for uniaxial products (Kroll, Lenz, and Wolberg 1989a, 1989b) and requires determining each component's assembly direction with respect to the base component. The component's relations (that is, mates), final assembly location, geometric center, and bounding box are used to make this determination. The result is an ordering of all components along the six possible three-dimensional directions.

From the exploded view, the assembly sequence can be determined. The program uses the heuristic that assembly should proceed along only one direction at a time whenever possible. This approach avoids reorientations. In addition, the sequence must meet the geometric, mechanical, and stability constraints previously discussed.

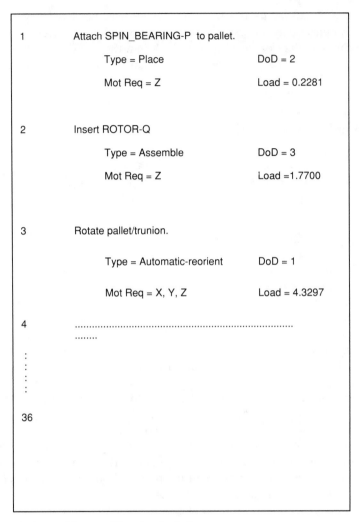

1	Attach SPIN_BEARING-P to pallet.		
	Type = Place	DoD = 2	
	Mot Req = Z	Load = 0.2281	
2	Insert ROTOR-Q		
	Type = Assemble	DoD = 3	
	Mot Req = Z	Load =1.7700	
3	Rotate pallet/trunion.		
	Type = Automatic-reorient	DoD = 1	
	Mot Req = X, Y, Z	Load = 4.3297	
4	....		
⋮			
36			

Figure 8. Partial Process Plan for the Seeker.

Assembly Process Planner

The assembly process planner builds a complete assembly plan for the sequences previously selected. Additional steps added by the process planner include orientation, attachment of fixtures, application of adhesives, oven curing of adhesives, and torquing of bolts. Moreover, each step in the process plan contains load, reach, and motion requirements. Heuristics determine task difficulty based on type of mate, sizes and weights of parts, and number of features that mate simultaneously.

The data necessary to add this information can be determined from the geometric features and information supplied by the designer. Figure 8 shows a plan for the seeker head. When the software finishes generating the process plan, the designer can review it and make any changes desired.

Assembly System Designer

The last step accomplished by the system is to convert the assembly process plan into a list of equipment and tools together with the plan steps that each piece of equipment will accomplish. The resulting plan should result in the lowest unit cost of assembly.

Candidate Equipment Selection

The system selects candidate equipment capable of completing the steps in the process plan. Possible equipment includes manual assembly, maintenance, robots, and conventional fixed-assembly automation. The selection process is carried out heuristically, using multiple sources of information as constraints on equipment costs and speeds. For example, bounding-box size of subassemblies, weight of parts, and type of mate are used to identify constraints on the type of equipment required. Larger, heavier parts might require longer reach or more stability and might use more costly equipment, more assembly time, or both. The estimated task difficulty is also used to rule out certain types of equipment and determine equipment cost. Finally, economic and production data, such as cost of labor, desired annual production quantity, and information on investment return requirements, are used as filters on equipment cost and speed. See Allan et al. (1990) for more information. The system also reasons about the trade-offs in cost, time, and flexibility arising from the assignment of several tasks to flexible equipment such as manual labor or robots that can do more than one task.

Feasible Workstations

A *workstation* is defined as a resource that can perform consecutive tasks. Feasible workstations can perform all their tasks within the maximum time allowable by system demand. The system finds all feasible workstations by taking into account the yearly production demand, the cycle time required for the workstation to complete each of its tasks, the time required to change tools, the time incurred in moving partial assemblies along workstations, and the amount of extra time the workstation needs for maintenance and repairs.

Assembly System Synthesis

The optimal solution can be calculated by finding the least cost combination of feasible workstations that can complete the product assembly.[1] The system searches the space of solutions incrementally by building the solution table for the system, beginning with the solution table for the null process plan. Solution tables (ST) are built from the workstations (WT) using the following relationships:

$$ST_0 = \phi$$

$$ST_i = \text{Merge}_{j=0}^{j-1} \left[ST_j + WT_{j+1, i-j} \right]$$

In these equations, the first index specifies the initial task of each workstation, and the second index specifies the number of tasks accomplished by the workstation. The merge function takes the lower envelope of the graph of the cost curves.

If the resulting solution table for the entire process plan is null, then no assembly system design can complete the process plan. This incomplete action can occur when there is a particular task that cannot be accomplished quickly enough by any resource to meet demand.

To find the optimal system, the solution table is scanned for the cycle time that minimizes the total system cost. This time corresponds to the workstation operation time that minimizes total system cost. For each workstation, the resulting plan identifies the resource used, the tasks performed, and the costs incurred. In addition, the user is provided with system characteristics, including production rate and capacity, number of shifts, unit cost, and system cost. Figure 9 shows the system design for the seeker.

This system is guaranteed to be least cost for single-resource workstations. However, the overall least cost system can include workstations with more than one resource. To find this system, the least cost single-resource workstation system is used as a benchmark. Then, each workstation cost table is repeatedly modified to reflect the addition of an extra copy of the original resource. When the total cost for each workstation exceeds the original benchmark, the augmented tables are combined. The resulting system is guaranteed to have the overall least cost. The previous procedure can be expensive computationally. Therefore, we have been considering modifying it to test the difference in cost for the workstations after each iteration. The process can then be terminated as soon as the difference gets small enough to be insignificant instead of waiting until the new workstation cost exceeds the benchmark. This technique would yield a near least cost system

Station	Begin-task	End-task	Resource	H-cost	T-cost
1	1	4	Prog	45000	98941
2	5	9	Fixed	0	77424
3	10	14	Prog	50000	115914
4	15	19	Prog	45000	104609
5	20	24	Prog	50000	113645
6	25	29	Manual	200	233892
7	30	34	Manual	200	233183
8	35	35	Fixed	0	60176
9	36	36	Manual	200	144805

Number of shifts	1.00	shifts
Unit costs	11.83	$
System cost	384546.54	$
Production rate	48.11	units/hr
Production capacity	277119.85	units/yr
Utilization	8.36	%
Number of stations	9.00	stations

Figure 9. Partial Final Assembly System for the Seeker.

that would be within acceptable limits of accuracy. Moreover, this limit could dynamically be set by the system user.

System Evaluation

The system described in this chapter provides users with an intelligent decision support environment linking feature-based modeling, computer-aided process planning, and assembly system design. The system required an effort of approximately eight person-years—four to develop the specifications for meeting the needs of the engineering team and four to implement and test.

The modules from the system have been used in consulting work on major industrial products both separately and in various combinations. We find that using the system results in increased productivity. Moreover, the ability to work on separate modules using a centralized database provides consistency of information and results in significant time savings.

Therefore, the engineering team is able to reduce the time required to evaluate product designs and recommend factory designs.

Our feature-based interface allows a complex sequence of solid modeling Boolean commands to be replaced by a single feature creation command, such as "insert chamfered hole." Subjective evidence with this simplified interface supports time savings in the model creation process. Furthermore, when features are used as a knowledge representation, considerable time savings can be achieved in downstream processes.

For example, in the seeker head example cited in the subsection on assembly constraints, the features were an essential knowledge representation for the automatic generation of geometric and mechanical constraints. The presence of these constraints allowed a reduction in the question count requiring user response from 203,754 to 58. Assuming that a typical question requires 15 seconds for a human response, the corresponding time reduction is from approximately 21 person-weeks to 14 person-minutes.

Our only analysis of the seeker head used our intelligent decision support system. We do not have time estimates regarding the seeker head without such assistance. However, such benchmark information is provided by an example assembly (De Fazio and Whitney 1987); this assembly is named *assembly from industry* (AFI). Furthermore, its complexity is roughly comparable to that of the seeker head, so we contend that it provides for a consistent comparison. A user of our system was able to select a preferred AFI assembly sequence within an hour. Previously, the required time was approximately eight person-weeks.

The cumulative efficiency gains can be translated into substantial direct monetary savings. Totaling the time savings as approximately 30 person-weeks and assuming that the analysis would be performed by a specialized consultant at a cost of $1,000 each day, a direct savings of $150,000 could be realized. Moreover, there are hidden yet significant savings that are difficult to directly represent in terms of dollars.

The richly expressive feature-based interface is much more natural for mechanical designers than the formal Boolean operators of solid modeling. This approach not only gives the designer greater confidence in a complex model but also permits verification of the functional aspects of the design.

The factor of 21 person-weeks of human interaction is so obviously prohibitive that in practice, all such constraint questions are not answered in the absence of our intelligent decision support system. However, the attendant cost is that the assembly system design is based less on comprehensive analysis and more on the designer's personal heuristics (often unarticulated), running the risk that a preferred assembly system design can be overlooked because of the complexity of the analysis. Thus, our system permits comprehensive analysis on assembly systems of greater complexity than might otherwise be attempted.

Each of the time savings cited can have a ripple effect through the product process cycle. All savings were achieved within the conceptual phase of the assembly system design. Hence, the entire product manufacturing cycle can begin earlier. Furthermore, the rigor of the analysis argues that the assembly system design is "right the first time." The attendant savings by avoiding redesign and rework can easily total months or even years. Recently, Boeing was able to able to utilize a digital preassembly method to halve the number of design changes required during production (Stix 1991). This preassembly software was far less sophisticated than our intelligent support systems. In fact, the Boeing software included only vendor available CAD tools, with no intelligent aids. Our more sophisticated system should provide even greater dividends.

In fact, the considerations of the subsection on assembly system synthesis will permit an optimal assembly system. Many existing assembly systems perform reasonably well but are not optimal. Their deviations from optimality can be so subtle that they are not even noticed by trained observers. However, this subobtimality reflects a real cost that is compounded over the life cycle of the assembly system. In summary, this intelligent decision support system can provide a significant competitive advantage in an arena where time to market is often the most critical variable in the success of a product.

An additional benefit is that the engineers report a greater level of confidence in their findings. By taking advantage of rapid feedback from the system, the engineers are able to explore alternate assembly opportunities, discover assembly problems inherent in the design, and correct them at an early stage. Finally, because only the cost models need to be updated to reflect industry-specific variations, the system is easily maintainable by industrial engineers with little if any assistance from knowledge engineers.

Future Work

An interesting opportunity is to enhance the functions of the system with other, existing technologies. Important work has been done on assembly design using both quantitative and qualitative techniques (Laszcz 1984; Poli and Fenoglio 1987; Boothroyd and Dewhurst 1983). These techniques could be added as a critic component that suggests improvements to the design created through the modeler. Because these techniques can lead to conflicting recommendations, the system can evaluate the suggestions using final system cost as the determining factor in deciding among conflicts. By using an intelligent control mechanism, the system could then iterate through this process, resolving conflicts among sets of recommended design changes to find the optimal set of improvements to the product design.

A research area of particular interest is the development of algorithms for deciding among alternate testing strategies (Pappu 1989). The choice of testing strategies has a significant impact on the design of an assembly system. In particular, in-process testing of partially completed assemblies can help detect problems sooner and more easily. This approach leads to earlier, simpler, less expensive repairs. However, choosing an appropriate strategy is a complex problem. It requires reasoning about trade-offs among the likelihood of failures, the cost of test equipment, the cost and time of repairs, and the interaction of test capabilities with possible failures. Further complications arise because some tests are not able to determine the causes of failures. Also, certain failures can only be detected after full assembly. Further empirical and theoretical work is needed to develop algorithms for making the correct choice.

An objective method to quantify total time saved would be to develop two assembly system designs—one using our system and the other not. Our fiscal constraints argued strongly against such an experiment. Thus, our measures of time savings were based on less comprehensive data. Although we believe that the examples cited are indicative of substantial time savings, it would still be instructive to conduct such a comprehensive experiment.

In summary, the system provides a robust, flexible, integrated environment for the design of assembly systems. The system has had the benefit of being useful for practical work. We believe the system provides users with a unique environment for making sophisticated decisions across many levels of the product life cycle. In the future, we hope to continue to increase the capabilities of the system.

Acknowledgments

The authors would like to thank C. S. Draper Laboratory for supporting the project and permitting those authors who have left the laboratory since this work was done to write this chapter. The authors also gratefully acknowledge the generosity of the researchers of the Alpha_1 Modeling System, University of Utah, Salt Lake City, Utah, for providing the chapter cover illustration depicting mating features in an assembly.

Note

1. See Cooprider (1989) for a good discussion of generic cost functions and Allan et al. (1990) for a more specialized study in the space industry.

References

Abell, T. E. 1989. An Interactive Tool for Editing and Evaluating Mechanical Assembly Sequences Based on Fixturing and Orientation Requirements," Master's thesis, Mechanical Engineering Dept., Massachusetts Institute of Technology.

Allan, D. C.; Denktsis, G. F.; Eppinger, S. D.; and Jakiela, M. J. 1990. An Engineering Model for Predicting Manufacturing Costs of Aerospace Components. Presented at the ASME Winter Annual Meeting, Dallas, Tex., 25–30 November.

Amblard, A. G. P. 1989. Rationale for the Use of Subassemblies in Production Systems. Master's thesis, Operations Research Program, Massachusetts Institute of Technology.

Baldwin, D. F.; Abell, T. E.; Lui, M-C M.; De Fazio, T. L.; and Whitney, D. E. 1991. An Integrated Computer Aid for Generating and Evaluating Assembly Sequences for Mechanical Parts. *IEEE Transactions on Robotics and Automation* 7(2): 78–94.

Boothroyd, G., and Dewhurst, P. 1987. *Product Design for Assembly*. Wakefield R.I.: Boothroyd and Dewhurst, Inc.

Boothroyd, G., and Dewhurst, P. 1983. Design for Assembly: A Designer's Handbook, Dept. of Mechanical Engineering, Univ. of Massachusetts.

Cooprider, C. B. 1989. Equipment Selection and Assembly System Design under Multiple Cost Scenarios, Master's thesis, Sloan School of Management, Massachusetts Institute of Technology.

De Fazio, T. L., and Whitney, D. E. 1987. Simplified Generation of All Mechanical Assembly Sequences. *IEEE Journal of Robotics and Automation* 3: 640–658.

Delchambre, A.; Coupez, D.; and Gaspart, P. 1989. Knowledge-Based Process Planning in Robotized Assembly. Presented at the SPIE Conference on Applications of Artificial Intelligence VII, Orlando, Fla., 27–31 March.

Dixon, J. 1988. Designing with Features: Building Manufacturing Knowledge into More Intelligent CAD Systems. In Proceedings of Manufacturing International, 51–57. Fairfield, N.J.: American Society of Mechanical Engineers.

Graves, S. C., and Holmes, C. H. 1988. Equipment Selection and Task Assignment for Multiproduct Assembly System Design. *International Journal of Flexible Manufacturing Systems* 1(1): 31–50.

Gustavson, R. E. 1988. Design of Cost-Effective Assembly Systems. Presented at Successful Planning and Implementation of Flexible Assembly Systems, Ann Arbor, Mich., 29–31 March.

Homem de Mello, L. S. 1989. Task Sequence Planning for Robotic Assembly. Ph.D. diss., Robotics Institute, Carnegie Mellon Univ.

Homem de Mello, L. S. 1988. Automatic Generation of Mechanical Assembly Sequences, Technical Report, CMU-RI-TR-88-19, Carnegie-Mellon Univ.

Ko, H., and Lee, K. 1987. Automatic Assembly Procedure from Mating Conditions. *Computer-Aided Design* 19:3–10.

Kroll, E.; Lenz, E.; and Wolberg, J. 1989a. A Knowledge-Based Solution to the Design-for-Assembly Problem. *Manufacturing Review* 1(2): 104–108.

Kroll, E.; Lenz, E.; and Wolberg, J. 1989b. Rule-Based Generation of Exploded Views and Assembly Sequences. *Artificial Intelligence for Engineering, Design, Analysis, and Manufacturing* 3(3): 143–155.

Laszcz, J. F. 1984. Product Design for Robotic and Automatic Assembly. In Proceedings of the Robots 8 Conference, 6.1–6.22. New York: Society of Manufacturing Engineers.

Luby, S. C.; Dixon, J. R.; and Simmons, M. K. 1986. Designing with Features: Creating and Using a Features Database for Evaluation of Manufacturability of Castings. *Computers in Mechanical Engineering* 5(3): 25–33.

Lui, M-C. M. 1988. Generation and Evaluation of Mechanical Assembly Sequences Using the Liaison Sequence Method. Master's thesis, Mechanical Engineering Department, Massachusetts Institute of Technology.

Pappu, S. 1989. A Dual Descent Algorithm for Finding the Optimal Test Strategy for an Assembly Sequence. Master's thesis, Operations Research Center, Massachusetts Institute of Technology.

Phillips, R. E., and Aase, J. 1990. An Integrated Environment for Concurrent Engineering. In Proceedings of the Second National Symposium on Concurrent Engineering, 487–499. Morgantown, W. Va.: Concurrent Engineering Research Center.

Poli, C., and Fenoglio, F. 1987. Designing Parts for Automatic Assembly. *Machine Design* 59(29): 140–145.

Pratt, M. J., and Wilson, P. H. 1985. Requirements for Support of Form Features in a Solid Modeling System, Final Report R-85-ASPP-01, CAM-I, Inc., Arlington, Texas.

Sriram, D.; Logcher, R. D.; Groleau, N.; and Cherneff, J. 1989. DICE: An Object-Oriented Programming Environment for Cooperative Engineering Design, Industrial Liaison Program Report, Massachusetts Institute of Technology.

Stix, G. 1991. Plane Geometry. *Scientific American* 264(3): 110–111.

Putting Knowledge-Based Concepts to Work for Mechanical Design

Ian C. Campbell, Kris J. Luczynski, and Steve K. Hood

CAMES (computer-aided mechanical expert system) is a tool for automatically designing material-handling equipment used in pulp and paper mills. Operational since 1988, it has designed over 700 machines in a total of 5 classes and, consequently, has influenced our principles for deploying all knowledge-based systems. Because it is being extended to other machines within our group of companies, it is becoming more closely integrated with other knowledge-based and conventional systems.

Principles for Deployment of Knowledge-Based Systems

The deployment of knowledge-based systems in our corporation follows some principles that are still evolving; the development of these principles is more important than the development of any individual system. The principles are that (1) we will develop knowledge-based applications that are directly in line with our corporate goals, strategies, and critical success factors; (2) knowledge-based applications must be introduced into our corporation slowly but surely, so that they neither are rejected by our organization nor destroy valuable aspects of our culture; (3) the corporate computing environment must encourage knowledge-based development; and (4) knowledge-based application must be under the direct control of the line operating manager who will most greatly benefit.

Prior History and the Current Environment

This chapter continues the case history of several expert systems, all intended to improve our company's ability to give well-rounded responses to customer needs by improving mechanical and electrical engineering specifications, engineering productivity, design quality, and proposal preparation. Our ultimate knowledge-based–engineering goal is to use less human effort to make our corporation more responsive to customer needs, thereby ensuring a more profitable corporation. Previous work on a programmable logic controller (PLC) system (CALES) is described in Campbell and Bukshteyn (1990). CAPES (computer-aided proposal expert system) is a proposal-preparation system that is dependent on the CALES and CAMES systems (so we know the proposed system is preengineered and, therefore, can accurately be costed and priced). An early version of CAPES is partially deployed. These knowledge-based systems are in direct alignment with our first principle and our corporate goals, strategies, and critical success factors (which are not included in this chapter for space considerations).

All these knowledge-based systems are being moved into an environment with a parallel Common Lisp object system (CLOS) on the corporate computer. This computer is a four-processor Sequent S27, which is the corporate fourth-generation language platform, running Informix. Integration between CLOS and Informix is by standard query language (SQL) calls. To implement the Information Technology Department's (ITD) first strategy—to contribute to "cross-functional and geographic integration"—CAMES and CALES are being ported to the corporate computer system, a Sequent S27 with 5 Sequent S3 computers operating an enterprisewide 56 kilobit/second networking environment. This architecture, supporting standards that include the X Window system, UNIX, TCP/IP, CLOS, and SQL, will help solve many integration problems between sales, engineering, business, and knowledge-based systems and is part of the implementation of ITD's basic mission. This hardware design partially implements our third principle, that the corporate computing environment must encourage knowledge-based development.

The Original Problem Defined

In 1986, some apparently intractable business problems were starting to hurt mechanical design sections of the company. Our company is located in a small western town, and skilled design engineers for pulp or paper machinery were hard to find. A continued corporate strategy of selling highly customized solutions to large, complex problems in the pulp and paper industry helped with our sales success but created internal problems and the need to improve engineering productivity and quality. These problems seemed intractable because inexperienced engineers, like all professionals, tend to make errors, and we simply could not afford to retain a full complement of human expertise from one business cycle to another, when the whole relearning cycle would start again. Therefore, we saw a need and an opportunity to transfer engineering knowledge between business cycles by using a knowledge-based system. We hoped that CAMES could make an impact on mechanical engineering productivity during the current business cycle (1985–1991). However, even if it did not, we thought CAMES would at least pay for its own development. Ultimately, our company would be able to handle more work with the same number of engineers, or if we were forced to lay off engineers, and business subsequently improved, we would not have to hire as many inexperienced staff members during the next business cycle.

Description of the AI Technology Used in the Application

This section describes the technology used in the CAMES system. We examine our decision to use Lisp and our initial problems with object-oriented Lisp, the design concept and the selection of the first machine to design, and initial problems.

The Decision to Use Lisp

One lesson learned from our CALES experience was that the Lisp environment contains a powerful development tool. We were prepared to attack problems in a rapid prototyping way without any clear plan of how we would handle the later parts of a large problem. We believed that if, as electrical or mechanical engineers, we could handle the engineering problems, then as Lisp programmers, we would be able to encode our mental processes after reasonable work. We knew we could not or would not explain our expertise to computer programmers, but we could and would explain it to a computer. This method avoided the serious problems of an uncooperative prima donna or an arrogant expert, the expert who is too busy, the expert who is inconsistent and has to be told so, or conflicting experts getting into a fight. We were all these things, so we just talked to ourselves a lot.

Our answer to the problem of selecting a development language was partly new and partly old: object-oriented programming using Lisp. Implementing this decision was slow but steady and illustrates our second principle, that important knowledge-based ideas be introduced only as quickly as the culture can accept them. We considered and rejected the use of rule-based systems after learning that serious software users were reporting problems of excessive complexity when the number of rules exceeded 1,000 or so. Conventional programming languages were too inflexible. Fearing that new languages would contain hidden problems that we would not be able to resolve, we rededicated ourselves to engineering solutions, not computer problems.

Initial Problems with Object-Oriented Lisp

In 1987, object-oriented systems were supposed to be available, but proven ones were so expensive that they were inaccessible to us. Our method of funding expert system work was by the *skunk-works method.* We think of a skunk-works project as one that is short of formally budgeted money but is allowed freedom from the normal checks and balances of bureaucratic organizations. The enormous benefit of this funding method was that although we could not plan or schedule progress because of the newness of the application problems and the relative strangeness of the technology being used, we did not have to. The price of this freedom was that we could not afford to buy a proven object-oriented Lisp.

We tried to use Object Lisp on an early version of Golden Common Lisp, but Object Lisp was not going to be supported. CLOS seemed too futuristic at this time, and GoldWorks was not available. Thus, we did the best we could and simply started programming in Common Lisp, using Golden Common Lisp. Because of the high costs for multiple copies of Common Lisp and the (to us at this time) specialized hardware, we decided to write a data-entry and initial calculation program in Pascal. This approach allowed multiple users to specify data on their own personal computers and then move this information onto one Lisp system. The ramps (our first) program, eventually grew to over 15,000 lines of Lisp code; the code was purely functional and did not include state-of-the-art ideas, such as case-based reasoning or constraint propagation, and was not object oriented. Figures 1 and 2 show drawings produced by the first ramps program. The reason for this brute-force approach to capturing ramp knowledge was that we were unable to develop a deep sense of comfort with any AI expert in any of these emerging research areas; any move to case-based reasoning, for example, seemed to require that our engineering staff turn over project control to an expensive AI expert who did not deeply understand our engineers or our corporation. For human and business reasons, this

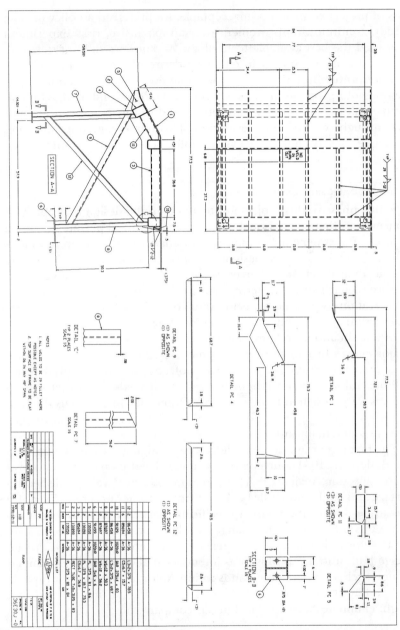

Figure 1. Ramp Drawings: Weldment.

loss of project control was unacceptable; we preferred a policy of slow, steady, continuous improvement over an expansive, risky experiment that used the best available technology. We knew we did not start with state-of-the art technology in either hardware or software, but this fact did not prevent a slow, steady growth that eventually resulted in implementing our programs in parallel CLOS, X Windows, and so on. Our corporate culture could never have progressed to this point without moving through years of lower evolution. This implementation illustrates principle 2, that knowledge-based applications should be introduced slowly.

First Phase: Design Concept

The first phase of this project was to agree on the design concept. This concept was that any reasonably intelligent technical person should be able to sit at a personal computer and answer specification questions about the machine to be designed; a specific instance of this machine should then be created. For example, if a person wanted a conveyor designed with certain economic, reliability, speed, and weight specifications, we would expect output consisting of complete mechanical weldment, assembly, and installation drawings.

In our situation, we knew that our equipment consisted of about 50 major classes of mechanical equipment connected by a custom-programmed PLC. Some of these pieces of equipment literally had an infinite number of possible instances, and it was seldom that two instances were designed to be identical. Other machine designs differed in only a small number of degrees of freedom, but all system designs were fundamentally different.

The first important decision dealt with changing the CAD system used for design. In 1984, our company standardized its use of a CAD program, selecting Anvil 1000. This program did not have a published interface and could not easily be driven from another program. Even if it was to be driven, the manual specifically warned against doing it because this interface might change in a later program release. In contrast, Autocad had a standard interface and even had an AutoLisp language built into it. AutoLisp was intended to allow users to do limited things, such as extend commands within Autocad, but was not capable of handling CAMES. We elected to use Autocad, starting a trend that might eliminate Anvil 1000 within our company.

Original Programming

The design program was written in Common Lisp, but the initial input program was written in Pascal so it could run on any 8088 or 286 com-

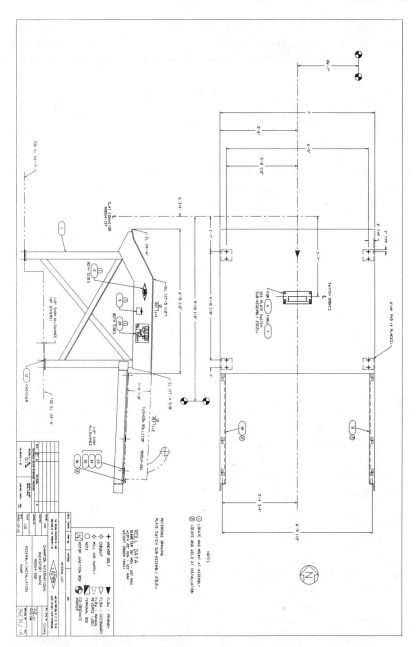

Figure 2. Ramp Drawings: Assembly and Installation.

puter (386s were not available at this time). The initial machine class, called ramps, was started in the fall of 1987. The first ramps were drawn within a few months and were relatively successful. However, to our surprise, we soon started to miss some production deadlines, creating serious problems. The main reason for this failure was that we had not mastered the breadth and depth of the options and complexities of our chosen machine. We elaborate on some of our failures in the next subsection.

Selecting the First Machine to Design

The fundamental criterion for selecting ramps as our first class of machine was economic. The class of ramps is the machine in our company with the greatest number of "same as but different" designs.

All experienced design engineers warned us not to attempt this generic design of ramps. The most skilled engineers claimed that although they looked easy, ramps were the most difficult machines to design because they were infinitely variable; any change in one specification would change almost all the design. Other, less experienced, or bystander engineers, believed that ramps were too easy to test the concept. These opinions seemed important, but what seemed more important was the hope of financial payback; we would handle the technical problems sooner or later, easy or hard. In addition, we believed that it was wise to start with the hardest problem first, so that each different instance is a simplification, not a complication. In retrospect, this approach was our first major error because the deep complexity of options nearly caused project engineers to lose confidence and commitment.

Initial Problems: Drafting Standards

The complexity of the task almost defeated us even before we started handling many variants of ramps. There appeared to be constant change in implied drafting standards. The different ways to write a number all have different meanings on engineering drawings; that is, 1, 1.0, 1.00, 1.000, 1.12, 1.125, and 1-⅛ all represent different concepts. The number 1.13 might not be in the allowable number set at a certain time. There are complex rules about rounding up or rounding down, some of which make little mathematical sense, but they are a part of our company culture. They could eventually be changed but not to accommodate a computer. As another simple example, the decision to record lengths in millimeters, decimeters, or meters or in inches or feet and inches was not primarily mathematical but the result of standards. The standards were not necessarily logical or stable. Humans could (at a cost) adapt to irrationally derived changes in standards, but our program could not. As a result, our business processes were gradually forced to become disciplined to handle CAMES. These changes were desirable in a manual system but were impossible to identify or implement before the use of CAMES. The process of changing business processes as a result of using CAMES is a valuable side benefit.

We started to realize, as we had with CALES, that we were dealing with a problem in translation. We were translating specifications into mechanical drawings, and we started thinking of a mechanical drawing not as a mathematical fact but as a description in a graphic language. The language has some standards, many dialects, and some major variants. These standards were policed by the department that checked the mechanical drawings, but the individuals in this department had differing views on standards and sometimes seemed to apply different standards to CAMES drawings than they did to human-generated CAD drawings or manual drawings. It took several critical months to work out satisfactory drafting standards for CAMES.

Initial Problems: Deeper Knowledge

This process of defining drafting standards for CAMES ironically was helped by the checking department after we started receiving drawings that were heavily *red lined*, that is, demanded many small corrections in red pencil. These small corrections were invariably proven to be correct in CAMES and incorrect when changed by the checking department.

CAMES now started to receive its first small measure of respect. No engineer or draftsperson normally had the time, inclination, or courage to challenge the checking department; we all just accepted its dictates because it was easier this way. However, with a knowledge-based tool, it was impossible to make superficial fixes. The design knowledge either had to be correct or had to be corrected. After some of the actions of the checking department were shown to be fallible, we started catching errors that would have cost between 10 and 100 times more money to fix in the field under the hostile gaze of a customer concerned about the late startup of his(her) billion dollar paper mill. As a reliable implementer of standards, CAMES became known as a useful tool. The greatest complaint became that "it takes too long and costs too much to transfer any machine into CAMES."

Details of the Operation of CAMES

The CAMES programs design the required machine and then automatically invoke Autocad to produce a drawing package for each machine processed. A manufacturing package consists of all the detailed weldment, assembly, and installation drawings and bills of materials required for a specific machine on a specific project. The system can produce drawings overnight using data entered during working hours or in a few minutes if necessary. In some cases, the Autocad drawing requires manual drafting corrections, but the average time for producing the ramp package was reduced by 50 percent or more. Figure 1 shows an example of a weldment drawing for a ramp. Figure 2 shows an example of an assembly and installation drawing for a ramp. These drawings were completely designed by CAMES and have not been touched by a human designer, although the task would be easy with the use of Autocad.

How CAMES Does What It Does

The ever-evolving design and frequent drafting standard changes consumed more and more programming time. Consequently, an attempt was made to structure the program in a similar way for each machine and rewrite the function library so it would approximate the Autocad drafting commands. This approach, we hoped, would allow users to make certain types of modifications themselves. In this concept, the drawing itself, with its three main views (plan, elevation, and front), is an object. The structure of the program for each drafting view is identical. Critical points (for example, the location of various elements, such as conduits, motor position, bearings) are associated with an object either by formulas or constants. Predrafted machine elements used as drafting blocks are assigned to the particular view by name and location relative to the view coordinates; so, the program always knows where to insert in relation to other components. The program uses a function library common for all the machines. The program maintains its own database of important machine components. If a new element, for example, electric motor, is specified, the program prompts the user for certain information about the new motor and its drafting representation (blocks); after recording this information in the database, the program is automatically ready to use it. A separate database is kept for important customer information, for example, bale dimensions and electric component specifications. The program also tracks the overall drawing database: If new requirements resemble previous designs, the user is alerted. The program uses an interface to Autocad and generates drawings using a set of standard or modified Autocad commands.

The Difficulty of the Design Problem

From the mechanical and drafting point of view, the machines completed to date in CAMES are not the most complicated in the machine line; however, their detailed design is subject to much change and is adapted to suit the other more complicated and standardized machines in the roll bale line. Almost all basic design criteria of the CAMES machines are subject to change, including main geometric dimension (length, width, height) and the position of motors, reducers, switches, and bearing types. These variabilities in the design propagate, to the drawing dimensions, changing patterns that must adhere to certain rules and be easy for the end user to read. For example, machine dimensions must be laid out differently for a motor on the left of a particular machine than for a machine on the right, greatly changing the structure of the dimension lines, not just the data for the dimensions. Problems are also caused when an additional machine is located on a CAMES machine. The design does not change, but the dimensioning must now accommodate both machines without "collisions." The rules governing the dimensioning have become complex and are one of the main reasons for an increase in programming time with design changes.

The Errors Found

The CAMES user answers between 30 and 80 questions pertaining to a particular machine. Most of the questions are simple, and the typing time should not exceed 10 to 15 minutes. However, for various organizational reasons, collecting the data before typing can consume a considerable amount of time. After data entry, the user usually reviews the CAMES-generated drawing in Autocad or plots it, marks the errors, and then corrects them in CAD. Most of the errors are caused by design and standard changes that usually keep ahead of programming. The usual area of error is line collision, for example, dimensions resulting from not updating the drafting blocks. There are few design or calculation errors.

Phase Two: Selecting the Second Machine

After our experiences with ramps, we wanted to design other classes of machines. The specifications for this second phase of our work were (1) the ability to handle interconnected systems of machines; (2) fast, correct manufacturing packages for each machine; (3) a friendly interface and database; (4) straightforward program design and structure; and (5) ease of modification when the design changes.

At this stage, CAMES was considered interesting but not proven. The next step was to automatically design whole systems of interconnected machines. However, the delays and disappointments caused by initial problems in ramp production had caused some hostility in the minds of the managers of our roll product line. Therefore, we decided to develop CAMES to handle whole systems of machines using our second most important product line, pulp baling. CAMES would be used with our most important line if it was successful on the second line. The class of pulp bale chain conveyors was selected as the next machine because it was the most frequently used machine in the pulp bale product line. This machine is designed in a wide variety of lengths, widths, strand spacings, and motor and reducer types. As with ramps, the basic layout of the program was completed in just a few months. Since this time, the program has constantly been modified with changing design standards and various requests for improvement. Figures 3 through 6 show designs produced at this stage of the project. There were signs in early 1991 that at least four to six product-line engineers wanted to learn CLOS to be able to extend CAMES in the future. It is psychologically important to them that they continue to control the basic knowledge, and some seem prepared to learn simple CLOS programs, if necessary, to retain their professional control of the product line.

Major Weaknesses in CAMES, Phase Two

A need for constant change and improvement leads us to the major weakness in the existing CAMES system: A Lisp engineer-programmer is required to modify the design engine, and the design engine is not extensible by the domain expert (a non-Lisp engineer). Much initial knowledge about the chain conveyor machine was collected from three relatively inexperienced engineers, who, in retrospect, did not have full knowledge of the whole design spectrum. With each new modification and addition, the design and program became more complex. Our experience (not unique) is that for each stage of the problem, it takes approximately 20 percent of the total programming time to complete 80 percent of the machine, but the remaining 20 percent of the work takes 80 percent of the total time. The last 20 percent of the work renders the project acceptable to the user and cannot be ignored. We also found that it is often economically correct to complete a machine with only about 95 percent of the options captured, leaving the remaining options to human correction in Autocad. This fact exists because the incremental investment in programming could not be recaptured for some infrequently used options. These issues

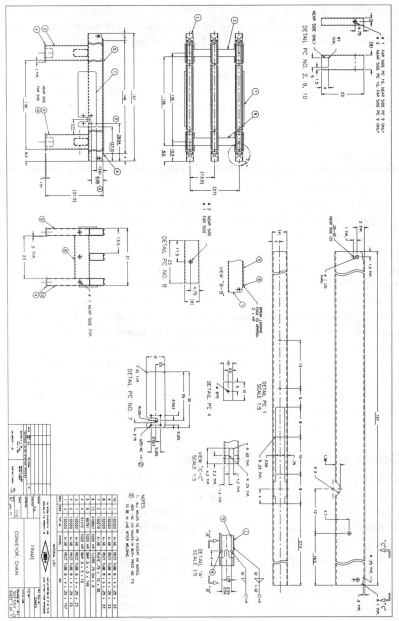

Figure 3. Chain-Conveyor Drawings: Weldment.

would be handled differently if CAMES were extensible by a domain expert and if these problems were in the hands of a project-oriented user and not a "staff stranger" with his(her) own time constraints.

CAMES creates and maintains its own dynamic database of various typical components, for example, motors, reducers, terminal boxes, and some customer data. In this way, we built in some extensibility, but this feature needs to be improved in quantity and quality, probably by using CLOS.

Moving toward Object-Oriented Programming and Extensibility

For this second phase of our work, we wanted to simplify the Lisp code and use a repeating programming structure for each new machine, moving in the direction of the objects and instances used in object-oriented programming. For example, libraries, variable names, and blocks were standardized for easy reusability, recognition, and maintenance. The system consists of three main units: data entry, design, and output. While designing a machine, the system searches its database for characteristics (for example, dimension or quantity) of various machine components. Drawings can be drawn to a specified scale with options for dimensions in metric, imperial, or both. Much of this second phase was done in muLisp. In retrospect, the main difficulty encountered in program development and maintenance is with knowledge acquisition and the frequent changes in design standards. Often, the knowledge that was used for design became obsolete once the programming was completed.

Details of Making the Drawings

Our first approach to making drawings was to represent a machine as a composition of a series of simple elements, build it in a three-dimensional space, and then project it onto three views on a two- dimensional drawing. It worked well for our first simple ramps; however, it became increasingly difficult to build more complicated ramp components or mechanisms with their intersecting lines and complicated shapes. It was also difficult to tell the computer which lines were important enough to be shown on the drawing and which were not. Human rules governing this information are often inexact. When we started even more complex machines, their projections in three dimensions became intricate for certain components. Therefore, we decided to use drafting blocks for each two- dimensional view. These blocks either were extracted from master drawings or were specially

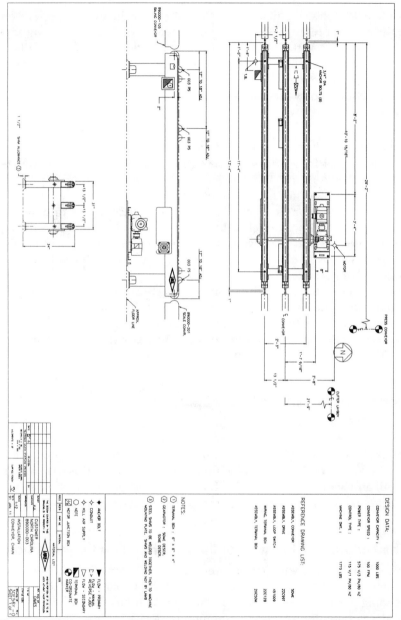

Figure 4. Chain-Conveyor Drawings: Assembly and Installation.

made by our drafting department. For some machines, we overreacted with block representations and had to revert to elementary programming. However, with time and experience, we developed artful skills in which blocks were used to represent certain design details, and functional programming was used to represent other elements of design. We do not yet know how to reduce this art to code.

Innovations Brought by the Application

As this chapter indicated, we believe that CAMES has improved our ability to check errors and improve design quality, increase human productivity for standard machines, increase drafting quality, and allow more time for innovation and creativity and has increased our options for using less skilled personnel. It has acted as a catalyst, even as a driver, for identifying and improving inefficient bureaucratic processes. We hope it will be a vehicle for transferring engineering knowledge between business cycles.

Our users want to continue our CAMES effort because they see personal and corporate benefits; we believe that this continued use is the ultimate endorsement. Some users consider themselves the best machine designers in the world and see CAMES as a natural evolution of their profession. We could not be more flattered.

Conditions for a Successful Application

Users demand that CAMES permit easy modification. However, a user must accept education about how CAMES works and upgrade his(her) general computer skills. For example, a user should have a good working knowledge about the machine being designed, the CAD system used, and some basic DOS skills. Users must actively be involved in the machine-designing process and not expect miracles from CAMES.

The Nature and Estimate of the Payoff to Our Organization

We estimate that by mid-1991, over 1,000 machines will have been designed by CAMES, saving a minimum of 16 hours each and, therefore, yielding a total savings of over 16,000 person-hours during the 5 years of development and use. At a minimum, we claim breaking even for the project to date. However, we don't think of strategic moves in terms of economic payout, and we consider CAMES to be a strategic initiative whose serious contribution will be most significant after the integration of all three systems: CALES, CAPES, and CAMES.

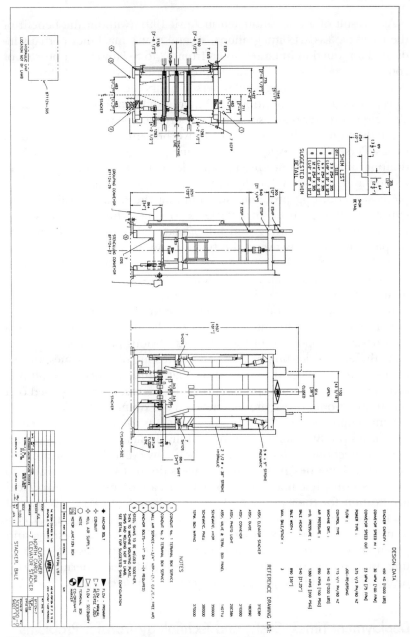

Figure 5. Stacker Drawing: Assembly and Installation.

As a result of a test conducted in April 1991 (without the benefit of the CALES-CAMES-CAPES integration), several CAMES machines perhaps indicated a reduction in target hours from 32 to 8. However, a process of continuing review was necessary to prove these figures and continue the downward trend to a target total person-hours reduction of 90 percent. This process involves monthly benchmarks and continuous incremental changes to programs and surrounding bureaucratic procedures.

Further qualitative and quantitative benefits can be credited to CAMES. Person-hours assigned to machine packages include design and drafting time but do not usually include plotting or material list completion and vary from 8 to 40 hours for each machine. There are simple cost-accounting problems surrounding the data we collected because the design time for CAMES is so small that operators take responsibility for plotting and bill-of-material tests, invalidating any simple comparison between the budget and actual costs. The design time shrinks, so that bureaucratic time becomes oppressive. Regardless of these problems, it takes only a few minutes for CAMES to produce a manufacturing package. The engineering data necessary for actual entry of the specifications, annual correction of drawings, preparation of bills of material, plotting, and other overhead operations consume a considerable proportion of the time. An obvious possibility is to automate these tasks, starting by using CAPES. In spite of these issues, the accounting data collected to date show that a time reduction of 50 percent was achieved with respect to previous processes. Activity-based cost accounting would reveal more benefits in our opinion.

Some engineers feel threatened by CAMES, as some felt threatened by the earlier proliferation of CAD. When fully implemented, CAMES will actually protect our corporation and jobs in any cyclical downturn of the economy. Some designers and engineers doubt CAMES will be able to process complex machines, but they can offer no theoretical justification for their position. As the developers of CAPES, CAMES, and CALES, we see no theoretical barrier to a complete mapping of customer needs into fully integrated electromechanical designs and preengineered proposals. Our company is in the process of committing itself to this concept of doing business and is considering restructuring and repositioning areas that might use these concepts.

Deployment Times, Costs, and Technology Transfer Problems

CAMES technology was developed in a branch of the Lamb companies in Vancouver, British Columbia, about 250 miles from the main design office. The location caused logistic problems concerning design changes,

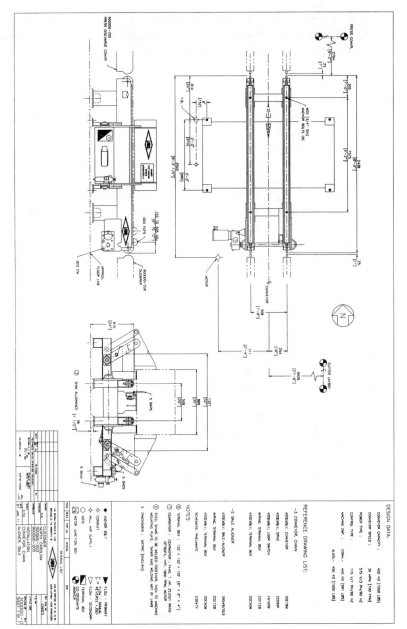

Figure 6. Aligner Drawing: Assembly and Installation.

program updates, inquiries, and user training. Now that most Lamb branches are connected through a comprehensive network system, communication between users and programmers was made much easier.

An attempt to transfer the CAMES ramps to the main design office was attempted but was unsuccessful. This failure was because the ramps were processed in a branch office and sent to the main office as a finished package in an established process no one wanted to change. The technology transfer of the chain conveyors and other machines took place in mid-1990 and was generally accepted by users. These users developed a plan to complete additional machines in the course of the next several months. It will take six to eight weeks to complete a new machine package with the system now in use. CAMES development took four years and an estimated six person-years of programming effort to create the existing tool. Because of continued change, the development of CAMES machines will never stop.

A critical move was made in 1990 by transferring the responsibility for the CAMES development to the line manager of the department that will obtain the greatest benefit from CAMES. This move illustrates the implementation of our fourth and most important principle, that the application must be under the direct control of a line operation manager, even if this person has no knowledge of AI or knowledge-based systems. This trend will continue as responsibility for implementing the CAPES, CALES, and CAMES systems is entrusted to line managers as part of a serious corporate reengineering effort by our group of companies, which involves empowering knowledge workers and is accompanied by organizational repositioning, delayering, and downsizing.

Acknowledgments

We thank Phil Parker for his long-term contributions and committment to CAMES.

References

Campbell, I. C., and Bukshteyn, I. 1990. Putting Knowledge-Based Concepts to Work for Generic PLC Programming. In Proceedings of the Second Annual Conference on Innovative Applications of Artificial Intelligence, 108–113. Menlo Park, Calif.: American Association for Artificial Intelligence.

QDES: Quality-Design Expert System for Steel Products

Yoshiteru Iwata and Norio Obama

Meeting customer demands for higher quality is a major business focus in the development of steel products. The quality of steel can be increased in many ways, for example, by improving its toughness or its resistance to atmospheric corrosion or by making thinner sections without sacrificing strength.

As the largest steel supplier in the world, Nippon Steel Corporation (NSC) receives many kinds of customer requests for new steel products with increased quality, sections of different size, and so on. Customer requests have become more complex, and their quality requirements have increased. At the same time, quality-design experts are expected to decrease the time to judge whether production of a desired product is possible and to design the product. Furthermore, fewer quality-design experts are available to design the new products.

Problems in the quality design of steel products have become important. To deal with these problems, NSC developed a design support system with a production database and a retrieval mechanism. Unfortunately, this system was efficient only for the design of products that were similar to products produced in the past. To overcome the limitations of the design support system, NSC undertook the challenge of developing the quality-design expert system (QDES). QDES is fully opera-

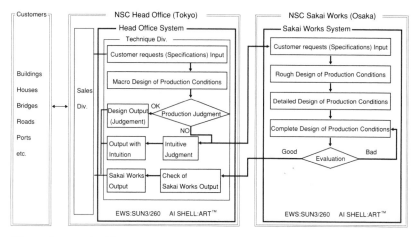

Figure 1. QDES Architecture.

tional and provides valid designs for shaped-steel products.

The application of AI to design problems is generally considered difficult in terms of knowledge acquisition and system modeling because of the combinatorial explosion that is inherent in a problem with a huge solution space. The achievement of QDES is a milestone in the application of AI to design. This chapter analyzes the experts' quality-design process and presents the technical points required to create the expert system model.

QDES Architecture

QDES runs on Sun engineering workstations within the ART environment and is integrated with the UNIFY database tool. QDES consists of about 3,000 rules, and about 500,000 lines of code. The system requires about 100 megabytes during run time.

QDES consists of two interconnected systems, as shown in figure 1: the head office system and the Sakai Works system. (Sakai Works is one of NSC's steel plants.) When specifications for a new product are input to QDES, the system assesses whether the product can be produced; if so, it creates a plan for the design, including operation conditions and cost.

The head office system performs an initial screening. When this system judges that a detailed design is needed, it transfers the product specifications to the Sakai Works system. The Sakai Works system develops a detailed design using many kinds of detailed data, for example, process data and test data. This system is able to design more complicated products than the head office system.

QDES performs the following functions: (1) system control, (2) reasoning, (3) maintenance, (4) explanation, (5) drawing management, (6) intelligent man-machine interaction, and (7) correspondence. The system-control function supervises the other functions and maintains coherence among them. Because the main function is reasoning, this chapter concentrates on the reasoning process.

Customer requests are primarily classified into two types: (1) requests for products made of a new material and (2) requests for H sections with new dimensions. (An H section is illustrated in figure 7.) For either type of request, the input to QDES includes information about the customer, the type of steel product, how and where the product will be used, and the deadline by which the customer needs results from QDES. Additional input for a request for a new material includes tensile strength; yield strength; yield point; elongation; temperature of charpy impact test; energy of charpy impact test; welding conditions; electric resistance; and upper and lower limits for the amounts of various ingredients, such as C, Si, Mn, P, S, Cu, Ni, Cr, Mo, Nb, V, Al, and Ti. Additional input for a request for an H section with new dimensions is flange height, web width, thicknesses of the web and the flange, corner radius of the shaped steel, length, quantity, weight, size accuracy tolerance, bending conditions, and squareness.

The customer requesting a new steel product provides the input data previously described. Using these data, QDES designs the operating conditions and assesses the ability to produce the specified product. The input to the Sakai Works system is the same as the input to the head office system.

Analysis of the Experts' Design Process Model

Prior to the development of the expert system, the design process of the human experts was thoroughly analyzed.

The experts at the head office go through the following four design stages: (1) macro design of production conditions, (2) production assessment, (3) intuitive judgment (for new materials only), and (4) check of Sakai Works output. Figure 1 shows the flow of control among these four stages.

In stage 1 (macro design of production conditions), the experts determine the essential issues based on input from customers, select the most similar past case, use parameters from this case in the initial design, and design the operating conditions without the local detailed knowledge of the plant where the product will be produced.

In stage 2 (production assessment), the experts judge production to be possible when they are able to design the operating conditions. If they are unable to design the operating conditions, the experts cannot judge whether production is possible. In such cases, they transfer the customer's input to the experts at Sakai Works.

Experts proceed to stage 3 (intuitive judgment) for a new material request when they are unable to judge whether the product can be produced, but a prospective customer needs to know whether the material can be produced. In this situation, the experts make intuitive judgments about whether the new material can be produced.

If the experts at Sakai Works are asked to design the operating conditions and judge whether the product can be produced, the experts at the head office go to stage 4 (check of Sakai Works output). In this stage, they check the output produced by the experts at Sakai Works.

The experts at Sakai Works go through the following four design stages: (1) rough design of production conditions, (2) detailed design of production conditions, (3) complete design of production conditions, and (4) evaluation. The flow of control among these stages is shown in figure 1. The experts' actions in each stage depend on whether the product is a new material or an H section with new dimensions.

For a new material, in stage 1 (rough design of production conditions), the experts determine the essential issues based on the input, select the most similar past case, and use parameters of this case as parameters of the initial design for the method of production. There are many parameters of the method of production, for example, whether the product needs continuous casting or ingot casting and whether it needs heat treatment.

In stage 2 (detailed design of production conditions), the experts design by quoting the test results from the most similar case. They use uncertain knowledge to evaluate whether the material can be produced given the charpy impact specification.

In stage 3 (complete design of production conditions), the experts use the ingredient combinations from the most similar cases. The customer specifications include acceptable ranges for the amounts of various ingredients. The experts decide what amount of different ingredients to use after trying as many combinations (within the acceptable limits) as possible.

In stage 4 (evaluation), the experts consider the production stability and judge whether the material can be produced. If the experts are able to design operating conditions, they judge production to be possible. If not, the experts then select the next most similar past case and investigate a different method of production based on this case. If the experts are not able to design the operating conditions after all alternative design methods are tried, they judge production to be impossible.

For an H section with new dimensions, in stage 1 (rough design of production conditions), the experts interpret the essential issues of the input and perform an initial screening. They judge production possible when the dimensions are within the range of dimensions of past products. When the new dimensions are outside this range, the experts select the most similar past case and use the parameters of this case as the parameters of the initial design. The production method for H sections is rolling. There are many conditions of the rolling operation, for example, vertical roll shape and horizontal roll shape.

In stage 2 (detailed design of production conditions), the experts design by quoting the conditions of the rolling operation from the most similar case and design the schedule of rolling passes, the mill spring, the shape of slab, and so on. At this stage, they consider conditions such as the number of passes through each rolling mill and the vertical and horizontal roll gaps of each rolling. The Sakai Works rolling process has 7 rolling mills. The experts design the pass schedule of each rolling mill by modifying the rolling conditions from the past case so that rolling will produce a product with the desired dimensions. If the experts cannot design the rolling pass schedule despite considering all alternative rolling pass schedule design methods, they judge production to be impossible.

In stage 3 (complete design of production conditions), the experts use other rolling conditions from the most similar case and modify them so that rolling will produce a product with the desired dimensions. At this stage, the experts consider conditions such as cooling conditions, rolling time, and rolling speed.

In stage 4 (evaluation), the experts simulate the vertical rolling load, the horizontal rolling load, rolling temperature, rolling length of each mill rolling pass, and so on, and judge the possibility of production. If the experts are able to design operating conditions, they judge production to be possible. If not, the experts then select the next most similar past case and investigate a different method of production based on this case. If the experts are not able to design the operating conditions after all alternative design methods are tried, they judge production to be impossible.

As previously described, the expert design process consists of various types of reasoning: (1) design based on the most similar past case, (2) consideration of as many alternative combinations of ingredients as possible, (3) intuitive judgments, (4) evaluations with uncertain knowledge, and (5) learning by experience.

Design Based on the Most Similar Past Case

Experts do not design based on theories only. Often, experts design based on past cases, in particular, the most similar case. In other words, experts use parameters of the most similar case as the initial parameters of a new design.

Experts can judge or design new cases using only theories. Why do experts design with past cases? The designs for past cases were created from a collection of many backgrounds, theories, and techniques. Often, experts can design more easily and more quickly when they use past cases.

Developing a design from first principles typically requires enormous cost and effort; these requirements can be reduced when a design is based on the designs of past cases with many pieces of potentially relevant information. The key issue for this type of reasoning is how to evaluate the similarity between new specifications and the past cases.

Consideration of as Many Alternatives as Possible

When experts are presented with acceptable ranges for several ingredients, they do not consider all possible combinations of different amounts of each ingredient. They do, however, try to consider as many combinations as possible, so they can design the optimum plan for new specifications. For this type of reasoning, it is important to know how to combine all feasible amounts of the various ingredients within the specified limits and to select the optimum plan from various points of view. It might be possible to build a system that is able to design better plans than the experts because the system can consider more combinations than the expert can.

Intuitive Judgments

Sometimes, the experts at the head office have to promptly judge the possibility of production for salespeople—before a detailed design is developed at Sakai Works. Hence, the expert often designs by intuition. The intuition is not clear enough to incorporate into an expert system; accordingly, the issue is how to represent the intuition and seek the answer.

Evaluations with Uncertain Knowledge

Experts often design efficiently while they reason with imprecise measurements, such as "small" or "rather big." The knowledge is not always exact enough to be put into an exact rules. The issue for reasoning with uncertainty is how to represent the uncertain knowledge and judgments.

Learning by Experience

Experts do not always have enough knowledge to design. They learn

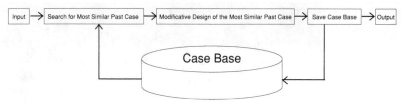

Figure 2. Case-Based Reasoning in QDES.

day by day and design the best plan given the current state of their knowledge. Experts try to acquire new useful knowledge to enable them to design for more complicated specifications they might receive.

The main issues are how to develop the acquiring function for getting the useful information, how to efficiently modify the knowledge, how to incorporate new knowledge into an existing knowledge base, how to assure the correctness of the knowledge, and how to keep the knowledge consistent.

Creation of the Reasoning Model

This section discusses the development of the QDES system in light of the five reasoning methods just presented.

Design Based on the Most Similar Past Case

QDES uses case-based reasoning (Schank 1982) because the experts themselves develop designs by adapting designs from similar past cases. Furthermore, a more conventional approach, such as ruled-base reasoning, might prove to be infeasible for a problem with such a huge solution space. Figure 2 illustrates how QDES uses case-based reasoning.

The most important issue for a system that uses case-based reasoning is how to evaluate the similarity between the past cases and new specifications. The similarity should be made clear through many interviews with the experts. For example, when the experts design H sections with new dimensions, they evaluate the similarity of the ratio of the flange thickness and the web thickness of the new specifications and past cases.

Case-based reasoning makes the system reasonably compact and, thus, is one of the most important techniques used in QDES. The number of rules is far fewer than if the system had been constructed using only theoretical rules, and the description of the design world is far smaller. Reasoning time is far shorter, and maintenance of the rules and the description is much easier. The efficiency of case-based reasoning is significant in QDES.

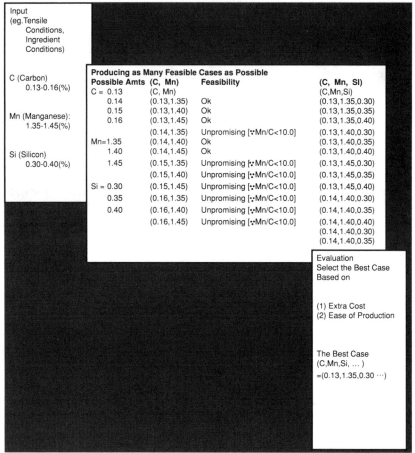

Figure 3. Example: Producing as Many Feasible Cases as Possible.

Consideration of as Many Alternatives as Possible

In stage 3 (complete design of production conditions) at the Sakai Works, the experts design the best combination of ingredients for a new material. They consider the most feasible combination in which the amount of each ingredient is within the specified limits. The experts do not try all combinations of possible amounts of each ingredient. They reject unpromising combinations along the way efficiently using an evaluating function of welding and design. Therefore, the issue is how to build a suitable structure that efficiently tries as many feasible combinations as possible.

To consider a large number of alternatives, hypothetical reasoning is a suitable technique. A more conventional approach might be to generate all possible combinations, evaluate each combination, and reject unsuitable ones. This approach would not be efficient. Instead, QDES uses the hypothetical reasoning capabilities of the ART environment. QDES recognizes unpromising partial combinations and does not expand these into complete combinations.

For example, figure 3 illustrates a request for a new material that must contain 0.13 to 0.16 percent of carbon, 1.35 to 1.45 percent of manganese, and .3 to .4 percent of silicon. (For simplicity, the required proportions of other ingredients are not shown.) QDES combines 4 different levels of carbon with 3 different levels of manganese to produce 12 partial combinations. Rather than combining each of these 12 carbon-manganese combinations with the 3 different levels of silicon, QDES evaluates the particle combinations. It eliminates 7 combinations in which the ratio of manganese to carbon is less than 10.0. QDES then proceeds to combine each of the 5 remaining carbon-manganese combinations with the 3 different silicon levels. This process continues until all ingredients have been added. After each ingredient is added, the partial combinations are evaluated. Only successful partial combinations are combined with the next ingredient.

The experts consider as many combinations as possible but not all combinations. Because QDES can consider more combinations, it can design a better plan with hypothetical reasoning than the experts can.

Intuitive Judgments

When a prospective customer has a request for a new material, the salesperson asks the experts at the head office whether the material can be produced. Sometimes, the experts must provide an answer before the detailed design is developed at Sakai Works. The experts must use their intuition to make the judgment. For this type of reasoning, the issue is how to represent the intuition and judgments.

The suitable structure of representation, judging, and learning with intuition is based on neural networks (Rumelhart, McClelland, and PDP Research Group 1986). In using a neural network, the main issue is the design of the network structure. The elements of the network, which are based on judgments, have to be obtained through interviews with the experts. When the experts judge the possibility of production, they consider the thickness of steel, the temperature of the charpy impact test, and the tensile strength. Hence, the thickness, the temperature, and the tensile strength are input conditions.

The network structure has to be developed by learning from training cases that contain input data and the experts' output judgments. Analysis of the results of some training cases showed that a three-lay-

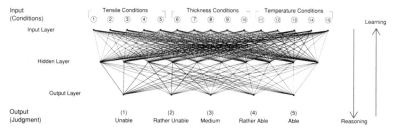

Tensile Conditions (1) $200N/mm^2 \leq$ Tensile Strength $\leq 400N/mm^2$ (2) $400N/mm <$ Tensile Strength $\leq 500N/mm^2$

Thickness Conditions   (6) 0.0 mm < Thickness $\leq$ 12.5 mm   (7) 12.5 mm < Thickness $\leq$ 25.0mm

Temperature Conditions   (11) –50 °C $\leq$ Temperature $\leq$ –40 °C   (12) – 40 °C < Temperature $\leq$ – 30 °C

Figure 4. Neural Network Model of Judgment in QDES.

ered network with a back-propagation algorithm is suitable. The network is shown in figure 4. When the number of layers was increased or decreased, the results of the training cases were worse. The optimal number of the hidden layer elements was found to be 10; when the number was increased or decreased, the results of the training cases were worse.

The neural network enables the system to reason with correlations that cannot be represented by exact rules. Although the technique cannot yield precise judgments, it is efficient for making rough judgments in such cases as described. The neural network approach is suitable for judgments in which there are no logical connections between input and output, the input and output are well defined, the patterns of input and output are limited to the cases that the system has experience with, and exactness is not required.

The limitation of this approach is generally a lack of accuracy in generating the output. Because the reasoning model is a black box to the experts, tuning it is difficult. Tuning the model can be accomplished only by teaching the system with new cases. The system can reason perfectly only in a case with the same patterns as a case that the system experienced. In QDES, a neural network was used only for stage 4 of the head office system (intuitive judgment) because more accurate reasoning models were applicable in other stages.

Evaluations with Uncertain Knowledge

The experts at the Sakai Works use sample test results to determine the steel plant's ability to produce steel with particular charpy impact specifications. Their decisions use imprecise classifications of the test results. For example, a change in temperature can be "small," "rather small," "medium," "rather big," or "big." Their decisions are also uncertain; they rate their ability to produce the desired steel product as "unable," "rather unable," "medium," "rather able," and "able." The issue for this type of reasoning is to develop a representation of these imprecise term expressions and a reasoning technique that is acceptable to the experts.

The suitable framework for reasoning with uncertainty is based on the fuzzy model (Zadeh 1965). In using the fuzzy model, the main implementation tasks are the fuzzy membership functions and the fuzzy reasoning mechanism. From an analysis of the experts' design process, the fuzzy membership functions were determined as shown in figure 5. Both premise parts and consequence parts of judgment rules have fuzzy membership functions corresponding to the experts' imprecise classifications of test data and uncertain decisions.

When the experts judge the ability to produce steel with new toughness specifications, they first consider a test temperature difference between a past case and the new specifications. They use inexact guidelines such as the following:

> If the temperature difference is big, then production possibility is able.
> If the temperature difference is rather big, then production possibility is rather able.

As figure 5, part 1, shows, a temperature difference of 14° C is rated as "big" with a strength of 0.4 and "rather big" with a strength of 0.6. The first rule uses the strength of "big" to rate production possibility "able" with a strength of 0.4. The second rule uses the strength of "rather big" to rate production possibility "rather able" with a strength of 0.6. Figure 6, part 1, shows that the peak of the membership function for "able" is 0.4. Figure 6, part 2, shows that the peak of the membership function for "rather able" is 0.6. Figure 6, part 3, shows the composition of the two membership functions. The center of gravity for the combined function is plus, so the final judgment is "able."

The fuzzy model permits effective reasoning with imprecise rules. QDES was able to use the fuzzy model for this reasoning task because the experts make logical (though imprecise) connections between the input data and the output conclusions. Without such logical connections, QDES would have needed to use a neural network, as described earlier. The fuzzy model is preferable to a neural network because the reasoning model can be understood by experts.

Learning by Experience

When the experts at Sakai Works judge the plant's ability to produce an H section with new dimensions, they perform an initial screening of

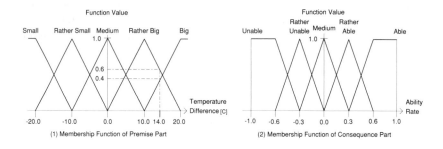

Figure 5. Examples of Fuzzy Rule Membership Functions.

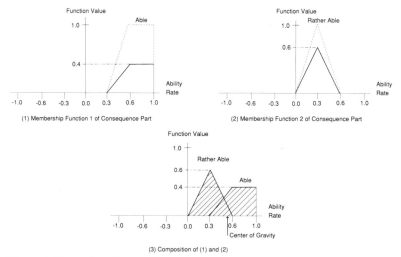

Figure 6. Examples of Fuzzy Reasoning.

the flange thickness, the web thickness, and the ratio of these two thicknesses. If the new dimensions are within the range of dimensions of past products, the experts can easily judge that the new section can be produced.

If new specifications fall outside the range of the experts' experience, however, the experts develop a detailed design by adapting the design of similar past cases. When they are able to design production conditions for the new specifications, they expand the range of dimensions that they will use in the initial screening in the future (figure 7).

In a similar manner, QDES learns by experience. The learning model reduces design time by increasing the number of specifications that

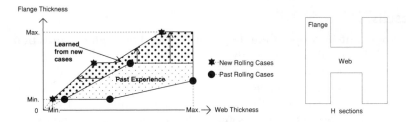

Figure 7. Learning Model of Judgments in Rolling Production.

can be accepted in the rough design stage without the development of detailed designs.

Support Functions

Although the main function of QDES is reasoning as described, its support functions are also important. This section describes two representative support functions: maintenance and explanation.

Maintenance Functions

QDES has two automatic maintenance functions. The first modifies the knowledge used in the rough design stage of the Sakai Works system to enable the system to learn by experience, as described earlier. The second maintenance function automatically adds new production cases to the collection of cases used for case-based reasoning. This function reduces design time but also increases the accuracy of design because the system has a wider range of similar cases to use. Both automatic maintenance functions operate frequently and save the daily maintenance work of the system operators.

QDES also has an interactive maintenance function that the system operators can use to update knowledge when the production process changes, when the standards are updated, and so on. The system operator checks, corrects, and accumulates data displayed by QDES. No updates have been needed since QDES has been in practical use, so this maintenance function has not been used yet.

Explanation Functions

QDES has two explanation functions. The first gives static, precoded explanations. The second generates explanations dynamically. These explanations trace the system's reasoning process and show how to develop designs. The explanations are shown in natural Japanese language; the system can be used as a valuable training aid for persons not already proficient in quality design.

Results

QDES was put into operation 18 months after knowledge acquisition began. About 350 person-months were required for development.

QDES has been in practical use since May 1990, and to date, no significant problems have been reported. NSC receives about 20 customer requests each month for shaped-steel products, and QDES designs all these products. QDES is currently running well, and the design space continues to expand. The payoffs are as follows:

First, QDES has reduced the design cycle time by 85 percent. The head office system takes about 20 minutes to design the production conditions and judge whether production is possible. The Sakai Works system takes about 40 minutes for a new material request and about 20 minutes for a request for an H section with new dimensions. This reduction in time allows NSC to accept more business, for example, steel products for multistory buildings and ocean platforms.

Second, the accuracy of design is 30 percent better than with the conventional method. For example, the use of hypothetical reasoning optimizes the combination of ingredients in a new material, thereby reducing the cost of the included ingredients.

Third, the more production experience that QDES acquires, the better the plans are that QDES produces. As described under Maintenance Functions, the system automatically learns from new production cases and collects new cases for use in case-based reasoning.

Fourth, QDES can particularly aid the novice who might not have a good working knowledge of quality design; it provides on-the-job training at the same time.

Fifth, QDES can serve as a resident expert, on hand 24 hours a day, 7 days a week.

QDES provides significant results and benefits in the quality design of steel products. QDES allows NSC to save or earn approximately $200,000 each year. QDES has the potential for tremendous savings in virtually all quality product design.

NSC is currently expanding QDES in two directions: QDES is being transferred to the other NSC Works, and it is being extended to assist with the design of new types of products. QDES will provide a much larger payoff in the near future.

Conclusions

This chapter presented the QDES approach to system development, which consists of the analysis of experts' quality-design process and the creation of a reasoning model consistent with the experts' planning process. It is important to build a system that is fit to experts. As a consequence, the thorough analysis and the development of knowledge representation and reasoning similar to experts' were crucial to the success of QDES.

The experts' design process uses various types of reasoning, so it is particularly important to combine the appropriate technologies for each type. This approach was effective in building QDES.

Although design applications are generally considered difficult to implement, QDES provides a useful framework for design applications. The main component of case-based reasoning is augmented with various other AI technologies to model the experts' reasoning: Hypothetical reasoning enables the system to generate and evaluate alternative combinations of ingredients, fuzzy modeling provides the mechanism for reasoning with uncertain knowledge when logical connections exist between input and output, and the neural network supports reasoning with intuition when no logical connections exist between input and output.

References

Rumelhart, D. E.; McClelland, J. L.; and the PDP Research Group. 1986. *Parallel Distributed Processing*, volumes 1 and 2. Cambridge, Mass.: MIT Press.

Schank, R. C. 1982. *Dynamic Memory: A Theory of Reminding and Learning in Computers and People.* Cambridge: Cambridge University Press.

Zadeh, L. A. 1965. Fuzzy Sets. *Information and Control* 8: 338–353.

Failure Analysis

CANASTA
Digital Equipment Corporation

NYNEX MAX
NYNEX Science and Technology

CANASTA: The Crash Analysis Troubleshooting Assistant

Michael S. Register and Anil Rewari

CANASTA (crash analysis troubleshooting assistant) is a Digital proprietary knowledge-based system developed by the Artificial Intelligence Applications Group (AIAG) at Digital Equipment Corporation in collaboration with Digital's customer support centers (CSCs). It is targeted to assist computer support engineers at CSCs in analyzing operating system crashes, traditionally one of the most complex types of problems reported by customers. Digital started work on CANASTA in January 1988. A version of CANASTA that assists in the analysis of vms operating system crashes was successful: It is currently deployed at CSCs in over 20 countries and is used to resolve over 850 crash-related customer calls each month. It is estimated that in time savings alone, it saves Digital over 2 million dollars each year.

CANASTA's success largely results from the innovative way in which it integrated different problem-solving modules that model the different types of problem-resolution strategies that experts use in this domain. These strategies include making quick checks (rule based) on whether the crash at hand is because of a known cause, using deeper analysis (decision tree–based) reasoning to resolve new types of crash problems, and checking for similarities among unresolved cases (a form of case-based generalization) that can lead to the identification of new hardware and software bugs. In fact, CANASTA's unresolved crash processor distinguishes it from other expert systems: It directly assists the expert in the generation of new knowledge regarding crash-causing bugs.

CANASTA also integrates different technologies that have not been combined before in this domain. It integrates a remote scripting package and rule-based inference to provide sophisticated automatic data collection that allows it to automatically gather data from the customer's machine thousands of miles away. It uses a rule-based system for quick checks on known problems. It uses a tool that allows experts to quickly encode troubleshooting knowledge graphically in the form of decision trees. It uses database technology to store case-related information that can be accessed later. CANASTA also includes an innovative distributed knowledge maintenance system that automatically collects knowledge from experts worldwide at all CSCs and automatically validates and redistributes this knowledge to all other sites. This approach facilitates the sharing of knowledge across various geographic sites.

In the following sections, we describe the crash analysis problem domain, the functions and architecture of the deployed system, details about the development and deployment stages, and the business payoffs.

The Crash Dump Analysis Problem

When an operating system detects an internal error so severe that normal operations cannot continue, it crashes. For many operating systems, this process involves signaling a fatal condition and shutting itself down in an orderly fashion by saving the contents of the registers, stacks, buffers, and memory at the time of the crash in a crash dump file. The underlying cause for the error can be a failure in user-written code, hardware failure, microcode failure, or an error in system software. *Crash analysis* is resolving the problem, whether it is in the hardware or software, and identifying a fix or a "workaround."

Analyzing crash-related problems is not an easy task because there is no fixed algorithmic method to identify the cause of the crash. Experience plays a large role in identifying the problem. Without CANASTA, the diagnostic process is as follows: First, the support engineer remotely connects (through modem servers) to the customer's machine to read the crash dump file on the crashed system. Once connected, s/he remotely scans the crash dump file and tries to identify the major symptoms of the crash.

The support engineer then checks to see if the symptoms match any known problems (bugs) that were already identified. Such problems are documented in over a dozen different textual databases. The support engineer usually does a key-word search over these textual databases based on the current symptoms. A significant number of problems being investigated by support engineers match previously identified problems. If an appropriate match is found, the support engineer notes the solution specified in the matched database article.

If the support engineer cannot match the current problem to a known problem, then s/he needs to do some deeper analysis. This process involves traversing the stack of procedure calls made prior to the point where the crash occurred, looking at the assembly language instructions and their operands, and locating where the error occurred. Knowledge of assembly language is required, and for many cases, knowledge about how the operating system works is required.

If the cause of the problem is identified, the solution is provided to the customer. For hardware-related problems, this solution usually involves replacing a hardware component. For microcode-related problems, it involves providing access to a new microcode revision level. For software-related problems, it can involve providing a new patch (a relatively small piece of software written to fix a specific problem in the system or application software), making recommendations to upgrade to a new operating system version, or correcting the software configuration of the system.

Unresolved cases are eventually seen by experts. They can try to resolve them by deeper analysis of the problem. However, based on their experiential knowledge about other similar crashes or an analysis of other unresolved crashes in the textual databases, they might be able to see similarities with other crashes and make generalizations that help them in resolving the crash at hand.

The process, as described, has several problems: Previously identified problems that are known to cause crashes are scattered in dozens of different textual databases. On the average, it takes about 30 minutes to scan the various textual databases to check whether the current crash results from a known problem. There are several reasons for this delay. First, many times one cannot identify a known problem because one does not scan the textual database where the right article lies. Second, even when known problem types are described in the textual databases, the descriptions might be incomplete. There is no set format for the articles. Finally, with the constant release of new products and software versions, it has become difficult for experts to document bugs, in a timely fashion, that are introduced by various hardware and software products.

Collecting symptoms itself requires knowledge. The techniques for collecting some of the symptoms are documented (Kenah, Goldenberg, and Bate 1988), but others are not documented and are difficult to obtain. Because of the amount of knowledge required to collect symptoms and identify bugs, often less experienced support engineers arrive at wrong conclusions and give wrong solutions. These errors invariably result in the customer calling back when the problem reappears, which results in increased calls to CSCs. Furthermore, support engineers follow no uniform approach in performing deeper analysis, and many of them have difficulty in performing deeper analysis.

Experts spend more time than necessary in looking at unresolved cases that are escalated to them because they do not have ready access to other similar cases seen in the company. Having access to similar unresolved problems allows them to make generalizations, resulting in faster resolution times.

These problems result in a substantial increase in the average time that a customer has to wait for a solution (also an increase in the time a customer's business can be disrupted), resulting in higher costs for Digital and a decrease in customer satisfaction. There are some tangible benefits to applying AI technology to this domain. Using an automated intelligent system results in quicker analysis times because it is considerably faster than manually searching through textual databases.

With an expert system approach, knowledge can be distributed and accessed easier than it was previously through the use of textual databases. Furthermore, expert system technology allows for much easier maintenance of the knowledge base than conventional software technology. This ability is especially beneficial in this domain because new bugs in hardware and software are identified on a continuous basis. Also, intelligent validation techniques can be used to validate the knowledge as it is entered into the knowledge base.

Using AI techniques also facilitates the generation of new knowledge. By using AI techniques to group similar unresolved cases, experts can now identify new problems faster because they have multiple instances (crashes) of the unresolved problems. This information also results in improved communications between the engineering development groups and the service delivery groups because now the service groups can send multiple instances of a problem to the engineering groups for resolution.

Finally, the automatic collection of data from the crash dump requires a significant amount of knowledge. Maintenance of this knowledge is difficult because it changes frequently. Encoding the knowledge in a rule base enables easier maintenance.

CANASTA provides an architecture that uses AI techniques to obtain these benefits.

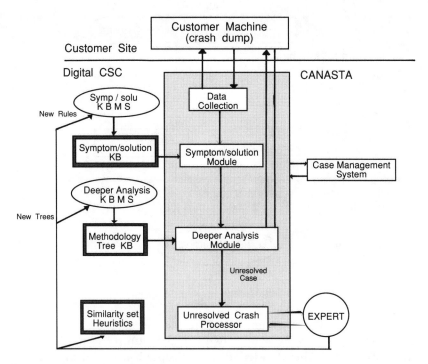

Figure 1. The CANASTA *Architecture.*

Architecture and Functions

In this section, we describe the architecture and functions of CANASTA. In figure 1, the horizontal line at the top separates the customer machine that crashed from the host machine at CSC where the support engineer works. The customer machine can be thousands of miles away. The crash analysis process begins with the support engineer establishing a remote connection to the customer system through a modem line.

Data Collection

The data-collection module extracts data from the crash dump file at the customer machine without transferring the entire dump to CSC. It uses a remote scripting package that enables it to remotely run commands on the customer machine. Figure 2 depicts the interaction between the data-collection module, located at the CSC machine, and the customer's machine.

A rule-based controller controls the sequence of information-gathering activities. It determines what information still needs to be collected

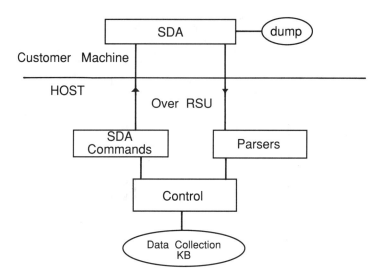

Figure 2. The Data-Collection Module.

and how. There is a large amount of knowledge regarding methods for extracting the relevant symptoms from the dump file for different types of crashes. The knowledge is represented in the form of about 750 OPS5 rules. When the controller determines that a particular piece of information is required from the crash dump at the customer machine, it sends a command to the customer machine over the modem connection using the remote scripting package. The commands usually involve running the *system dump analyzer,* a tool that formats binary crash dump files into ASCII text and displays particular parameters of interest. Output from the system dump analyzer at the customer site is automatically sent back to the data-collection module at CSC by the remote scripting package. This information is parsed, and then based on the parsed value, the controller decides which command to send next to the customer machine. It collects 15 key symptoms that CANASTA uses to make an initial hypothesis about whether the problem is because of a known bug. In case the crash is not resolved by the symptom-solution or deeper analysis modules (described later), it later collects additional parameter values and saves them with the unresolved case so that these additional symptoms are available to experts who look at the unresolved cases.

Using AI techniques (rule-based data collection) has resulted in considerable leverage. Initially, we started out with a procedural representation of the knowledge, but later, it was found easier tomaintain and add data-collection knowledge by representing it declaratively in the form of rules. It was difficult to represent the data-collection techniques using algorithms because too many exceptions had to be dealt with. Using a rule base allows CANASTA to represent this knowledge more conveniently and collect only the parameters that it needs to meet our goals of completeness and speed.

The goals for the data-collection module were to automatically collect data for 95 percent of the crash types with 99 percent accuracy and to collect the initial 15 symptoms within 3 minutes over a 1200-baud modem line. All these goals were met.

Symptom-Solution Module

After the initial set of symptoms are collected, CANASTA invokes the first of its analysis modules. The *symptom-solution module* uses a knowledge base of symptom-solution rules to see if the given crash matches a well-known hardware or software bug. A sample rule is shown in figure 3. If the combination of initial symptoms in the current crash matches a rule, then a hypothesis (the "description" part of the rule) is displayed to the support engineer. For many cases, this hypothesis is, in fact, the conclusion. However, for other rules, a further test is required (the "technique for confirmation" part of the rule) to actually confirm whether the current hypothesis is true. This determination involves running further commands remotely on the customer machine, that is, probing the dump file in more detail. If the test results are positive, then the hypothesis is proved to be correct, and a solution is then displayed (the "solution-recommendation" part of the rule). The rationale for having techniques for confirmation tied to particular rules is to save the overhead costs of performing such tests for every crash when they are only required to confirm specific bugs.

Rule-based pattern matching and heuristic identification of problems give considerable leverage in trying to quickly identify the cause of the problem, especially in a domain where almost half of the problems seen are repeated problems that were previously seen by others. This module is implemented in FOXGLOVE, a rule-based shell developed internally in our group. Currently, there are over 630 symptom-solution rules in CANASTA-VMS. Almost 75 percent of the rules point to software problems that cause crashes. There are rules for problems caused by system software bugs, application software bugs, hardware faults, faulty system configuration parameters, and microcode bugs.

Deeper Analysis Module

If a match is not found in the symptom-solution knowledge base or if

IF:

VMS-VERSION	= (one-of 5.0 5.0-1 5.0-2 5.1 5.1-1)
BUGCHECK-TYPE	= INVEXCEPTN
MODULE-OF-CRASH	= ETDRIVER
MODULE-OFFSET	= x1546

THEN:

DESCRIPTION:
"The crash occurs due to a synchronization problem in the
ETDRIVER while it is stepping down its list of UCB."

TECHNIQUE FOR CONFIRMATION:
"Check to see if R5 = FFFFFFFF. This tells us that the UCB
has already been severed."

SOLUTION-RECOMMENDATION:
"You should first recommend the customer upgrade to VMS
version V5.2 because this patch and 6 others are included in
this major release!

If the customer cannot upgrade then send them patch
number 0055."

Figure 3. A Symptom-Solution Rule.

the confirmation test does not succeed, then the *deeper analysis module*
is invoked. This module uses a *methodology tree knowledge base*, containing
knowledge of how experts troubleshoot crashes, to guide the user in
analyzing the crash dump. This module suggests the most appropriate
tests to be performed given the particular crash type and eventually in-
dicts a hardware component in the case of hardware problems or nar-
rows the list of possible software causes.

Currently, the deeper analysis module's troubleshooting knowledge
is organized into several decision trees that are separated on the basis
of high-level symptoms. A graphic view of a portion of the length violation tree is shown in figure 4. At the top of the tree, we only know that
this particular crash was caused by a length violation. At run time,
CANASTA asks the user questions to determine the reason for the length
violation. By the time CANASTA reaches a leaf node in the tree, CANASTA
has either isolated the reason for the crash or significantly narrowed
the list of possible reasons.

Currently, the tree knowledge base covers a small breadth of crash
types but one that captures 80 percent of the problem types seen at

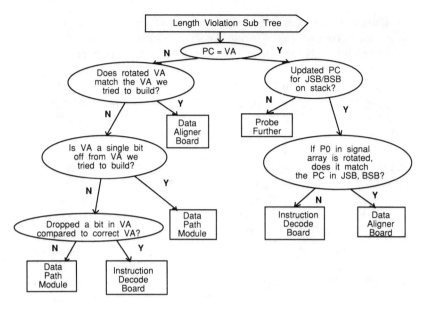

Figure 4. The Length Violation Decision Tree.

CSCs. In some places, the tree knowledge base lacks depth. Some of the conclusions it reaches are of a high level, and further probing (by the support engineer) is required to identify a cause at the hardware component level or software module level. Experts at CSCs were provided with a maintenance tool for expanding the depth and breadth of the methodology tree knowledge base.

Unresolved Crash Processor

CANASTA's unresolved crash processor periodically collects unresolved crash cases from all CSCs that run CANASTA and, using heuristic knowledge, groups similar unresolved crashes into similarity sets. It attempts a high-level classification of the cause for each similarity set. These sets are then made available to users worldwide, although the main beneficiaries of this module are the much-overworked expert-level support engineers and the engineers in the software and hardware development groups to whom the unresolved cases are escalated. AI techniques such as the heuristic grouping of cases into similarity sets and the heuristic classification of these sets are the basis of making the unresolved crash processor a powerful tool that is crucial in expediting the process of experts generating new knowledge about crash-causing bugs.

The unresolved crash processor design consists of three subcomponents: the back end, the browser, and the matcher.

The Unresolved Crash Processor Back End. The *back end* collects all the unresolved crash cases and groups them into similarity sets, providing a high-level classification for each set. First, it collects the unresolved crash cases from CSCs all over the world. It then uses a heuristic rule base to group similar cases into sets. The rules in this heuristic rule base are domain specific and include knowledge such as "crashes occurring in the same software module with very similar offsets are most probably due to the same underlying cause." Once the sets are formed, it infers a high-level characterization of the cause for the crashes in each similarity set. It uses a set of heuristics to perform this function; for example:

> If all the crashes in a set occurred in the same minor release of VMS, then the problem seems to be in that minor version of the VMS software (as opposed to hardware or the microcode).

If several of these heuristics are applicable, then the similarity set can have several possible causes attached to it. The back end then removes all sets that have a small number of cases in them, treating them as noise. The remaining sets correspond to the most common types of problems remaining unresolved, as seen at CSCs worldwide.

Finally, the unresolved crash processor back end builds a set of rules, one for each similarity set, that are used by the unresolved crash processor matcher module. As described later, the matcher is used by users during run time to check whether the current unresolved case corresponds to a known set of similar cases. To form a rule that represents a match with a similarity set, the back end takes certain key symptoms of the cases in a set and includes them as conditions in the left-hand side of a rule. Three symptoms—the software module, the offset, and the VMS version—are always included as conditions in the left-hand side of the rule because they are vital to detecting similarity. If there is a single value for this symptom in all the cases in the set, then the left-hand side of the rule will simply have an equality test. If there are multiple values, then a condition of the form "(one-of <symptom> '(<symptom-value1> ...))" is generated. If multiple causes are listed in a similarity set, then a rule is formed for each possible cause.

To illustrate, on the left-hand side of figure 5 is an example of a similarity set. In this example, only the symptoms deemed significant in identifying the problem are included. The right-hand side of the figure contains the two rules that would be generated from this problem description. Two rules are generated because there are two potential causes associated with the problem. The first rule identifies the problem when caused by a microcode problem. The left-hand side includes the basic symptoms (module, vms-version, offset) as well as another

```
((PROBLEM-TEMPLATE:          IF:
cpu-type:    NAUTILUS          module-of-crash = CTDRIVER
vms-version: 4.4, 4.2          vms-version     = (one-of 4.4 4.2)
module:      CTDRIVER          module-offset   = (one-of AA9 A7E)
offset:      AA9, A7E          cpu-type        = NAUTILUS
image:       NETACP)          THEN:
                              Cause seems to be due to the microcode
                              version on this CPU family.


(CAUSED-BY MICROCODE IMAGE)  IF:
                              module-of-crash = CTDRIVER
individual instances follow ...)   vms-version     = (one-of 4.4 4.2)
                              module-offset   = (one-of #xAA9 #xA7E)
                              current-image   = NETACP
                              THEN:
                              Cause seems to be related to the
                              image running at the time of crash.
```

Figure 5. A Similarity Set (left) and the Two Rules Derived for This Set (right).

symptom that is critical in isolating microcode problems (cpu-type). The second rule is identical to the first except that cpu-type is replaced with current-image. In this case, the current image is critical in isolating software problems that occur when this specific image is running on the system.

Unresolved Crash Processor Browser. The *browser* is an interface meant primarily for expert support engineers viewing the sets of unresolved cases. To the expert support engineers, the automated grouping into sets saves substantial effort and time. When manually looking at unresolved crashes, they do not have other similar unresolved cases available to compare them with. If they did have other such cases, it would be much easier for them to make generalizations and resolve the current unresolved crash. Having similar unresolved cases as a comparison helps in strengthening hypotheses and discarding others. It significantly shortens the resolution time and, thus, accelerates the generation of new knowledge about known crash-causing problems that goes into the symptom-solution or deeper analysis knowledge bases.

Unresolved Crash Processor Matcher. The *matcher* is available to all users during run time. When the symptom-solution and deeper analysis modules do not assist in resolving the current crash, then a user has an unresolved case. S/he can quickly check whether the current crash corresponds to a set of similar unresolved crashes in the unresolved crash processor database. If a match exists, then the user knows that such cases have already been seen at CSCs, and by looking at the comments attached to the particular similarity set of unresolved cases, s/he might find information that would assist him(her) in proceeding further. For example, an expert trying to resolve a set of similar unresolved crashes might place a comment stating that any support engineer seeing similar crashes should get some further parameters to store along with the case that will help the expert in further analysis.

The unresolved crash processor matcher consists of a rule base, with one rule for each similarity set. A rule fires if the symptoms of the current crash match with certain key symptoms of the crash cases in a particular similarity set. The user can then look at the individual crash cases in this set and the comments attached to this set.

Implementing the Unresolved Crash Processor. The unresolved crash processor was written in VAX Lisp, Digital's implementation of Common Lisp (Steele 1989). The unresolved crash processor matcher rule base uses FOXGLOVE rules.

In the latest run of the unresolved crash processor back end, it collected approximately 2500 unresolved cases from 20 CSC sites worldwide. With a threshold of 4 (at least 4 cases in a set), about 90 similarity sets were formed. Our main expert estimates that over 50 rules were generated by him alone within the short time of 8 weeks as a result of accessing these sets through CANASTA. As a comparison, in the previous year when the unresolved crash processor was not available, it is estimated that the knowledge generated by all experts at the U.S. CSC during the course of the entire year was less than 100 bugs (rules).

Case Management Module

All crash cases that are seen by support engineers are saved in a case database. It allows them to browse through both the resolved and unresolved cases seen at their site. There are several important benefits of saving case-related information in a database. CANASTA always saves the status of a case before exiting, including information about whether the crash was resolved using information from outside CANASTA's knowledge bases. Experts can now retrieve all such cases resolved by non-CANASTA means and fill the holes in the CANASTA knowledge bases by adding information about such problems and their solutions. Also, a history of crashes seen on a particular machine is available and can be used when analyzing new crashes on this machine. Finally, it is easy to generate statistics from the database. For example, the most common crash types being encountered or the number of crashes caused by a particular software module can now be generated.

Knowledge Base Maintenance

A knowledge-based application such as CANASTA is only as good as its knowledge base. Critical to CANASTA is the timely and periodic update of its various knowledge bases. New bugs in hardware and software are continuously identified, and previously identified bugs frequently extend to new releases of software or might have better solutions available at a later date. CANASTA has two main types of knowledge bases: a rule base where well-known symptom-solution rules are encoded and a decision tree–based knowledge base where the troubleshooting methodology that experts use is encoded. The development team provided tools and processes to allow the support engineers to maintain these knowledge bases on their own.

For maintaining the symptom-solution knowledge base, a tool was developed that allows experts to enter knowledge of known problems in the form of templates into an exclusive crash-related textual database. The templates are basically textual renditions of the rules in the knowledge base. The CANASTA template consists of essential symptoms that identify a problem and textual attributes such as a description of the problem, the technique for confirming the problem, and the solution. The user first enters the values of only the minimum set of symptoms that are relevant to identify the problem. The tool dynamically checks whether the values being entered are valid (it has validation routines attached to each symptom slot). It also checks for consistency among different symptom values (there are constraints in the relationships between some of the different symptoms). The checks are based on domain-dependent information. For example, version 5.0 of the VMS operating system is valid for the newer central processing units (CPUs). If the user types in VMS 5.0 as the VMS version and then types in the CPU type as VAX 780 (an old CPU that is incompatible with VMS 5.0), then the system indicates a warning. Therefore, even though the value 780 is valid as a DEC CPU, this value is inconsistent with the value of the VMS version already filled in. This type of checking ensures that the conditions in the rule are consistent with each other. The maintenance tool resides at CANASTA sites worldwide, so that crash analysis experts from various locations can enter knowledge into CANASTA. Once the template is filled, the maintenance tool automatically forwards it to a central site where all such templates are collected.

All templates received at the central site are parsed and translated into rules and are then compared for consistency with all the existing rules in the knowledge base. The central-site software has both domain-dependent, as well as domain-independent, heuristics to check for consistency. A new rule is added only if it is found to be consistent with all the other rules in the knowledge base. In this case, the corresponding textual template is also added to the exclusive crash-related textual database, allowing the experts to view the rules in a textual format. They can modify textual entries in the textual database, resulting in corresponding modifications to rules in the rule base. The updated knowledge base and the corresponding textual database are then copied over Digital's internal network by demon processes running at CANASTA sites around the world. The knowledge and textual databases are updated and distributed on a weekly basis.

The symptom-solution knowledge base of previously identified bugs has been exclusively maintained by the experts since September 1989. New rules are added when new bugs are identified in software or hardware. Rules are modified when bugs are found to extend to other CPUs, operating system versions, or software modules; the techniques for confirming the bugs are changed; or better solutions become available. On the average each week, about 5 new rules are entered, and about 10 existing rules are modified.

The deeper analysis knowledge base is maintained using DECtree, a tool developed by Digital. DECtree provides a graphic user interface that allows one to create or modify decision trees. It translates the decision trees into C source code that is compiled and linked to the rest of the CANASTA run-time system.

Development

Early in the project, based on a set of requirements and discussion sessions with several experts, a high-level architecture of the system was designed. We followed many of the suggestions in Kline and Dolins (1987) for identifying the knowledge representation schemes to use. During the first year, we went through several design-implement cycles, similar to the iterative cycles mentioned in Buchanan et al. (1983). The development schedule was tied to base-level releases, with each base level having increased functions or knowledge. By the time we released base level 4 in April 1990, all the modules had been implemented with full function.

The CANASTA team had the full-time commitment of one of Digital's leading experts in crash dump analysis for knowledge-acquisition purposes. The knowledge acquisition was undertaken in two ways: We periodically interviewed the expert, and he scanned the textual databases and placed knowledge about crash-causing bugs into CANASTA using the maintenance tool previously described.

The initial development costs included about six person-years for software development and about two years of expert time for knowledge acquisition.

Testing and Deployment

After each base-level release, CANASTA was tested by both the developers in Marlboro and experts at the U.S. CSC in Colorado. Several types of testing were performed. Each module was tested to check that it was behaving correctly. The developers extensively tested all the modules, except the data-collection module, to verify that they were working as designed. The data-collection module was extensively tested by several of the experts. The experts generated several hundred dumps to test the data-collection module.

After testing module behavior, the different modules in CANASTA were tested on actual customer crashes to verify that they arrived at conclusions that were similar to ones that expert-level support engineers had arrived at. The data-collection module was run on some difficult crash dumps to verify that it could collect all required symptom values. The symptom-solution module was tested on different types of cases to find out how it compared with experts in identifying known problems, both in terms of accuracy and time. To test the unresolved crash processor, our expert collected a number of unresolved cases that he had grouped into similarity sets and had provided high-level classifications for. We ran these unresolved cases through the unresolved crash processor to compare its results with the expert's results. The validation heuristics for the maintenance tool were tested by entering inconsistent symptom-solution rules.

Several criteria were used to measure the success of the deployment effort. First, CANASTA had to be installed at all the major CSCs worldwide. By October 1989, this effort was accomplished: CANASTA was installed at over 20 CSCs in the United States, Europe, Canada, Australia, and Japan. We also wanted CSCs to receive training in using CANASTA. This goal was met by April 1990, with training being offered at most of the major CANASTA sites. We also wanted support engineers to use CANASTA on most crash-related calls seen at CSCs. Current figures indicate that in most CSCs outside the United States, almost all crash-related calls are run through CANASTA. During the summer of 1990, almost 200 crash-related calls were being run through CANASTA every week. We see this goal as being met.

Because CANASTA runs on existing CSC hardware and requires only Digital software, the main deployment cost at CSCs was training. To date, at the U.S. CSC in Colorado, 2 instructors have spent 1 week training about 105 engineers to use CANASTA.

Nature and Estimate of Payoff

There have been a variety of business payoffs since CANASTA's deployment. The bottom line is that the use of CANASTA at CSCs has resulted in substantial savings to Digital in handling crash-related calls. It is estimated that in time savings alone, it is saving Digital over two million dollars each year. Most of the savings directly result from the savings in call-resolution times and increased first-time-correct resolutions. Some of the types of payoffs are hard to quantify, although they are clearly felt by users and managers at CSCs. The most significant of these payoffs are described below.

The average time for handling crash-related calls has decreased. The automatic data-collection module collects the symptoms in less than 3 minutes for most crashes and does so with greater accuracy than most engineers. Cases where a technique for confirmation is not necessary are directly identified within 10 seconds. The rest of the cases require a further test to confirm the initial hypothesis. It usually takes a few minutes to perform the additional test. In both cases, a great deal of time is saved over the previous method of scanning a dozen databases to find a match, which on the average took over 30 minutes.

Experts are able to identify the causes of unresolved cases much faster now by using the similarity sets of unresolved cases generated by the unresolved crash processor. This step leads to a significant decrease in time for identifying bugs in new software and hardware products. Furthermore, the sharing of a common-case database and knowledge base among the engineering staff (the developers of software) and CSCs has resulted in quicker dissemination of knowledge about existing problems and quicker resolution of unresolved cases.

More accurate identification of software problems has resulted in a decrease in the unnecessary replacement of hardware. Besides the cost of the boards, some of which are expensive, this step also saves in the fixed cost associated with sending a field engineer to replace the board. Recently, an expert discovered with the help of the unresolved crash processor that a set of similar unresolved cases was the result of design faults in a hardware product. Catching such hardware design faults early in the release period saves Digital a significant amount of money because a reduced number of hardware components have to be replaced in existing installed systems.

The presence of a case-management facility, where all cases, resolved and unresolved, are saved, has resulted in several advantages: First, support engineers can retrieve cases relating to those that they are investigating by features, such as symptoms, customer ID, dates, and type of resolution. Also, by running the cases in the case database at a site against the weekly knowledge base updates, many unresolved cases are flagged as resolved because rules are modified or added. Support engineers can go back to customers and on a proactive basis suggest changes to their systems that will prevent a repeat of the problem. This sort of tracking was not possible earlier. Furthermore, support engineers at CSCs can now trace the crash history of each customer machine for which calls were reported. Having the crash history of a specific machine can help in isolating the cause of the latest crash in this machine.

The introduction of a distributed knowledge maintenance system allows the incorporation of expertise from multiple sites worldwide. The smaller CSCs in Europe and Asia can now benefit from the large volume of crashes seen at the U.S. CSC. They now share a global case database and the same knowledge base.

CANASTA is perceived as a good training tool at CSCs for new support engineers working on crash analysis. The symptom-solution module, which identifies almost 45 percent of the cases as known bugs, has confirmation techniques for many rules that indicate to the engineers the type of tests that are required to confirm different hypotheses. The decision trees help new engineers in learning about the sequence of tests that are required to confirm different conclusions.

Customer satisfaction has increased because of the quicker resolution of problems and the accurate identification of problems the first time around. The U.S. CSC has been experiencing a reduction in the gross volume of crash-related calls. Several of the expert engineers are attributing this reduction to the increase in first-time-correct resolutions by support engineers who are using CANASTA.

Summary

CANASTA represents a major breakthrough in the way crashes are analyzed at Digital. Using AI technology, CANASTA integrates multiple problem-solving strategies into a single architecture. CANASTA not only assists in initially analyzing a crash, it also provides assistance in the generation and distribution of new knowledge about crash-causing problems.

The success of CANASTA has led us to believe that we can develop diagnostic systems with architectures similar to that of CANASTA to assist support engineers in the resolution of various types of computer hardware and software problems. In fact, an effort is already under way to develop CANASTA-ULTRIX to handle crashes in the ULTRIX operating system (Digital's implementation of UNIX). As we gain experience with several other domains, Digital might well build a shell that is based on this architecture. Such a shell would allow us to release a series of quickly built AI-based diagnostic systems that could be of great use at CSCs.

Acknowledgments

The CANASTA project has been fortunate to have the enthusiastic support of Steve Brissette, one of the leading experts in Digital in the domain of crash dump analysis. We are also grateful to Charlie Gindhart and Mark Fisher, who contributed much of their time toward developing the initial version of the automatic data-collection module. Shanti Subbaraman worked with us during the first year of the project, and we thank her for her efforts in the project during this critical time period. Mark Swartwout, the CANASTA project manager, played a crucial role in helping us access the right people and acquiring the necessary resources.

References

Buchanan, B.; Barstow, D.; Bechtal, R.; Bennet, J.; Clancey, W.; Kulikowski, C.; Mitchell, T.; and Waterman, D. 1983. Constructing an Expert System. In *Building Expert Systems*, 127–167. Reading, Mass.: Addison-Wesley.

Kenah, L. J.; Goldenberg, R. E.; and Bate, S. F 1988. *VAX-VMS Internals and Data Structures*. Burlington, Mass.: Digital.

Kline P. J., and Dolins S. B. 1987. Choosing Architectures for Expert Systems, Technical Report, Corporate Computer Science Center, Texas Instruments Inc., Dallas, Texas.

Steele, G. 1989. *Common Lisp: The Language*. Burlington, Mass.: Digital.

NYNEX MAX: A Telephone Trouble Screening Expert

Henry Rabinowitz, Jack Flamholz, Erica Wolin, and Jim Euchner

No one likes to wait long when the telephone is out of order. Maintaining customer telephones is a significant problem for telephone operating companies because delays in fixing troubles mean dissatisfied customers. Moreover, the high costs of maintenance adversely affect the profits of the telephone companies.

The Problem: Telephone Maintenance

Within NYNEX (a regional Bell operating company and the parent company of New York Telephone and New England Telephone), improving the maintenance process is a strategic priority. The problem of diagnosing and fixing customer-reported telephone troubles has been made more difficult in recent years by the proliferation of new kinds of customer premise equipment, such as answering machines and cheap telephones, nonstandard equipment that was not anticipated by the diagnostic systems designed during the predivestiture days of the Bell System.

The goals of improved maintenance are: a shorter time to diagnose and fix a trouble; fewer handoffs from one person to another when analyzing and repairing the trouble; a reduction in *repeat complaints*—complaints that resurface after the trouble was cleared; a reduction in

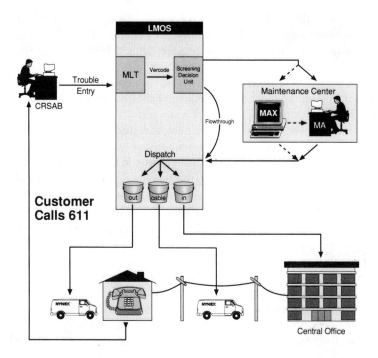

Figure 1. Trouble Flow with and without MAX.

false dispatches—the sending out of a repair technician when the problem is actually in the customer premise equipment, or there is no trouble found at all; and a reduction in *double dispatches*—the sending out of a repair technician to the home when the problem is in the cable, the central office, or some permutation of these locations.

Customer troubles are currently recorded by a Centralized Repair Service Answering Bureau (CRSAB) that answers calls to 611.[1] The troubles are then screened in a maintenance center where they are diagnosed by *maintenance administrators*, who then dispatch the troubles to technicians in the field or the central office. The maintenance administrator first diagnoses where the trouble is: the customer premise equipment, the customer's wiring, the cable facilities (underground or aerial), or the central office (switch, frame, or program control).[2] If the trouble is in customer premise equipment, the maintenance administrator can talk with the customer to help diagnose the trouble.

The entire operation runs on 1970s-style automation: A mainframe computer system, the loop maintenance operation system (LMOS), which was introduced by AT&T in the early 1970s, replaced an earlier operation based on paper slips and dispatch wheels. The CRSAB clerks enter the troubles into LMOS; the maintenance administrators receive the troubles from LMOS and dispatch them through LMOS to the field technicians; the technicians receive their assignments on hand-held LMOS terminals and enter the final status of the troubles back into LMOS.

LMOS has access to a mechanized loop test (MLT) facility. A clerk in CRSAB invokes MLT as soon as the customer identifies the telephone number in trouble. MLT creates an electrical profile of the wire pair, or *loop*, between the customer's telephone and the central office. MLT results are the primary source of information for diagnosing the trouble.

Opportunity for an Expert System for Telephone Trouble Diagnosis

To the Expert Systems Lab at NYNEX, the diagnosis of telephone troubles provided a clear opportunity for an expert system for the following reasons: First, some people are much better at analyzing troubles than others. Second, diagnosis involves the analysis of much information—the electrical test data, the type of switch equipment, and the distance of the trouble from the central office. Third, the diagnostic reasoning process must at times proceed with incomplete or inaccurate data. Fourth, new types of equipment are always being introduced in the network, requiring an evolution of the diagnostic rules.

Historically, diagnosis was performed by test desk technicians, or *testers*, whose training enabled them to perform electrical tests using specialized test equipment on a customer's line. Testers had a good understanding of the electrical principles of telephone operation. As part of the first generation of automation, the work of testers was largely replaced by the MLT facility, which automatically carries out the tests and reports their results to LMOS. The diagnosis could then be performed by maintenance administrators, who no longer needed as deep an understanding of the electrical basis of the telephone network, but knew how to read the MLT screen and apply its information in a formal way to the diagnosis of a customer trouble.

In a second stage of automation, LMOS Generic 3 included a *screening decision unit*, a primitive rule-based system for diagnosing troubles based on a condensed version of MLT data called the *vercode*, a two-character code intended to summarize the MLT results. Unfortunately, the vercode does not preserve enough information to allow the screening decision unit to make an optimal decision. Some locations rely on the screening decision unit to make dispatch decisions because their heavy load of troubles makes human screening difficult. Those locations that rely on the screening decision unit to diagnose their trouble load generally show a higher rate of double and false dispatches.

MAX was designed to emulate the work of a human maintenance administrator, that is, to use the MLT test results, together with other information such as the weather, to make a screening diagnosis. The only exception is that MAX would have the option of referring difficult troubles to a human maintenance administrator. A goal of MAX is to reduce the number of double and false dispatches.

Knowledge Acquisition

Part of the problem in building a knowledge-based system in an already automated field is that much of the knowledge in the domain is disappearing. Only seasoned veterans who once worked as testers have deep knowledge of the telephone system from the ground up. We turned to one such expert from New England Telephone, Ed Power, who was able to suggest rules that were more subtle than those used by many maintenance administrators today. For example, his rules are based on a three-point electrical test, but most maintenance administrators use data from the less reliable two-point test.

The series of interviews with the expert lasted several months. After modeling Power's diagnostic ideas in a knowledge base using the ART expert system shell, we compared the results of the rules on a set of troubles with Power's diagnosis. The comparison led to further refinements in the knowledge base. This process continued through several iterations.

External Architecture

MAX emulates a human user sitting at an LMOS terminal. MAX receives a trouble on an emulated LMOS terminal screen, obtains MLT data on another emulated terminal screen, makes an expert diagnosis, and enters the recommended dispatch instructions on the original LMOS screen. MAX's recommendations take the form of a status code, which directs the trouble to the correct dispatch pool, and a narrative in which MAX explains what it thinks is the cause of the trouble.

The advantage of emulating a human maintenance administrator's interface is that no changes in the host systems or the maintenance center's operations are necessary. Because MAX works on one trouble at a time, even if it fails, it cannot disrupt the operations of the maintenance center. The host system tracks each trouble; if a trouble assigned to a maintenance administrator or MAX times out, LMOS reassigns it to another maintenance administrator.

Because MAX emulates a human maintenance administrator, it is easy for management to track its performance. All the management tools for monitoring a maintenance administrator's performance can be used to monitor MAX's performance. For example, managers can monitor MAX's performance by checking the pending trouble queue for MAX's employee code or, retrospectively, by checking the results of troubles screened by MAX's employee code. Thus, the integration of the expert system can proceed with minimal change to the maintenance center's work flow. When people ask, as they always do of a new system, "Did MAX cause this problem?" we can always answer by saying, "Could a human maintenance administrator have done this?" MAX cannot do what a human cannot do. This design decision helped to smooth MAX's deployment. The ability of a workstation to emulate several terminals and run an expert process simultaneously makes this design possible.

The disadvantage of using terminal emulation as the interface to a host application is that the majority of the work in implementing the system is devoted to getting the communications right; the design of the knowledge base was by far the easiest part of the system. We are forced to use terminal emulation because the host system, LMOS, was purchased from another company, AT&T, and offers no application-to-application communications interface. Terminal emulation is complicated by the fact that screens change periodically, with each new release of the host application. In general, screens are not designed for computer "users" but for human users, who can more readily adjust to changes in the position and contents of a field. Unfortunately, at the moment, there is no alternative to terminal emulation. For an expert system to be of strategic significance, it must interact with host databases; to do so, it needs to use terminal emulation until host systems provide better interfaces.

To the host system, MAX looks like just another maintenance administrator with a distinct employee code. To cause LMOS to feed troubles to MAX, MAX executes an administrative LMOS command that establishes a queue of pending troubles for MAX's employee code and modifies the LMOS screening rules to send appropriate troubles to this queue.

Internal Architecture

Internally, MAX consists of an *expert agent* that communicates with LMOS through a *session manager* that handles multiple emulated terminals. MAX is implemented on general-purpose UNIX workstations. We chose UNIX workstations over Lisp machines because of their relatively low cost and because UNIX with windowing forms a good environment for software deployment and user interface design. We used Sun 3/60 and

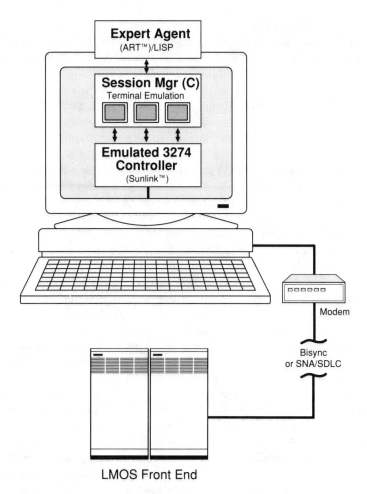

Figure 2. The MAX *Internal Architecture.*

Sun Sparcstation 1+ workstations to deploy MAX. The MAX expert agent's knowledge base is implemented in ART with additional Common Lisp code. The communications interface between LMOS and the MAX expert agent is handled by the session manager, an application-level protocol interface-building tool that was designed for use in MAX. The session manager has proven to be such a valuable tool for implementing host-workstation dialogues using multiple terminal emulation sessions that it has already been reused in four other applications. We used Sun's Sunview interface to build the user interface to MAX and FrameMaker to provide an online hypertext help facility.

ART-Lisp Expert Agent

The heart of MAX is the expert agent's knowledge base. The expert agent is written as a set of about 75 rules that follow the human expert's reasoning process. The MAX expert agent bases its diagnosis on five elements: First is the MLT electrical signature, including voltage, capacitive and longitudinal balances, and AC and DC resistances. MLT sometimes also provides the distance of the trouble from the customer and from the central office. There can be more than one invocation of MLT. Second is the type of switching equipment to which the customer's line is attached. (Each type of switch has a distinct electrical signature, and MLT can be fooled by certain signatures on certain switches, drawing the wrong conclusion from its own data.) Third is the class of the customer's service. Fourth is the weather. Different rules pertain in wet and dry weather. A human user must tell the computer what the weather is like outside. Fifth is the number of stages of cable facilities between the customer and the central office.

The expert agent reasons by forward chaining from the available trouble data. If more than one diagnosis is reached, an arbitration phase chooses the best diagnosis. The arbitration phase works as follows: First, select the diagnosis derived from the highest-authority rule. Rules are assigned authority as members of rule groups. The authority of a rule group is based on the type of information involved. For example, rules based on water have higher authority than rules based on the type of equipment. Second, if two diagnoses have the same authority, choose the diagnosis that is cheaper to implement. For example, it is cheaper to dispatch a technician to the central office than to dispatch to the customer's home. The rules are designed conservatively; if there is insufficient information to choose a firm diagnosis, MAX passes the problem to human maintenance administrators for further diagnosis or testing.

Under certain conditions, MAX can decide that the original data from MLT, performed when the trouble was called in, are inconclusive. The expert agent can request a fresh MLT. It can then base its diagnosis on the combined information from the old test and the fresh test. To request a fresh test, the expert agent sends a request to the session manager, which sends a request to LMOS by typing on the emulated terminal.

The MAX expert agent's diagnosis is expressed in a canned narrative that is used by human screeners and repair technicians who subsequently receive the trouble. It might say, for example, "check for open in drop wire" or "needs talk test; possible CPE trouble." The diagnosis is also expressed in a status code that tells LMOS where to send the trouble. The trouble can be sent to a human maintenance administrator for further testing, a cable technician, a technician who will go to the customer premises, or a technician in the central office.

MAX's rules can be customized to local conditions by a set of parameters, which the individual maintenance centers can change and tune over time. In designing the rules, our philosophy about parameters was that they should be as few as possible, they should enable all sites to use the same set of rules, and they should each have a physical meaning. These goals proved difficult to attain; we began with 8 parameters and, after a second release, ended with 29. However, the enhanced set of parameters allows the MAX administrator to more closely tailor MAX's operations to local conditions.

Session Manager for Terminal Emulation

The session manager is a tool for writing application-level protocols between various hosts and processes. In MAX, we used the session manager to communicate between the expert agent process and three emulated terminal sessions associated with Bisync LMOS terminals. The Bisync communication is implemented using Sun's Sunlink package, which allows a Sun to emulate a 3270 controller. We also ported MAX to a VTAM-SDLC communications environment using Sunlink SNA.

The session manager is a data-driven program. It allows the programmer to specify a set of agents, each of which controls a dialogue between the application and a host application or other external process. Each agent is specified as a set of messages to be recognized and a finite-state machine that controls its actions. Each agent has a device, which controls its communication with the external host by means of, for example, terminal emulation, printer emulation, or UNIX pipe.

For each agent with a terminal emulation device, its messages are specified as a set of screens, or *masks*. The masks can be specified using fields, which are regular expressions anchored at particular row and column positions. A mask can also be specified as a Boolean combination of fields and other masks. A mask can be relocated to different parts of the screen so that a complex set of masks can be constructed from common components.

Each agent has two mailboxes: an external mailbox that receives events corresponding to incoming masks on the agent's device and an internal mailbox for receiving messages from other agents, allowing the agents to cooperate and coordinate their work.

In the original implementation of the session manager, the agent specifications were written in Lisp-style S-expressions. A Lisp preprocessor converts these specifications into object-oriented C code, which is then compiled with the generic session manager code.

The session manager also contains a timer facility that allows an agent to send a message to another agent (or itself) after a specified time interval. This facility is useful in emulating a maintenance administrator's ability to periodically hit a key to request a new trouble.

Because of the many users of the session manager, we reimplemented it in C++, using LEX and YACC for preprocessing the agent specifications. The rewrite was necessary to thoroughly disentangle MAX from the session manager. We successfully used the session manager in four other applications, using Bisync, SDLC, and asynchronous terminals as well as UNIX pipes.

The session manager offers a number of useful tools for debugging, including a log file from which the entire session can be replayed. The log file created by the session manager contains all input events from external sources and all timer events. In playback mode, the session manager can replay the events from the log file, possibly choosing some sources from live input and some from playback input. This approach enables the programmer to recreate communications problems and analyze them in the lab, where a greater number of debugging tools are available. We have also played back log files on site and over the phone for rapid troubleshooting.

Current Deployment and Benefits of MAX

MAX is currently running in 42 maintenance centers in New York Telephone and New England Telephone (virtually every residence-oriented maintenance center). It screens 38 percent of all troubles, that is, about 10,400 troubles every day.[3] Because each maintenance center can control how many troubles flow through MAX, some centers make greater use of MAX than others. Some centers have over 50 percent of their troubles flowing through MAX.

Part of the variation in the percentage of troubles screened by MAX is because MAX currently handles only residential and small business troubles. The variety of customer premise equipment in large businesses makes diagnosing their troubles more complex. A version of MAX for large businesses is under development.

Another reason why MAX does not handle all troubles is that LMOS can correctly screen certain troubles on its own, using its screening decision unit. We did not need to replicate this capability. Also, troubles with certain "handle codes" assigned in CRSAB bypass the screening decision unit and, hence, MAX. For example, when a troubled line is identified as a component of a damaged cable, it is automatically attached to the cable failure ticket for this damaged cable, without passing through MAX.

Locations that formerly relied heavily on the LMOS screening deci-sion unit, primarily in New York Telephone, find that MAX's greatest benefit is in reducing false dispatches in the field. Locations that for-merly relied heavily on human screening of troubles, primarily in New England Telephone, find that MAX's greatest benefit is in reducing the number of maintenance administrator hours needed for screening troubles in the maintenance centers.

As with other expert systems, the measurement of MAX's benefits is not a simple matter. We performed studies with small samples and highly accurate data and studies with large samples but somewhat noisy data. With few exceptions, MAX's diagnostic accuracy was universally ac-cepted. In each location where MAX was deployed, employees would challenge MAX's more unusual diagnoses and were often pleased to find that MAX reasoned correctly, if unconventionally, in making its conclusions. A comparison of MAX's diagnoses with those of human ex-perts found 96-percent agreement.

One way to measure the benefits from MAX is to review a set of trou-bles diagnosed by MAX and retrospectively examine their final disposi-tions. One such study was performed on a set of troubles randomly se-lected from a base of 5158 MAX-handled troubles in 4 maintenance centers—2 in New York, 2 in New England—over a 1-week period. Such a study required careful analysis of each trouble by an expert, precluding a large sample of troubles. The final dispositions of MAX-di-agnosed troubles were contrasted with the way these same troubles would have been diagnosed by the LMOS screening decision unit before MAX was installed. The purpose of the study was to see how much human testing (maintenance administrator work in the maintenance centers) and how many unnecessary dispatches (technicians in the field) were saved by MAX. The results at the four maintenance centers are shown in table 1.

Maintenance centers 2 and 3 are in New England, and 1 and 4 are in New York. Note that in maintenance center 4, MAX actually increased the amount of maintenance administrator testing. Even a small-per-centage savings in the number of dispatches translates to significant dollar savings because each dispatch typically involves at least one hour of time by a highly trained craft worker.

The aggregate results for these tests are as follows:

Number of troubles examined:	593
Number of tests saved:	23
Number of dispatches saved:	25

Similar studies were performed in other maintenance centers with equally promising results.

Center	Tests Saved (%)	Dispatches Saved (%)
1	9.1	5.3
2	3.8	0.8
3	5.7	4.2
4	-3.7	10.6

Table 1. Test Results Comparing MAX and Human Testers.

However, the accuracy of individual decisions is not the only way to measure MAX's benefit. Another way is to observe changes in the false dispatch rate in the maintenance center as a whole. Because MAX sometimes passes its diagnosis of the trouble to human maintenance administrators for further screening, it is not sufficient to view MAX's performance in isolation from the maintenance center.

A large-scale study was performed involving nine maintenance centers in New England. With a database query system associated with LMOS, data were pulled for two seven-week periods, one from a pre-MAX baseline and one from a period exactly one year later with MAX in place. The one-year-later time period was selected so that weather and other seasonal factors would have minimal impact. The results are as follows:

	Troubles Screened	False Dispatches
Baseline	177516	16663 (9.39%)
With MAX	178832	15669 (8.76%)

The drop in false dispatches from 9.39 percent to 8.76 percent constitutes a 6.7 percent improvement and represents nearly a thousand saved dispatches in 9 maintenance centers over the 7-week period. To these savings must be added the savings in maintenance administrator testing, which in New England locations is significant.

These studies, combined with other similar studies, conservatively place the savings in maintenance center operations at several million dollars each year—at a minimum.

Implementation History and Effects on the Maintenance Centers

The initial design of MAX began in December 1986. The knowledge base was first tested against a set of troubles in mid-1987. The first live test of MAX in a maintenance center occurred in Manchester, New

Hampshire, in February 1989. MAX was programmed by 3 people, taking 2-½ years from inception to first deployment. Then, fate intervened in a curious way. Just before the scheduled deployment of the first production version of MAX, NYNEX underwent a strike by its unionized employees. MAX was drafted to help the management staff run the maintenance centers without their normal complement of craft workers.

We had not intended to deploy rapidly. In fact, we had developed software and a strategy for prospective preinstallation assessment of MAX site by site. We had planned a careful, slow rollout of MAX, with time to evaluate its performance in each maintenance center, carefully tune its parameters to local conditions, train local users, and build the trust of management and workers before moving on to the next site. Under the circumstances, these steps had to be deferred.

Because of the strike, MAX was deployed in 23 maintenance centers within 5 months. The strike conditions enabled a rapid deployment because normal operating procedures were temporarily bypassed. The rapid rollout of MAX enabled the maintenance centers to cope with the volume of troubles encountered during the strike. The users of MAX found it was especially helpful in identifying customer premise equipment troubles that could be handled by talking to the customer, thus saving dispatches to the field.

Once the strike was over in December 1989, we began to revisit the MAX installations. The most striking observation we made was that certain features of the MAX system, designed and tested in New England, did not work appropriately in New York City. New England differs from New York in its weather, the age of its plant, its operating procedures and regulatory rules, and its trouble load.

New York City is exceptional in many ways, including its telephone network. For example, MAX correctly identified most of the problems in many areas of New York City as lying in the cable facilities. However, this diagnostic fact, although correct, was not useful to the maintenance centers, which lack the personnel to correct all the cable problems in the city.

In one particularly tense and memorable meeting, the management of three New York City maintenance centers told us that if we didn't reduce MAX's propensity for cable dispatches, they would shut it down indefinitely. They had grown accustomed to dealing with the chronic shortage of cable splicers by *swapping pairs*, a procedure that quickly restores service but defers cable maintenance. MAX was actually creating extra work for them, forcing them to manually restatus a large portion of its cable dispatches as swaps.

We found ourselves faced with a dilemma: Either retain the purity of the knowledge base and face shutdown in the centers, or make MAX an automated accomplice to a practice that senior management did not want to encourage. Our solution was a compromise. We agreed that a subclass of the cable troubles, namely, cross-battery troubles, would always be marked for cable dispatch, with a new voltage-threshold parameter provided to control MAX's sensitivity to cross-batteries.[4] The remaining cable troubles would default to cable dispatch, but the maintenance centers could restatus them for pair swaps inside MAX by setting a parameter. In this fashion, we supported the maintenance centers' need for an established "workaround" without compromising the knowledge base.

Regulatory differences between New England and New York created another crisis. In New York State, troubled lines marked "out of service" must be fixed within a certain time interval, or the customer is entitled to a rebate. The out-of-service indication is piggybacked onto a three-digit code on the trouble ticket that MAX receives, a fact that the New England expert was unaware of. MAX was unwittingly overwriting the out-of-service indication in certain New York troubles. As a result, some New York centers were charged with undeserved rebates and shut MAX down for a few weeks. We addressed this problem by introducing a parameter to allow local control.

Our solution to most regional differences was to enlarge the set of parameters that allows each maintenance center to tune MAX to its local needs without changing the knowledge base itself. Thus, one knowledge base can still suffice for all our installations.

Maintenance of MAX

The Expert Systems Lab at NYNEX Science and Technology found that maintenance of MAX is an issue that cannot be ignored. Terminal emulation means that MAX is vulnerable to changes in corporate networking policies and host application screens. New kinds of customer equipment or switch equipment and changes to operating procedures require changes in MAX. The fact that it is embedded in the day-to-day operations and communications of the company makes MAX more vulnerable to change than management information system–type applications—the knowledge in knowledge-based systems ages quickly. Moreover, the Lisp and ART languages involved in MAX make it difficult to hand off to a management information system organization. Therefore, the Expert Systems Lab chose to assume the responsibility of maintaining MAX, with the idea that this process will help us channel MAX's evolution in a direction desirable to the users. We brought some people from the operation side of the telephone companies into our lab to help us support the product. Their presence not only helps us support the existing product but also anticipate the future needs of the users in the maintenance centers.

A second release of MAX in March 1990 greatly increased the number of parameters that are controllable by the individual maintenance centers. Increasing the number of parameters allows MAX to more flexibly meet local needs without requiring changes in the knowledge base. The problem with introducing more parameters is that eventually a second expert system might be needed to help set the parameters! In reality, we followed the release by having a human expert visit each maintenance center to tune its parameters based on local needs. The increase in the number of parameters can point to gaps in the knowledge base, which, if filled, would reduce the parameter set to a manageable size.

Reactions to MAX

Skepticism of MAX's abilities accompanied its arrival in each maintenance center and was generally dispelled by the examination of a few of MAX's diagnoses. The opposite problem appears over time: People begin to trust MAX too readily. Its status as a computer lends it undue authority; the users assume that MAX makes the right decisions without carefully evaluating MAX's performance. Changes in the operating environment that would affect MAX's rules are not always entered into MAX. MAX requires continued vigilance by the system administrator and local management. Some centers continue to question MAX's value and have configured it to process few customer troubles, but they are a small minority.

Workplace Issues

In general, management is drawn to expert system technology by its promise of increased productivity, but clerical and craft workers see it as having a destabilizing effect on their work environment. Management might find it easier to initiate change in the workplace by introducing obedient, pliable computer systems than by changing policies, operating procedures, and contracts.

Although NYNEX does not traditionally lay off employees, MAX will lead to some reassignment of employees. Many maintenance administrators are concerned that MAX will be used to reduce the number of maintenance administrator positions. They understandably see MAX as computerized competition—MAX can diagnose a trouble in 10 seconds, but a human maintenance administrator takes about 3 minutes.[5]

Automation does not always reduce workload and jobs despite our impression to the contrary. For example, MAX is conservative in its dispatching strategy, leaving certain kinds of troubles for human analysis. In table 1, note that MAX increased the test load in maintenance center 4, which meant more work for the maintenance administrators. However, MAX also cut the dispatch rate, thereby enabling maintenance center 4 to reallocate outside craft workers from ongoing to preventive maintenance. The center subsequently experienced a decrease in new troubles. Although it was MAX that initially reduced the load on the outside craft workers, the consequent drop in report rate resulted from a decision by local management on the best way to reallocate these people.

Another example of the complex outcome of introducing MAX into the workplace is in the cable dispatch area. The fact that MAX identifies many problems in the cable facilities lends greater weight to these problems, even though the problems were well known beforehand. Thus, paradoxically, MAX might lead to creating more jobs in some areas (cable splicing) and reducing jobs in others.

The choice of how to reallocate maintenance administrators and field technicians after MAX's deployment is a significant management decision. The presence of MAX can allow maintenance administrators to move to positions where they can focus on more preventive maintenance work. However, the pressure to reduce costs in the maintenance centers might push managers to see the presence of MAX as an opportunity to reduce the number of maintenance administrators.

Centralize or Decentralize?

MAX is designed as a locally based workstation tool. Currently, the local users interact with MAX primarily by turning it on and off, announcing the weather to it, changing local parameter information, and checking its performance during the day. The developers of MAX would like to use its presence in the maintenance centers to provide more interactive, cooperative tools for analysis and training. Management and data processing operations staff are understandably concerned about having 42 UNIX workstations performing critical tasks at widely dispersed geographic locations that lack local system expertise. They prefer to centralize all the MAX machines.

Those who favor remaining decentralized argue that the company should pay the higher administrative cost of distributed workstation maintenance to realize much greater cost savings in customer loop maintenance. Given that MAX already takes a significant amount of work and, with it, some control away from the centers, the proponents of remaining decentralized question the impact of taking away the machine itself.

The proponents of centralization counter that loop maintenance is a highly reactive, pressured job that leaves little time for analysis. Thus, no matter how powerful and sophisticated the workstation tools are, the benefits are limited by the job and the environment. They argue that one might as well at least enjoy the benefit of centralized hardware maintenance. The centralization-decentralization debate has not been resolved.

Future Enhancements

An enhancement that is under way will make the MAX knowledge base available as a server to other client applications. For example, when a new telephone is installed, the line is tested on the morning before the installer goes out. The installation process would benefit from using MAX's diagnostic abilities to analyze the test results. Similarly, if the operator in CRSAB had MAX's expertise available, s/he could possibly close out certain troubles during the initial contact with the customer. Moving MAX's expertise into the initial customer contact can transform the work environment by reducing the number of handoffs of the trouble. Both these applications are actively being pursued. In each case, MAX's knowledge base would have to be restructured to separate MAX's knowledge from the policy requirements of MAX's current job as a trouble screener.

We are actively investigating an adaptive MAX that uses machine-learning techniques to improve performance. The greatest problem in this effort is obtaining a reliable feedback mechanism; the data on final disposition of closed troubles can be noisy. We are examining inductive, neural net, and explanation-based learning approaches.

A further area for future enhancements is giving maintenance administrators more tools to examine MAX's performance. A maintenance administrator should be able to inquire how MAX handled a particular trouble on a particular date and ask MAX why it made this diagnostic decision. This inquiry feature would be useful both as an educational tool and as a means of improving user feedback. Such a tool would make MAX friendlier to human maintenance administrators and might improve their perception of it.

We would like MAX to be able to read the free-form comments entered by the clerks in the original interaction with the customer. They use common codes for complaints, such as "HOOL" (hears others online). These codes could be incorporated into the evidence that MAX can sift for diagnosis.

One future enhancement that has often been requested is to connect MAX to more host systems so that it can incorporate more information in its decisions. For example, if MAX connects to the billing system, it can determine whether the customer has lost service because the bill was not paid.

Conclusion

MAX demonstrates the practicality of using an expert system to diagnose telephone troubles. MAX is now a mature and widely deployed expert system whose integration in the NYNEX telephone companies' maintenance operation has been smoothed by its emulation of the human maintenance administrator's interfaces. The deployment of MAX has shown the value of a workstation-based expert that can talk to multiple host screens through terminal emulation. Although MAX emulates a human maintenance administrator's computer interfaces, it uses a knowledge base with a deeper knowledge of the electric basis of telephone diagnosis than is possessed by many human maintenance administrators. MAX's design included reusable components that have since proven their value in other expert systems as well.

Notes

1. In some areas, the Centralized Repair Service Answering Bureau has a different telephone number.

2. Troubles lying between the central office and the drop wire to the customer premises are said to be in the cable facilities. Cable can be aerial or underground.

3. This estimate is for all NYNEX locations as of October 1990. New York Telephone alone sends 29 percent of its troubles through MAX, about 6,100 troubles each day. The percentage is based on the total number of customer-reported troubles for residential and small business telephones.

4. Cross-battery troubles are caused by an undesired completion of the customer's circuit with a foreign battery, often indicating trouble in the cable. MAX's sensitivity to these types of troubles can be controlled by setting the threshold of the voltage at which such a problem is noted.

5. MAX can take as long as two minutes to diagnose a trouble if MAX needs to ask for a retest of the telephone line. Most of this time is spent just waiting, so that the retest does not immediately follow the initial test.

Finance

AES
SunAmerica Financial & Inference Corporatiog

AL^{2}X
AL^{2}X Development Corporation

The Credit Clearing House
Dun & Bradstreet Corporation & Inference Corporation

CUBUS
Swiss Bank Corporation

AES: SunAmerica's Appointment Expert System

Richard Levine, Gary MacKinnon, Frank Angrisani, and Lew Roth

SunAmerica is a major financial services company that primarily sells fixed and variable annuity products. Its assets (owned or under management) currently total approximately 11 billion dollars.

SunAmerica was confronted with the industrywide problem that all agents, broker-dealers, and corporations must be appointed to the State Board of Insurance in each state for each product line to be sold. Fixed-rate annuity products are state regulated, variable-rate annuity products are state and federally regulated, and appointment regulations for each state are unique. The process was paper and labor intensive and, subsequently, error prone.

Additionally, SunAmerica was in the process of moving its administrative operations from Atlanta to Los Angeles. As part of the move, reductions in office staff, including the Licensing Department, were planned, and most of the Los Angeles staff would be hired locally. Years of in-house appointment expertise would be lost with the closing of the Atlanta office. Therefore, the appointment expert system (AES) was an excellent solution to capturing and codifying the expertise before it was lost and allowing the small and untrained Los Angeles staff to maintain appointment processing in the growing company.

In addition, AES took an internal process that averaged two weeks to perform and reduced it to two days. This process is often an agent's first impression of the insurer's service and can influence the agent's attitude toward the insurer's products. Because high-speed, high-quality service is often the margin of difference when agents choose an insurance carrier, AES provided SunAmerica with a significant achievement in retooling its appointment procedure, thereby gaining strategic advantage.

In this chapter, AES refers to the core expert system, and the term *licensing system* refers to the aggregate of AES and the software that connects to the associated systems, printer, and appointment processor terminal. AES was jointly developed by SunAmerica and Inference Corporation in less than a year, starting with a proof-of-concept model and ending with a fully deployed production system. Inference Corporation built the core expert system, and SunAmerica built the connectivity to the associated systems and supplied the domain expertise.

The Appointment Process: A Business Perspective

Appointment requests are received from agents, broker-dealers, agencies, and corporations through a *preliminary data sheet* (PDS), the SunAmerica appointment request form. PDS requires the applicant to indicate the type of appointment desired (for example, individual or corporate), corporate affiliation, demographic information, character data, and current licensing information for the state(s) in which the appointment is requested.

The submitted forms are read by an imaging system in the mail room and indexed. The documents can be accessed from the imaging system by all internal offices. In the Licensing Department, two terminals are set up at each appointment processor's desk, one tied in to the imaging system, the other connected to AES.

The appointment processor types the pertinent data from the imaging system into the licensing system. The appointment data-entry screens are window and form based, allowing the user to map data into forms in the licensing system that essentially correspond in a one-to-one manner with physical forms received from the agent or the state's licensing departments. (Currently, the pattern-recognition talents of a human appointment processor are necessary to transfer data from the imaging system into a machine-readable form for the licensing system. When the technology allows, even this tiresome task will be automated.)

After data entry, AES is invoked to reason on the submitted data for compliance with the pertinent regulations. Input errors and data or form omissions are brought to the attention of the appointment processors for immediate corrective action. If some errors cannot immediately be corrected, AES is again invoked with a request to write the missing requirements onto SunAmerica's work queue system for followup. Later in the day, staff members will "work the queue," attempting to solve the open issues by phoning or writing to the agent or state.

When no errors remain, AES will order a check to be generated by the check disbursement system (CDS) by providing CDS with the state-required fee amount, name and address of the state insurance agency, and the payee of the check. The checks are run in batch mode and delivered the next day to the Licensing Department. The appointment processor then reactivates AES, which informs the appointment processor which state appointment form to load into the Smart Printer. AES then automatically completes the form with the appointment-specific data and provides additional instructions, such as having the form signed or notarized.

The Smart Printer is key to the labor-saving benefits of the system. The software built for the system allows the printer to automatically print over 100 different state forms and minimizes the chances of typographic errors that would result in state rejections of applications.

The form is matched with the previously ordered check and mailed to the state for approval. Depending on the state, the agent is either appointed at this time or must wait for an acknowledgment from the state. In either case, when all conditions are met, AES communicates with the automatic letter generation system to send a congratulatory letter informing the agent of the appointments for particular states and products that s/he can now sell.

The Appointment Process: A Technical Perspective

An expert system solution to the appointment problem was clear from the beginning because of the extreme variability between appointment requirements coupled with the need to frequently modify the procedures as states change their requirements. Indeed, an individual appointment process is relatively straightforward, consisting primarily of filling out and submitting proper forms and fees to the state. The amount of reasoning on an appointment is minor. However, any error in the forms or fees can cause delays of weeks. The real problem is classifying the appointment into the right appointment category so that the procedures that pertain to this category are properly applied. Some of the issues of the classification problem are outlined in the following paragraphs.

Each state has it own language and semantic definitions for agent appointments, so that part of the solution was to create abstractions of the state's definitions and then attempt to fit the states into these categories. The states themselves make no attempt to cooperate with each other in the definitions, so it was not unusual for us to not only add categories but also to redefine existing categories and the rules that applied to them as we learned more during development. Some of the state variability is outlined in the description that follows:

What is an appointment? Nominally, an appointment is not a license. A *license* typically represents an ability to sell a type of insurance. An *appointment* represents the ability to sell a particular insurance company's insurance products. In most states, these elements are two separate concepts, with the licensing component preceding the appointment component. In some states, the licensing and appointment are one and the same, and the term appointment is not even used by the state.

What is an agent? In general, an *agent* can be a corporation, an individual working independently, or an individual working for a corporation. (Some states add the concepts of general agent, solicitor, or broker-dealer, which we won't define here except to say that they are exceptions and, typically, need special case handling.) An agent (particularly a corporation) can have different names in different states. An individual can be licensed differently as an individual, a corporation, or an individual within a corporation among the various states in which s/he does business. All states appoint individuals as agents. Some states do not recognize corporations as entities that can be appointed and require that the members of the corporation get individual appointments. In some states, the employees of the corporation are carried on the corporation appointment; in others, they must be separately appointed. In some states, the requirements for a license do not parallel the requirements for an appointment; for example, in some states, corporations are licensed but not appointed.

Where is the agent? Agents must get *resident appointments* in the state in which they are a resident and *nonresident appointments* in any other states. In general, an agent is resident in the state where s/he lives and has an office. Complications arise when the agent works in a different state from where s/he lives. Corporations, however, can obtain resident appointments in more than one state.

What can the agent sell? In general, precedence requirements exist for an agent to sell a particular brand of insurance in a particular state. One relatively simple requirement is that the agent be licensed to sell the type of insurance. In addition, if this state is a nonresident state, the agent typically is required to be successfully appointed in his(her) resident state first. Often, a letter of certification from the resident state addressed to the nonresident state is required for proof of the resident appointment. An appropriate fee must accompany this request.

Some types of insurance require that the agent be licensed successfully and appointed in other certain types of insurance before appointment in this type is allowed. If the agent is part of an agent hierarchy within an agency, the agents above this agent must typically be successfully licensed and appointed.

When can the agent sell? This question is really two questions. One concerns when the agent can solicit business, the other when the agent can receive commissions from sales. For each of these areas, there are several milestones that are significant, with the significance varying between the states. The milestones are the internal processing of the paperwork by the insurance company; the mailing of the forms from the state; a fixed time in days after the forms are mailed; and, finally, the receipt of an acknowledgment by the state. In some states, no paperwork needs to be sent to the state at all, and the agent can do business as soon as the insurance company internally processes the paperwork.

How long can the agent sell? Appointments are typically for one or two years or an indefinite period of time. Renewals or terminations can happen automatically at the end of this time, depending on the state, and the insurance company must take some action if it desires some other outcome.

What is the fee? Typically, fixed fees are required for an appointment. In some states, the fee is based on each product; in others, it is based on appointments. For nonresident appointments, some states retaliate against other states' nonresidence fees, so that the fee charged is the higher of the two. One state is reciprocal, and charges whatever the other state charges. For these nonresidence situations, sometimes the resident state is determined by where the agent lives. In others, it is where the insurance company is located. Also, some fees are dependent on the time of year the appointment is made.

Where can the agent sell? Most states appoint and license agents on a statewide basis. Some states require separate appointments for individual counties or cities within the state.

Where are the forms sent? Most states have one address for applications. Some states have different addresses for different product types. Others have different addresses for appointments and terminations.

Miscellaneous: Some states require that the forms be handwritten; others require a number two pencil be used; most require that the forms be typed. Some require a notary signature. Some require the agent's signature. For some lines of insurance, the states require various types of federal licenses.

What is an agent's address? The variability of the appointment process even applies to mundane issues such as the agent's address. Typically, an agent has three addresses: residence, office street address, and office

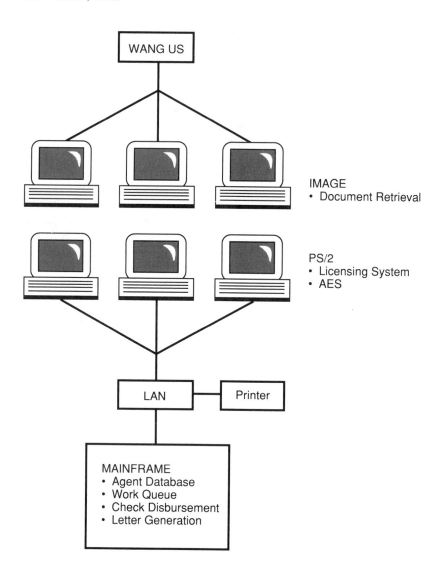

Figure 1. System Architecture.

mailing address. When a form requires an address, a selection from these three, based on state requirements, must be made.

Although not complete, this listing represents more than half of the current variations found in the appointment process. Undoubtedly, the list will grow as time goes on, and states invent new complications. The technical challenge was to find a way to accommodate these variations in an architecture that was sufficiently transparent to be maintained by the insurance company staff and flexible enough to readily accommodate changes to state regulations.

System Architecture

As described earlier, two major software systems are used together in the processing of appointments, although at this time, they are not physically connected. The first is an imaging system that holds images of all documents associated with an agent. This information includes licenses, applications, and other forms and correspondence. The second system, the licensing system, contains machine-readable data associated with an agent (figure 1).

The licensing system itself resides on approximately 10 IBM PC model 80s running OS2 with 16 megabytes of memory. The personal computers are connected on a local area network, which serves primarily as a gateway to the mainframe and the Smart Printer as well as a distribution vehicle for software upgrades. In regard to the licensing system, the personal computers do not talk to each other except by passing data through the mainframe.

Each workstation is connected to a mainframe computer that serves as a gateway to other systems used by the licensing system:

First is the *agent database system*. This system contains information about the agent and the current status of the appointment, including missing information or documents.

Second is the *work queue tracking system*. Problems associated with processing an appointment are recorded and tracked on this system.

Third is the check disbursement system. This system writes a check on receiving an electronic request from AES.

Fourth is the automatic letter generation system. This system automatically writes congratulatory and other letters on receiving an electronic request from AES.

Software Architecture

One approach that was initially considered was to represent the state data as tables and have processing done as table lookups. This approach would yield a working system but at an enormous loss of flexibility and maintainability. For example, the state addresses could nominally be placed in a table of length 50. However, this length is not sufficient. The addresses currently vary along at least two other dimensions because of exceptions in a few states: type of product and type of action (appointment or termination). One can conceptualize other dimensions that states can add in the future, such as type of agent (corporate or individual) or resident versus nonresident. Adding or removing these dimensions as they came and went would require extraordinary modifications to the tables.

Instead of placing the appointment procedures into tables whose access keys represent the appointment situation, each appointment procedure is represented as an ART-IM (ART-IM is a commercially available expert system development language from Inference Corporation) schema that not only describes the particular procedure but also contains all the information identifying where it is applicable. The advantage of this approach can be shown with an example: If the state of Ohio splits its insurance address from one into two, depending on whether the agent is a corporation or an individual, then the one data schema in the system is copied by the programmer into two schemas, one with each address; the one requirement limiting the applicability to the state of Ohio is amended to add a second requirement based on agent type. This change is relatively simple and can readily be made by a programmer who is not versed in the overall system architecture but is given a simple maintenance manual.

The following example is a typical procedure schema in the system written in pseudocode:

```
Schema Mississippi-individual-appointment-procedure
    tasks                    Appointment
    states                   MS
    companies                Anchor or Sun
    agent-types              Individual
    resident?                ANY
    product-types            ANY
    required-output-forms    MS-life-form-1
    fee-schema               MS-appointment-fee
    required-internal-forms  appointment-acknowledgment
    mail-schema              MS-address
```

In English, this schema states that if this entry is an appointment (not a termination or a renewal), the state is Mississippi, the insurance company is either Sun Life of America or Anchor National Life (subsidiaries of SunAmerica), the agent is an individual, s/he is a resident or is not, and it is for any type of product s/he is requesting, then the form MS-life-form-1 must be submitted to the state, the fee information in the schema MS-appointment-fee applies, an appointment acknowledgment is expected from the state, and the address information in the schema MS-address applies. This procedure is only one of many that apply to this situation. Other procedures specify license requirements, details on how to fill out form MS-life-form-1, and so on.

Given this general data architecture, an agent appointment is processed by AES by first formulating a schema describing the task at hand. This task is next broken into subtasks because agents typically want to be appointed in more than one state for more than one insurance line. The description of these subtasks includes type of agent, resident status, state for appointment, and types of insurance products. An example of a subtask in pseudocode follows:

```
Schema Subtask-1234
    agent-type      individual-in-corporation
    task-type       appointment
    company         Anchor
    product-type    fixed
    state           MS
    resident?       no
```

The heart of the system is a rule engine that uses ART-IM's pattern-matching language to match procedures with the subtasks they apply to. Conceptually, the procedures themselves direct the process. They appear to always be on the lookout for subtasks to match and attach themselves to this subtask.

When the matching process completes, the procedures that attached themselves to a subtask are gathered and converted into actions to be taken by the system, such as requesting a check made out to the state or printing application forms to be sent to the state.

The deployed AES system contains over 2500 permanent schema and about 100 rules. Some additional schemas, for example, representing subtasks, are created and deleted at run time.

Operation and Maintenance

AES processes between 100 and 200 appointments each day. There are approximately 10 appointment processors, each with their own terminals. The one printer is shared between them.

State and federal regulations, forms, and fees change frequently. Each month, listings of state regulation changes are received through an industry service that tracks the regulations. Because AES is a vehicle for process and regulatory compliance, changes must be made immediately to avoid state appointment rejection and subsequent rework. Although the original system was built by Inference Corporation, system maintenance is handled by the in-house SunAmerica management information system staff, usually within 48 hours, including coding changes, model office testing, user approval, and production release. AES has run successfully since August 1990, and numerous updates to state regulations, forms, and fees were processed during the first five months of production.

Innovations

AES innovations include the use of expert system technology to facilitate a corporate relocation without a transfer of staff, the only real-time expert system deployed for insurance appointment processing, and a system that encompasses a PS2-OS2 expert system deployment working with image processing.

Payoff

AES has enabled SunAmerica to solve an industrywide problem, retool the appointment process, and achieve the following successes: (1) as a high-speed appointment service, a reduction in processing time from 2 weeks to 2 days; (2) a reduction of appointment staff by 70 percent; (3) the elimination of rework and the optimization of time to obtain appointments because of state rejection of applications; (4) a reduction in training requirements; (5) the automation of regulatory compliance; and (6) the fast assimilation of state regulation changes.

Acknowledgments

The authors want to acknowledge the invaluable contribution of expertise from Carol Ann Howard, formerly of SunAmerica. The authors also want to thank the following knowledge engineers for their professionalism and hard work in writing a unique system under tight time constraints: Elizabeth Ralston; David Subar; and especially, Mark Clark, Eric Hestenes, Barbara Starr, and Gary Vrooman.

AL²X: An Expert System for Off-Site Evaluation of Commercial Bank Financial Stability

John R. Segerstrom

> *Doctors spend their lives treating patients, who come to them in a never-ending stream, and they inevitably see the answer to any disease in terms of treatment rather than prevention. Nonetheless, historically, progress against disease has come from prevention and vaccines, not cures.*

> —John Cairns
> Department of Cancer Biology
> Harvard School of Public Health

By substituting "bank regulators" for "doctors" and "troubled banks" for "patients," Cairns's insight can be applied with equal generality to the U.S. banking system. The regulatory establishment has traditionally sought to fulfill its role as watchdog of the public's interest in the banking system by reacting to problems in individual banks and treating them to restore the bank to health. Unfortunately, in the 1980s, the bank mortality rate soared. Traditional "treatment" failed to protect the public interest, and taxpayer dollars were allocated through bad investments by financial institutions rather than through public policy.

These diversions of public resources are almost unbelievably huge. The mistakes of about 1,000 savings and loans diverted $300 billion, or $1200 for every man, woman, and child in the country. In 1990 dollars, this amount is roughly 6 times the cost of the Marshall Plan, which rebuilt Europe after World War II. Conservative estimates of the cost of commercial bank errors run about $5 billion each year for at least the next 2 years; some estimates are much higher. The Federal Deposit Insurance System is generally agreed to be insolvent in its current form, with some form of subsidy required soon. It is clear that the bank treatment system has been overwhelmed and is no longer adequate for the task of protecting the public interest. An effective prevention mechanism must be found and implemented if the banking industry is to return to stability.

The treatment paradigm on which bank regulation has been based focuses on the emergence of troublesome symptoms, particularly deterioration in loan repayments. The underlying critical assumption is that loans are made conscientiously: "They're all good when they're made," the banker's saying goes. A bad bank loan, in this view, is considered an anomaly.

Until about 1980, this assumption and the resulting model were adequate, and bank failures averaged about four each year. Since this time, however, the bank failure rate has skyrocketed, and there is considerable evidence that failures today are resulting not from good loans gone bad, as before, but from loans, actually bad when made, gone undiscovered by regulators. Rather than being an aberration, bad loans appear to have become the rule in some banks. Because bad loans might not develop symptoms for as long as two years, a fatal volume of such loans can already be in place when traditional regulatory treatment is triggered by symptom presence. By this time, failure of the bank is virtually inevitable.

Genesis of the AL²X Prevention Paradigm

AL²X (pronounced "Alex") was originally intended to assist private-sector auditors (CPAs) in making recommendations to clients. It began as a rudimentary expert system with 150 rules and a 20,000-word structured vocabulary. It produced an essay-style analysis of a bank's financial reports based on the early-warning research available at the time (Koch and Cox 1983). All methods of distinguishing one group from another are subject to two kinds of error: type 1 errors, in which a member of the target group (in this case, a future problem bank) is identified as a nonmember (a strong bank), and type 2 errors, in which a nontarget member is included in the target group. To adjust AL²X to achieve low type 1 error levels, identifying a high percentage of future problem banks, it was necessary to accept the identification of a large number of strong banks as possible future problems, creating an excessive type 2 error rate. Users complained that the original AL²X "cried wolf" too often to be credible.

More seriously, no actionable recommendations were available because the identification of the troubled banks came too late. A typical suggestion might have been, "To help this bank, make good loans starting two years ago and continue to do so until the present." This second failing led to the withdrawal of the original model. AL²X Development Corporation was formed in 1984 to identify and market a more effective bank analysis paradigm. The objective was to find the root cause of an individual bank's abandonment of industry norms and consequent acceptance of excessively risky loans.

First Hypothesis: Risk Sought to Offset Weak Earnings

In 1984, research identified several financial ratios for identifying troubled banks: loan losses as a percentage of total loans, nonperforming loans as a percentage of total loans, and actual losses as a percentage of expected losses, to name three. The second AL²X model retained some of these ratios from the original AL²X design.

Sophisticated cost measures were added to these straightforward calculations. These measures are used to identify banks that require a large amount of income from loans to cover high expenses and also make a profit. The hypothesis is that excessive loan risk can be expected in banks configured to require high loan income; cost pressures can force the bank to make loans that, although riskier over time, produce immediate income.

The cost rules in AL²X cover four distinct areas of expense: overhead, interest, yield curve placement, and nonloan asset yields. Each expense level is estimated, relative to industry norms, by an algorithm in the model and assigned a relative level. All the levels are then combined using a weighted factor analysis system that produces a *loan income pressure score* (LIP score), which is compared to a standard in the model's knowledge base. In general, higher LIP scores create more concern in AL²X about the quality of the loan decisions being made.

Field tests of AL²X were encouraging. Banks with high LIP scores did, in fact, have a tendency toward loan problems after a one- to two-year lag. The correlation was not perfect, however; banks with identical LIP scores apparently respond differently. Robert Long, a well-known bank observer and futurist, suggested that the source of the differences in response is cultural; that is, each bank has a unique predisposition to take risk under pressure (Long 1988). To test this suggestion, a subfactor analysis system that measures risk taking was added to the LIP scoring system. In this subsystem, noncredit risks that surface promptly in the bank's financial statement (funding risk, investment risk, interest rate risk, and regulatory risk) are measured with additional algorithms and aggregated using factor analysis. The resulting *risk propensity score* (RP score) is added as a factor in determining the LIP score. By adjusting factor weights and knowledge base standards, the model can now be tuned to provide a measure of pressure for loan income relative to the bank's cultural resistance to loan risk rather than to a fixed threshold.

The addition of the RP score dramatically improved the performance of AL²X in identifying banks at high risk. The model is now able to identify situations in advance of actual loan deterioration and make recommendations for current action to relieve the pressure for loan income. The system also identifies cultures that are most likely to accept risk and, therefore, are most in need of monitoring by regulators.

A significant retrospective field test of the AL²X first-hypothesis system was conducted in the state of Michigan in early 1988. In the 20 years preceding 1987, Michigan had had 1 bank failure. Using 1985 data, AL²X identified 4 of 250 Michigan banks as seriously unstable. The actual 1987 failure was 1 of the 4. The result was cause for optimism for both the hypothesis and the actual paradigm underlying the AL²X model.

Second Hypothesis: Risk for Its Own Sake

The effectiveness of the first hypothesis was tarnished in other field tests by the appearance of banks that either failed or experienced significant problems but maintained a relatively low LIP score. Every effort was made to eliminate the effects of dishonesty and economic fluctuations, but the inconsistency remained.

In discussions with regulators and insurance companies writing bank insurance, it was suggested that small risks in banks have no natural enemies and rapidly grow into large risks with no apparent bounds. The experts felt that this potential for risk explosion was especially true for risks with which the banker had little or no experience, such as those new risks created by the deregulation of the banking industry beginning in 1979 and 1980.

The process begins with the banker assuming a small risk. If s/he "wins," s/he becomes overconfident and plays again for higher stakes. If s/he "loses," s/he raises his(her) bet, either assuming that the law of averages is now in his(her) favor (the infamous "gambler's fallacy") or simply acting in desperation to recover his(her) loss before it is discovered. In either case, win or lose, the size of the risk balloons until it exceeds the capacity of the bank.

To test this second hypothesis, the new banking risks from deregulation were listed, and measurement algorithms were developed. A separate risk progression model was then added to the LIP model in AL²X. Rerunning the field tests and tuning this segment of the program resulted in a two-screen process with impressive accuracy. Furthermore, the second hypothesis lent itself to practical recommendations for breaking the chain of risk progression. The resulting paradigm was dubbed *stress mechanics* (Segerstrom 1987). The enhanced AL²X system was released in early 1988.

The Question of Risk Capacity

Because banking risk is not symmetrical—that is, because a bad decision involves a loss as much as 50 times greater than the gain from a good decision—and because some losses are inevitable in a risky environment, it was necessary to consider risk capacity in the AL²X model. After further consultation with bankers and other experts, certain levels of capacity were established as minimums, and additional algorithms were added to provide base measures of a bank's ability to accept normal banking risk.

These algorithms were developed heuristically. The capacity to accept risk translates into the ability to incur loss and continue in business, and the capacity measures in AL²X are ranked accordingly. The most serious conditions are those that can result in the immediate demise of the bank (low liquidity, for example: if a bank runs out of cash its demise is immediate). The capacity measures range from liquidity (cash) to equity level to potential profitability and are ranked in descending order of severity. The minimum levels of each are determined by AL²X on the basis of heuristic rules using demographic factors for each individual bank, including size, type of market, and legal environment.

AL²X System Structure

The AL²X model applies the two hypotheses and the heuristic capacity rules to bank data and produces an analysis at one of five levels:
1. Is capacity adequate?
    a. IF yes, proceed with analysis.
    b. IF no, stop and report.

2. Is trouble evident now?
   a. IF yes, revise minimum capacity and go to 1.
   b. IF no, proceed with analysis.
3. Is loan pressure high?
   a. IF yes, stop and report.
   b. IF no, proceed with analysis.
4. Is risk progression evident?
   a. IF yes, revise LP max. and go to 3., ELSE
   stop and report.
   b. IF no, proceed with analysis.
5. Are strategic improvements available?
   a. IF yes, stop and report.
   b. IF no, summarize and stop.

The system reports on the most serious observations; that is, it does not make recommendations for high-level strategic improvements if the individual bank lacks the basic capacity to survive in a normal banking environment.

The appropriate level at which to report is first estimated by applying broad rules of the form "IF (data) THEN (estimate)" to the results of preliminary algorithms. This estimate is then confirmed by secondary, more sophisticated algorithms and rules of the form "IF (estimate) THEN (data)ELSE (fail)"; failure of the confirmation process generates an adjustment to the preliminary and secondary algorithms and the reprocessing of the data, followed by reapplication of the broad rules and reconfirmation. The process continues until a confirmed estimate (conclusion) is identified, allowing the system to generate a report.

The AL^2X report is written from the system's vocabulary on the basis of the final output from the primary and secondary algorithms, using syntax rules in a report assembler in the AL^2X program. The vocabulary is stored in phraselike parcels, which are available to the report assembler by coded reference.

The user has the option of bypassing the written AL^2X report and directly viewing the results of the system's algorithms on the computer screen. In this mode, the system operates as a specialized calculator, performing complex mathematics for the user who is responsible for interpreting the results. This approach allows the system to support the expert, as well as the novice, user.

AL^2X normally accepts data from bank financial statements through the computer keyboard. Data are updated quarterly by the user, and the system retains data for 1 year for trend analysis. Fewer than 50 pieces of data are required each quarter, and data entry requires less than 5 minutes, as does processing. Large-scale users, such as regulators, have the option of acquiring preformatted data about a large number of banks in computer-compatible form, accessible by key code, which eliminates manual data entry altogether.

The AL²X system contains 55 separate analytic algorithms and 3,500 decision rules. It draws its output report from a 60,000-word vocabulary and supports its conclusions with statistical exhibits comparing the actual results of the bank with the standards in the model. AL²X draws initial data from public financial reports prepared by each commercial bank in the United States and allows the user to inquire about the potential impact of changes in the bank's activity on the AL²X analysis.

The AL²X system is written in Borland, Inc.'s TURBO BASIC compiler for MS-DOS–compatible personal computers. The software is designed to be acceptable to the broadest possible range of computer and peripheral device configurations: The minimum requirements are an MS-DOS computer with 256K of random-access memory and a single floppy diskette drive.

The current evolutionary system represents 6 years of development and a combined development and deployment investment of $450,000. The AL²X software is currently used nationwide by over 300 banks; 6 state bank regulatory departments; and a sampling of attorneys, accountants, investment advisers, and other professionals.

Automatic Data Acquisition and Mass Testing

In 1988, just following the public release of the current AL²X system, data from 31 December 1987 (the most current then available) from federal bank reports was purchased on magnetic tape and decoded. AL²X was asked to analyze each bank in the country within its domain (banks with less than $1 billion in assets). The results of the AL²X analyses were summarized for each bank in the form of an index, called the <STAR> index (Segerstrom and Meadows 1989). The number of high-risk banks as a percentage of total banks was computed for each state, and the states were then divided into quartiles by the resulting percentages.

The southwestern states, already troubled, figured prominently in the lowest quartile. This result could have been anticipated by the inclusion of traditional measures of loan problems in AL²X. However, Massachusetts, Connecticut, and Rhode Island were also in the lowest quartile at a time when the "Massachusetts Miracle" was being touted as the potential economic salvation model for the country. Skeptics of the AL²X model were easy to find, including then-Governor of Massachusetts and presidential candidate Michael Dukakis. By late 1988, however, the *American Banker* and the *New York Times* featured stories about the decline of the New England economy (Bartlett 1988;

Matthews 1989). The prescience of the AL²X prediction for New England has since been proven beyond debate.

The AL²X system has correctly predicted problems in the Mid-Atlantic states, particularly North Carolina, and beginning in June 1989, the model began predicting serious problems in California that are, in fact, currently unfolding.

Since 1987, the year of the first nationwide application of the AL²X system, no serious deterioration in a state banking system has taken place that was not predicted, and no prediction has proven to be groundless. In each case, the AL²X system identified specific banks requiring attention and made practical recommendations for action in each of these banks 18 months to 2 years in advance of the appearance of traditional symptoms of trouble in the bank.

AL²X System Deployment: Real-World Lessons

There are approximately 14,000 banks in the United States, about 12,000 of which are within the domain of the AL²X system. The federal and state bank regulatory agencies monitor the stability of each of these banks to protect the public interest. Because of the previously mentioned failure of traditional off-site analysis methods, emphasis is currently being placed on increasing the frequency of on-site examinations in all banks at tremendous expense. A bank examination typically costs $25,000 or more; so, the cost of examining each bank in the AL²X domain once each year would be at least $300 million. Based on the results of the AL²X stability study of 30 June 1990, approximately 70 percent of this cost ($210 million each year) could be avoided by examining only those banks too large or too complex to be included in the domain and those banks within the domain that AL²X indicates are unstable. The necessary antecedent to realizing these savings is confidence on the part of the regulatory establishment in the reliability of the AL²X analysis and conclusions.

Although it was not the original mission of the developers of the AL²X system, it is clear now that individual banks can also benefit from the expertise embodied in AL²X. Empirical observation led to the conclusion that reversing the focus of the hypotheses in AL²X (from risk measurement to risk avoidance) defines a management discipline that produces both stability and high profitability in individual banks. William M. Reid, president of a $650 million (assets) bank in Richmond, California, observes:

> The major impact of AL²X on the investment or structural decisions of the bank came from understanding the powerful financial concepts that are embedded in the model. Most important among these are the long-

term predictable relationships between the various rates that affect the bank. Not all loan, investment, and deposit interest rates change by the same amount or at the same time when interest rates in general rise or fall. By understanding and being able to study these relationships, we realized that the bank was actually positioned to earn substantially less money if interest rates fell. We saw the need to make longer term, fixed rate loans and purchase longer term, fixed rate investment securities. We also saw the trade-offs between various types of risk our bank faces: credit, liquidity and market valuation.

By our acting on these convictions, we saw bank earnings rise immediately as longer term investments and loans yielded higher returns than the shorter term instruments we were previously using. More important, however, is the fact that as interest rates have fallen and as a positively sloped yield curve has been reestablished, the bank's interest spread on a ratio basis has been maintained. This was precisely the bank's objective—to maintain strong and stable income levels regardless of the interest rate environment in which we happened to be operating. Had we used traditionally accepted methods, our income in 1991 would almost certainly have suffered by as much as a million dollars.

Because AL²X is not based on a previous hypothesis, its methods and conclusions are unfamiliar to bankers and regulators alike. AL²X Development Corporation, with significant assistance from the Office of the Comptroller of the Currency, which regulates the 4,200 federally chartered banks in the United States, undertook an extensive study to compare AL²X's results with those produced with the theory being used by this office. The results were substantially different: There was virtually no correlation. The regulator's conclusion was that AL²X failed the test. Ironically, the standard used—the regulator's existing theory—had already itself failed in the real world. As the challenger, AL²X faced several barriers in the study's design, many of which could not be overcome because of legal protections applying to information about banks. No barrier, however, was greater than the fact that no accepted theories or results are appropriate to test the AL²X methodology.

AL²X is an *orphan* expert system: There is no one expert or group of experts whose knowledge is embodied in the system. Lacking this credibility, the AL²X system relies on empirical results to demonstrate its utility. Mention has been made of the demonstrated success of the AL²X methodology in New England, the Mid-Atlantic states, and California since 1987; empirical credibility is high and still growing. However, acceptance remains slow. It is now believed that the system is hindered by two aspects of its design, neither of which bear on the performance of the expert system itself: (1) the potency of the system and (2) the interface between the system and the user.

The word potency describes the power of the output. AL²X is forceful in its reporting; the output is conclusion oriented and concise. The AL^2X bank report emulates a consultant's report, usually producing 10 to 12 pages of text—expert opinion—with supporting statistical exhibits. However, this opinion is often contrary to prevalent theory and, thus, seems threatening to a user whose knowledge and experience are based on this theory. The empirical success of AL^2X only adds to user discomfort because there is no ready means for discounting its results.

The acceptance of an expert system with new capabilities seems to require that the system's output use implication and suggestion rather than conclusion. To succeed, the output must rely on skillful design to guide the user to the proper conclusion on his(her) own. This theory is the current thrust of AL^2X's evolutionary development, and it is proving as difficult as, if not more difficult than, the development of the knowledge base itself. The AL^2X knowledge base is maintained by the developers, and the redesign of the output routines can be integrated into the maintenance effort as new knowledge is gained. If AL^2X were a learning system, the output design would certainly be much more complex than the development of the knowledge base.

At a less abstract level, the use of a written report creates comprehension problems for the user with this kind of expert system. The written word is assimilated serially, one word at a time; the AL^2X algorithms work in parallel. A high percentage of these algorithms determine the structure of other algorithms, in addition to developing conclusions that are often based, in turn, on the results of yet others. The AL^2X report is carefully crafted to describe this parallel analysis, but in the process of reading, users almost inevitably make an effort to imply simple causality in the conclusions. This approach can appear successful in an isolated case; however, users become frustrated when they attempt to generalize the same inferences from one analysis to another because they rarely succeed.

Interestingly, the transition from serial to parallel processing in human cognition is synonymous with becoming an expert in a complex field (Buffington 1987). It is probable, then, that written output from a complex expert system can only be used by an expert in the field. The newest challenge in redesigning the AL^2X system is to find a way to display, in quasi-real time, all the algorithms or syntheses at the same time on the computer screen but provide the user with access to financial variables through the keyboard (or perhaps a mouse-type interface). This banking "flight simulator" would provide a vehicle through which the non-expert AL^2X user could communicate with the AL^2X parallel system on a trial-and-error basis until, like a pilot, the user becomes more comfortable with simultaneous interactions. This sort of display module, combined with less intimidating written output, might bridge the existing gap between accepted theory, discredited but entrenched, and the AL²X methodology, proven but unfamiliar.

The AL²X Model: Prospects and Perspectives

A representative of the Xerox advanced research facility in Palo Alto, California, once said that a new technology cannot be integrated into society in less than 10 years and, then, only if it attracts a significant competitor. The AL²X paradigms, if viewed as new technology, are 4 years and 1 competitor away from acceptance. As a product, the AL²X system is a growing commercial success; as a useful technology, the potential benefit has been denied to the general public, to some extent because of the design of the system itself.

The knowledge base in which the details of the AL²X paradigm exist has not been copyrighted or offered for license, nor have the details been published. They are maintained as trade secrets. It is the particular and circular dilemma of small-company research that wide use requires acceptance; acceptance requires competition; and competition, in turn, endangers the small developer. The development of AL²X provided a tremendous amount of insight into the workings of the banking industry in the newly deregulated environment and could have tremendous value to bankers, regulators, and legislators in the immediate future. AL²X Development Corporation now seeks a vehicle that allows the dissemination of the details of AL²X's knowledge without committing commercial suicide. Success in this quest will, it appears, finally determine AL²X's contribution to the prevention of further banking disasters in this country.

References

Bartlett, S. 1988. Bad Real Estate Loans Hurt Northeast Banks. *The New York Times*, 15 November.

Buffington, P. 1987. Experts: Who Says? *Sky*, June 1987.

Koch, D. L., and Cox, W. N., eds. Early Warning Systems and Financial Analysis in Bank Monitoring. *Economic Review* 68(11): 6–48.

Long, R. H. 1988. Secrets of High-Performing Bankers, Thinking Technology Associates, Phoenix, Arizona.

Matthews, G. 1989. Economic Downturn Seen for Northeast. *American Banker*, 31 October.

Segerstrom, J. R. 1987. Stress Mechanics: Understanding How Deregulated Independent Banks Work. *The Supervisor* 24(4): 2–7.

Segerstrom, J. R., and Meadows, G. D. 1989. Why Is AL2X Saying That about My Bank?" AL²X Development Corporation, Portland, Oregon.

The Credit Clearing House Expert System

Roger Jambor, Sylvia Jow, Dan Meder, and Philip Klahr

The Credit Clearing House (CCH) is a division of Dun & Bradstreet (D&B) Business Information Group's Business Credit Services. CCH functions as the arm of Business Credit Services' Product Marketing Group, dedicated to serving the risk management needs of the apparel industry by assigning credit ratings and dollar-specific credit limit recommendations.

CCH has several thousand customers that use its services. It recommends a credit limit that the D&B subscriber can safely extend to a given client. An example customer of this service is an apparel wholesaler who receives an order from a retailer with which they are not familiar or an order with a high dollar amount that raises some credit uncertainty. The wholesaler would request an evaluation of the retailer and a maximum credit recommendation from CCH.

CCH credit ratings have historically been based on the information found in D&B business information reports. The quality of the CCH service is dependent on three primary factors: (1) the ability of CCH analysts to apply consistent decisions to diverse business situations, (2) the ability to respond rapidly to customer requests, and (3) the ability to update ratings and recommendations with the most current data.

To meet these criteria, CCH was required to maintain a process that was both time consuming and labor intensive. This manual process presented CCH management with certain business problems that resulted in lost revenue. As an example, a staff of 15 credit analysts was required to maintain a database of ratings and recommendations on roughly 140,000 businesses, but it was estimated that another 60,000 businesses could be of interest to customers but were not reported on because of production constraints inherent in maintaining the existing database. Often, a customer inquiring about one of these "no hits" would abandon the inquiry rather than wait for a CCH analyst to investigate the case and return a rating and recommendation, a task that could take from three days to three weeks.

Lost revenue opportunities based on a lack of account coverage are among the more quantifiable of the problems. Less tangible but certainly as much (or more) of a problem was customer satisfaction with the quality of the analysis for those cases already in the CCH database. The quality issue is really several issues. First, the analytic ability of the most expert credit analysts should be applied to all ratings and recommendations considered. Second, these decisions should be based on the most up-to-date data available. An analyst can do his(her) finest analytic work on a case, but if the data s/he is reviewing are not the most current in D&B's files, it has a direct impact on quality. Third, all analysis topics should be considered and evaluated for each case; that is, evaluation of all data and all areas of analysis should occur for each case. If not properly handled, each of these issues could result in decreased customer satisfaction, which, in turn, could lead to problems when it is time to renew a customer's contract. It became necessary for CCH management to address these quality issues and arrive at a solution that could provide both quality enhancement and cost avoidance.

In further defining the problem, it should be understood that the CCH analyst staff was affected by turnover. The average analyst's tenure is about two years. It is difficult to build expertise in a staff when the life expectancy of an analyst is so limited. The turnover issue also affected the ability of CCH to maintain a completely up-to-date database on existing accounts. It took some time for a new analyst to reach the necessary level of understanding for the job to keep up with the new information coming in each day on the businesses in his(her) area of responsibility. Obviously, training was considerable, and there were many associated costs.

In investigating a solution to these problems, it became apparent that any solution should address the following objectives: (1) improve product quality by developing a pool of analytic expertise that would be impervious to turnover; (2) increase productivity to update existing cases in a more timely fashion and capture those cases that were formerly defined as "no hits"; (3) improve quality by including new information as soon as it becomes available; (4) improve the consistency of the ratings and recommendations provided to the customer; (5) enforce the evaluation of all data available to improve both quality and consistency; and (6) as a by-product of the solution, provide a foundation for new and enhanced product development opportunities.

One solution might have been to increase staff beyond the 15 analysts that were currently employed. This solution would have allowed increased account coverage but at an obvious expense to CCH, and it would not have addressed the turnover issue. In addition, the consistency issue would have been compounded by an increased number of individuals creating the credit-evaluation product. It became evident that the solution to the CCH problem would have to be an automated one. Unfortunately, the analytic process had elements of relative complexity that did not conveniently lend the potential application to traditional data processing approaches.

Expert System Investigation

In May 1987, Information Technology Research (ITR), a department within Information Management (IM, the data processing division of the Business Information Group), began investigating the use of expert systems in commercial applications. ITR, which was formed to identify, evaluate, and introduce new technologies, published a study in June 1987 recommending that a pilot application be developed within the Business Information Group as a means of researching expert system technology.

The following criteria for choosing an application were set forth in the study document: (1) the business problem must be well understood; (2) the business problem must have a practical solution, with application development in months rather than years; (3) the application should have a clear benefit and a return that is potentially large; (4) the focus should be on an application that can be developed and tested independently and can later serve as the kernel for other applications; and (5) the business problem has not successfully been automated or cannot be automated cost effectively with conventional technology.

The study also went on to detail hardware and software requirements for a development project. A number of vendor tools were evaluated as well as different technical approaches. Developing expert systems from scratch, using either an AI programming language or an AI programming environment, was determined to be too time consuming and would require a certain degree of AI experience and expertise. Therefore, the study recommended developing expert systems by building knowledge bases with a commercial shell, exploiting the shell's user interface and inferencing logic. In terms of hardware, the study recommended the use of AI workstations or personal computers for their response capabilities and also the separation of the expert system from the mainframe to avoid a possible unfavorable impact on existing mainframe systems. AI workstations were preferred to personal computers because of the perceived limitations of personal computer capabilities at the time.

Within the Business Information Group, ITR was able to identify candidate projects from Business Credit Services, Data Resources, and Information Management for expert system applications. Among these candidates was CCH. Besides fitting the aforementioned attributes, CCH also represented an analytic process that was deemed relatively complex and well defined in terms of both input and output and that required mainframe database inquiry and update without being completely embedded in an existing application. Coincidentally, CCH was then embarking on a redesign of its database and input-output system architecture, providing the advantage of being able to integrate the expert system into the new architecture rather than having to retrofit and rewrite an existing application.

Prototype Development and Evaluation

Following the selection of the CCH analyst's function as the application with which to research the use of expert systems, work began on developing a prototype. In October 1987, the ITR group started the CCH Expert System (CCH-ES) Prototype Project in conjunction with Coopers & Lybrand (C&L), which functioned as a consultant. Using C&L's proprietary expert-apprentice simulation technique, the project team articulated and decomposed the mental processes of CCH credit professionals as they performed their analytic tasks. By restricting communication to questions and answers, the expert was forced to externalize the individual analysis steps and components, as well as the information, algorithms, and rules used and the assessments generated, for each step associated with a particular case.

Once the simulation phase was completed, the project team began constructing a credit- analysis model using C&L's FFAST knowledge-modeling tool as a front end to a run-time version of Inference Corporation's ART running on a Symbolics workstation. The initial version of the knowledge model was coded in FFAST based on the simulation results. With a rough model completed, model refinement took place over the next several weeks. This process involved bringing the experts in to review each step of the analysis process as captured by the initial model. Based on the experts' feedback, the knowledge engineers were able to further refine each of the analytic phases, effectively externalizing in greater detail the experts' thought processes. By early December 1987, sufficient model development had taken place to allow the entry of test cases for further validation and refinement of the system.

In January 1988, with the initial prototype developed, demonstrations of the knowledge model were given to senior management within various Business Information Group divisions, including IM, Business Credit Services, and Data Resources. After reviewing the work accomplished, the following conclusions were established by the business units:

First, the specific expert system approach used and the functions developed for the CCH-ES prototype were appropriate for their business needs and could be used to improve their products and services.

Second, many components of the CCH credit analysis captured in the model were generic and could be reused for a variety of products. Furthermore, because they were generic, they could be consolidated into a centralized process to generate assessments that could be shared by many products.

Third, the level of analytic sophistication achieved by using expert system technology was significantly superior to what was in existing computer-generated products.

Fourth, the time required to develop system requirements for analytic products can significantly be reduced using the knowledge-modeling approach (the CCH-ES prototype knowledge model was developed in 11 weeks by about 3 full-time programmers).

With the initial prototype completed and following positive feedback from management, fine tuning of the system continued for the next few months. To make the expert system as comprehensive as possible, it was necessary to manually enter over 100 test cases reflecting a wide variety of circumstances. Based on the evaluation of these cases, certain rules were changed, and certain modules were revised. One example was in the area of trend analysis. Because of the flexibility provided by FFAST, this recoding was completed and tested in one week.

Hardware and Software Selection for the Pilot System

When it was determined that the prototype performed within CCH operational standards, work began on expanding CCH-ES into a pilot (pre-production) system. At this time, there were no mature mainframe-based software platforms to support an expert system application. In addition, there was no in-house experience in gauging the resource requirements and operational and environmental impact of this type of system. Therefore, it was decided to pursue a nonmainframe approach in implementing the system to gain experience with this technology without affecting the normal production environment.

Because FFAST was not a commercial package, it could not be used for the CCH-ES pilot. Because FFAST was merely a front end to ART, and most of the FFAST rules were translatable to ART rules with a minimum of recoding effort, the choice of a pilot software platform was leaning toward ART-IM, a C-based implementation of ART. Several other factors involved the selection of ART-IM as the software platform, including the fact that is was C-based; C had advantages over Lisp, which was considered undesirable in D&B's production environment because of its memory management characteristics. Other considerations included efficiency; availability of both development and run-time versions; flexibility in platforms, including the ability to run in an IBM personal computer environment; availability for porting to a DEC environment; and a planned IBM-MVS version. A development tool was needed that would be IBM compatible because of the immediate availability of IBM equipment in the Business Information Group.

DEC was chosen as the production hardware platform because it offered an environment in which processors could easily be upgraded without modifying the application. Also, DEC had a proven IBM link that would eventually be used in an integrated production environment.

Expert System Design

With the prototype stabilized and the pilot system hardware-software issues resolved, the research staff (now named Applied Research [AR]) began designing and coding the knowledge base in ART-IM. In September 1988, two consultants were brought in from Inference to help in this process. The consultants were able to effectively make the system modular and determine which modules were best done in ART-IM and which would be implemented more efficiently in procedural language (C). With the support of the Inference consultants, the AR project team was able to code the entire knowledge base on personal computers by mid-November 1988.

The four principal modules identified and implemented are shown in figure 1. They include *payment analysis*, which analyzes the credit and payment history of a business; *financial analysis*, which analyzes the current financial statements and three-year trends of a business; *business analysis*, which analyzes the strengths and weaknesses of a business, including prior business history; and *ATB rating and recommendation*,

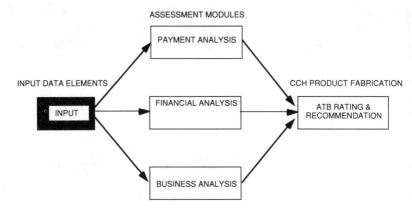

Figure 1. CCH-ES Assessment Modules.

which determines the final rating and overall recommendation. (ATB stands for *Apparel Trade Book*, which is published four times a year by CCH and which now includes the ATB ratings produced by CCH-ES.)

Because of the large amount of data required to process the payment analysis, as well as the statistical nature of this module, it was coded in C. The other modules, primarily analysis and decision rules, were coded in ART-IM.

Generating an analysis and assessment in CCH-ES consists of forward chaining from the initial data through intermediate assessments to final recommendation. As shown in figure two, 167 initial primary (raw) data elements are extracted from the mainframe databases. Rules process these data elements and form a set of 57 intermediate assessments and, from there, form final assessments for the capital rating, payment rating, and financial rating. The final dollar-specific recommendations and ATB rating are then produced.

An example of this assessment process is shown in figure 3.[1] The example shows two financial analysis assessment rules. One rule takes four intermediate assessments (already determined by rules that take raw data and determine initial low-level assessments) and infers a high-level intermediate assessment; another rule takes two high-level intermediate assessments and infers a final assessment for working capital.

While the CCH-ES pilot was being developed, the data requirements to run the system in production were identified and given to an ad hoc development group within IM. In turn, this group developed a temporary data-extraction program that extracted data from several IBM 3090 databases and created a flat file for volume testing the knowledge base. An interface to the mainframe was written that read the data

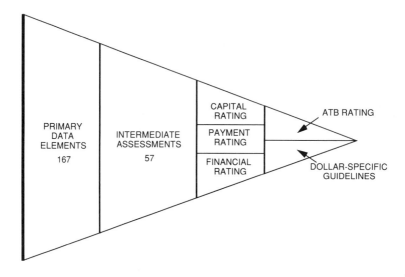

Figure 2. CCH-ES Processing.

from the flat file and preprocessed them for input into CCH-ES running on a Digital MicroVax III. CCH-ES code developed on the personal computers was simply transferred to the MicroVax III, where it was compiled, and a run time CCH-ES system was generated.

Volume Testing

By early December 1988, all the pieces were in place to begin a volume test of 2800 cases, roughly 2 percent of the total number of cases in the CCH database. These cases were input into CCH-ES, and the results were reviewed by a quality control team of 4 CCH credit analysts. Because of commitments related to the day-to-day operations of CCH, the quality control team was not able to devote full time to the quality review process. Consequently, this stage of the development process was not completed until the middle of April 1989.

During this testing phase, over 30 CCH customers were given demonstrations of CCH-ES, and their opinions on the workings of CCH-ES were solicited. This "reality check" was an integral part of the system evaluation process.

Initial review of the volume test results showed a 92 percent agreement rate of the experts with CCH-ES. The volume test revealed the need for some further system modification. By the end of the fine-tuning process, this rate was raised to 98.5 percent. (In most of the other

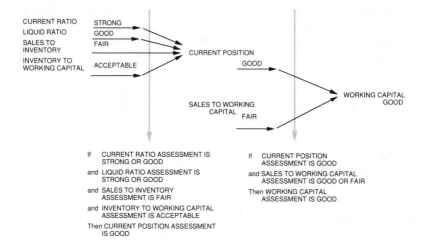

CURRENT RATIO
LIQUID RATIO
SALES TO
INVENTORY
INVENTORY TO
WORKING CAPITAL

STRONG
GOOD
FAIR

ACCEPTABLE

CURRENT POSITION
GOOD

SALES TO WORKING
CAPITAL   FAIR

WORKING CAPITAL
GOOD

If CURRENT RATIO ASSESSMENT IS
    STRONG OR GOOD
and LIQUID RATIO ASSESSMENT IS
    STRONG OR GOOD
and SALES TO INVENTORY
    ASSESSMENT IS FAIR
and INVENTORY TO WORKING CAPITAL
    ASSESSMENT IS ACCEPTABLE
Then CURRENT POSITION ASSESSMENT
    IS GOOD

If CURRENT POSITION
    ASSESSMENT IS GOOD
and SALES TO WORKING CAPITAL
    ASSESSMENT IS GOOD OR FAIR
Then WORKING CAPITAL
    ASSESSMENT IS GOOD

Figure 3. CCH-ES Assessment Example.

cases, analysts did not agree with each other, so there was no consensus on a correct decision.)

Also during this period, certain knockout rules were defined. *Knockouts* are CCH-ES–evaluated cases that D&B forwards to a credit analyst to review or audit. The principal reasons for a case being a knockout include incomplete or missing data, possibly conflicting data, borderline cases, and possible internal inconsistencies. When it determines a case to be a knockout, CCH-ES provides its usual analysis but does not publish (record in the CCH database) its results until an analyst approves. It is then left to the analyst to decide whether to accept the system decision or opt for his(her) own analysis.

Transitioning the Pilot System into Production

In mid-April 1989, CCH management gave AR the final sign-off for CCH-ES deployment. Concurrent with CCH-ES development, CCH was undergoing a redesign of its mainframe system and database architectures by an IM project team. The plan was to incorporate CCH-ES into the new architecture by July 1989. To help facilitate this integration, AR assigned a project team member to the IM project team for four months. It was this person's responsibility to ensure that the interfaces between the mainframe case-selection and data-extraction programs, being developed by the IM team, and CCH-ES were correctly implemented in both online and batch modes. This responsibility also extended to the interface between the output of CCH-ES and the new CCH database, where the CCH-ES decisions would reside for delivery to the customer. In addition, the AR consultant assisted a Digital programmer in customizing the communications software between the IBM 3090 and the DEC platform.

The delivery platform hosting CCH-ES is the VaxStation 3000. Three VaxStations are currently in use: one for continued CCH-ES maintenance and testing and two for production use.

In the CCH-ES production version, the payment module was moved from the expert system to the mainframe and recoded from C to COBOL. This move was principally made for ease of maintenance because D&B has many more COBOL programmers than C programmers. Thus, the payment module output (intermediate assessments on payment history) is sent to CCH-ES along with other information. CCH-ES uses the payment assessments, along with the other intermediate assessments CCH-ES generates, to determine the final recommendation.

By mid-July 1989, CCH-ES and the new architecture were put into full production. At this point, all cases requiring review each day were passed through CCH-ES. CCH-ES recommendations were automatically uploaded to the CCH database without any human intervention and made available to the customer. Each knockout case would be delivered online to an analyst who would review the case; results of the review would then be uploaded and made available.

The following timetable summarizes CCH-ES development and deployment:

1987

May-June	Expert system study; potential applications identified
June-September	Applications assessed; CCH-ES to go to prototype
October-December	CCH-ES prototype development

1988

January-August	Internal selling; fine tuning; testing and evaluation
September-December	Pilot CCH-ES design and development

1989

December-April	Volume testing
April-July	System integration; fine tuning
July	CCH-ES in full production

CCH-ES cost approximately one million dollars (internal and external costs) to develop and deploy.

Use and Performance

CCH-ES has been in continual production use since July 1989. It currently contains approximately 800 ART-IM rules and is invoked either through online transactions or batch transactions as a result of database changes.

Online transactions occur when CCH customers call in for service or when analysts want to review knockout cases. Batch transactions result when there is new business information (updates in the *report file*, D&B's principal business information repository, or the *case summary database*) or when there is new trade information (payment updates in D&B's *trade file*). Whenever such changes occur through updates in the various databases, the applicable cases are run through CCH-ES the next morning. On a typical day, there are 300 online CCH-ES transactions and 2,500 batch transactions.

Figure 4 shows the relationship of CCH-ES to D&B's database systems. The other files not previously mentioned include the *sales conversion file*, containing industry sales norms for various company types and sizes; the *payment output file*, containing the intermediate payment analysis assessments produced by the payment program COBOL module; and the *CCH database*, containing the CCH-ES output. The preprocess program is a COBOL driver that packages the data for shipment to the expert system.

As was previously discussed, CCH-ES produces an ATB rating, a recommendation, and a dollar-specific guideline. (Figure 5 shows an example screen output produced by CCH-ES.) CCH-ES also displays *reason codes*, which provide an explanation of the most salient decision-supporting elements used by CCH-ES to produce its recommendation. Each letter (or numeric number) is a code for a particular supporting element. CCH-ES creates as many as 114 such supporting elements that are available to the analyst for review online. They are also saved with the case to provide an audit trail.

CCH-ES produces its recommendation in subsecond response time. A total response time of 3 to 5 seconds includes IBM 3090 mainframe data extraction, the communication and sending of data from the mainframe to CCH-ES on the DEC, CCH-ES processing, the communication and sending of results back to the mainframe, and the formulation and display of a screen.

All cases are run through CCH-ES. Approximately 89 percent of the cases are automatically handled by CCH-ES without any human involvement. In 1 percent of the cases, there is not enough current background information in the database to make a credit decision. User-defined knockouts currently total about 10 percent of all cases, but this

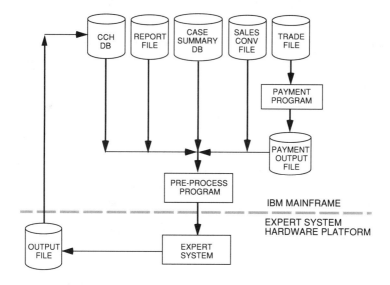

Figure 4. System Flow.

number is expected to gradually be reduced over time. Analyst agreement with CCH-ES continues to be at approximately 98.5 percent on an ongoing basis.

Maintenance

CCH-ES undergoes a few rule changes every month. These changes typically involve a refinement, a consolidation, or an addition of knowledge. A significant example of an addition is the rules that use new data elements. CCH-ES has helped D&B identify what additional data could be used to improve the decision-making process. In turn, this assistance prompted D&B to make such data available in a retrievable format; new rules are added to intelligently process the new data. There is a new CCH-ES production release each month. The CCH-ES knowledge base has expanded from its initial base of 750 rules in July 1989 to slightly over 800 in January 1991.

CCH-ES is being maintained by one of the system's original developers. Because of the complexity of the system environments involved (C, COBOL, ART-IM, communication links), end users do not have sufficient computer expertise to perform maintenance on their own.

Benefits

Major benefits from the use of CCH-ES include those for the customer and those internal to CCH and D&B. Customer benefits include the following:

```
┌─────────────────────────────────────────────────────┐
│           CCH RECOMMENDATION SCREEN                   │
│                                                       │
│     NAME                    COMPANY-X                 │
│     DUNS NUMBER             00-123-4567               │
│                                                       │
│     MERCHANDISE CODE        WGZ                        │
│     ATB RATING              B2C                        │
│     RECOMMENDATION          RECOMMENDED               │
│     DOLLAR GUIDELINE        $1,000,000                │
│     REASON CODES            BEGHJ                      │
│                                                       │
└─────────────────────────────────────────────────────┘
```

Figure 5. CCH-ES Example Output.

First is improved decision quality and consistency. CCH-ES ratings and recommendations are based on the experience and expertise of the most senior CCH credit analysts. Reaction from CCH customers has been extremely positive. They feel that CCH-ES ensures them that all relevant issues will be analyzed; that is, all the rules will examine all the data. ("CCH-ES never has a bad day.")

Second is the increased timeliness of the information. The ratings and recommendations provided are based on the most up-to-date information available.

Third is faster response. Customers get an analysis and recommendation in three to five seconds instead of the one to three days it typically took analysts in the past.

Fourth is expanded coverage. Approximately 20,000 new cases have been added to the CCH database (increased coverage by approximately 15 percent). When a customer requests a new case, information existing in normal D&B files is extracted and sent to CCH-ES, which generates an evaluation and stores the result in the CCH database.

Internal CCH and D&B benefits include the following:

First is the lower cost for each rating and recommendation.

Second is reduced vulnerability to turnover.

Third is reduced staff expenses. The number of CCH credit analysts was reduced from 15 to a smaller number of senior, highly experienced analysts.

Fourth, it allows analysts to work on the most complex cases.

Fifth is the expanded coverage at a minimum cost. CCH-ES automatically evaluates a new case from information in D&B's files. Done manually, the processing of a new case takes from three days to three weeks to accomplish.

Sixth, it helps explicitly identify how data elements are used in the decision-making process and what additional data might be important.

CCH-ES also demonstrates the software development benefits in using expert system technology. These benefits include the following:

First is increased user involvement. Because the expert system is more knowledge intensive than conventional software, it required more user involvement, which ensured that users provided the ongoing monitoring and evaluating of functional requirements and system performance.

Second is decreased development resources. A development team consisting of a knowledge engineer, a software specialist, and an expert credit analyst built the production version of CCH-ES. Software systems at D&B of similar but non-expert scope require significantly more resources.

Third is decreased maintenance resources. Changes to conventional software that can take hundreds, maybe even thousands, of hours can be done in an expert system in one day (including changing rules, implementing, testing, and putting in production).

Fourth is increased responsiveness. Changes can be made more frequently, with faster turnaround into the production environment.

An important benefit not previously given is the improvement in D&B's legal position. D&B requires all systems that affect what is delivered to customers be approved by D&B's legal department before full production. This approval is to protect D&B, its customers, and the subjects of D&B's reports. The legal department felt that CCH-ES would significantly improve D&B's legal position by providing the following benefits:

First, CCH-ES has no bias. All rules are applied automatically and consistently in all cases. There is no possibility of any favoritism, either positive or negative.

Second, it provides an audit trail of recommendations. Pertinent facts, intermediary assessments, and reasoning steps leading to a conclusion are stored with the conclusion and, thus, can easily be retrieved to explain how a particular recommendation is reached. D&B would no longer be dependent on someone's memory to explain a past decision.

A final benefit involves technology transfer. The system provides a successful and highly visible use of expert system technology at D&B. The Business Information Group has begun to disseminate, among other operating units, the means to build other expert systems. This technology transfer has resulted in a number of new expert system projects at D&B.

Conclusion

CCH-ES has been a major success at D&B. It has provided CCH with an automated credit analyst expert system that can provide expert-level credit analysis decisions consistently and at a high-quality level. Customers have uniformly praised the system. Customer service is enhanced because of the consistent expert-level recommendations, expanded coverage, faster response, and reliability. In addition, CCH internal expenses have been reduced as have the problems associated with staff turnover. Finally, technology transfer has occurred at D&B because a number of new efforts using expert system technology have been initiated.

Note

1. The rules shown in figure 3 are exemplary only. Actual rules cannot be shown for proprietary reasons.

CUBUS—An Assistant for Fundamental Corporate Analysis

Michael F. Wolf, Dieter Wenger, and Klaus Kirchmayr

Granting credits to commercial customers is one of the central activities of a bank. Avoiding incorrect credit decisions and minimizing the required effort are crucial factors for the economic success of a bank. The basic task of credit granting is a *correct valuation* of the customer, which includes the analysis of his(her) annual account and the estimations of the customer's solvency. The bank is increasingly forced to deal with nonfirst-class debtors to keep and, perhaps, improve its market share. This situation leads to two main problems: (1) the increasing risk of loss because of the activities itself and (2) the increasing costs connected with the supervision of solvency to control the risks. With knowledge of these facts, it becomes evident that a bank is required to possess innovative means to check and supervise the solvency that allow an immediate and efficient realization of risks, that is, reduction in costs, in terms of solvency as well as the rational use of personnel.

Only a minor part of the knowledge that is necessary for the analysis and valuation of commercial customers is available in a well-documented form. Individual experience is of great importance considering the fact that there are only a few standard procedures and few generally accepted valuation guidelines. Therefore, the quality of the valuation depends on the abilities of the credit specialist.

The interpretation of an annual account requires analyzing the relations between many different items. A final judgment has to be based on the integrated consideration of all these relations, which often contain conflicting information. For these reasons, it takes a considerable amount of effort to even analyze the necessary information to get a first impression of a company. Too much time is wasted on the valuation of evident cases, and often, the complicated cases receive incomplete analysis. In addition, a request often has to pass more than one department in the bank; that is, the information available has to be analyzed and judged by several specialists. On the way from one department to the final department (general management), each credit specialist analyzes the balance sheet, gives his(her) opinion, and refines and adds the information that s/he believes is missing. For example, the specialist who has direct contact with the company contributes information on the quality of the management, and a specialist in the back office might add his(her) knowledge about the regional characteristics of the economic branches. A lot of time is wasted with these repeated analyses.

CUBUS **Overview**

The program CUBUS (computerunterstütztes Bonitötsuntersuchungssystem = computer-supported system for analyzing financial solvency) was designed to solve some of these difficulties and support the decision procedure in terms of decision quality and reduced cost. The system gives a general valuation and a first global impression of a company. It also draws the user's attention to the most critical items. In addition, a detailed analysis and valuations of each annual account item (that is, the position of the balance sheet and the profit and loss account) are provided.

The existing solvency analysis systems often provide (sometimes after elaborate calculations) general valuations of important abstract concepts such as solvency or capital structure, but the detailed valuations at a concrete level are missing. It is assumed that such systems will never be perfect, and the users always have to check the results provided by the system. Thus, this approach does not fulfill the requirements of practical decisions: A credit specialist usually does not think in terms of highly aggregated, mathematically calculated concepts, meaning that s/he cannot evaluate the results of such a system or say why his(her) own results might differ from those produced by the system. The user, however, knows a great deal about the quality and adequacy of concrete items in the annual account; for example, s/he knows whether a company has too much stock or whether the proprietary capital is high enough in a specific case. If a system is to be transparent and meaningful for the user, results and valuations should be provided at this concrete level. Essential for the practical usability of the system is that it allows the user to overwrite specific single valuations and include this input in further automatic processes. In this way, the capabilities of the system and the user's additional knowledge and information can efficiently be combined.

Information about the specific economic branch is insufficient for the construction of norms that constitute the base of all valuation processes because it is the aspects of the company's individual annual account that must be studied. For example, norms for the liability side cannot be defined without knowing what the asset side looks like. All norms that only refer to the customer's branch are doomed to fail, which means that an individual norm (dynamic pattern) has to be defined for each company. This self-calibrating process is a critical success factor for the usability of the system across a variety of branches, regions, and countries. The dynamic pattern approach was a theoretical breakthrough that is now studied at universities. It contributes to the avoidance of branch-specific norms. The construction of such an individual norm (see Domain-Specific Task: Technology and Basic Algorithm for Solvency Analysis) requires so much knowledge of business economy and so much computation that it cannot be done manually in daily work. Even the theoretical model for the dynamic pattern generation could not be transferred from existing economic theories but could only be built iteratively with system prototypes. Before cubus was available, the norms based on branch data were intuitively modified by the credit specialists.

To be useful not only for an isolated one-shot analysis but for the whole institutional decision process, which concerns several organizational instances (departments), all the contributions of all the specialists involved have to be represented by the system and included in the automatic analysis. This approach means that a multiperson decision process is to be supported. The system is useful to experienced experts as well as less skilled staff. It is up to the user to decide whether s/he merely wants to obtain a rough overview of the most important elements or whether s/he seeks details that are of special interest to him(her). The handling of the system is easy, so that even persons who are unfamiliar with computers have no problems in using the program. The system provides the following functions: autonomous valuations, reactive assistance, active consulting, and interactive cooperation (see Human-Computer Cooperation). The system must apply to about 300 local Swiss Bank Corporation (SBC) branch offices and run in a commercial computer environment. The facility to communicate with a host computer is important, especially the downloading of the customer's annual account data, which are already available on a central database.

CUBUS Architecture

In this section, we discuss the CUBUS architecture, analyzing the elements we used and the steps we followed in developing and deploying the system: knowledge representation, process control, the task concept, truth maintenance, fuzzy logic, the user interface, maintenance and modification.

Knowledge Representation

The technology applied can be described as a combination of a data-driven production rule and a frame approach. To avoid an accumulation of dissipated superficial heuristics with all the problems of extension and maintenance, as much knowledge as possible is represented as data: In a deep modeling approach, frames and other hierarchical relations are used to represent relations and dependencies between objects and attributes. Even the regulations for numeric operations are represented as attributes of the elements. This approach allows formulating general rules and applying object-oriented programming in an efficient way. New objects can easily be included. Even if they affect many procedures, changes are only required on the data level, which is how a high-flexibility system is reached, and changes can easily be made without having to rewrite the processing rules. This approach allows delegating modifications of the application to a system administrator.

Data-Driven Process Control as a Prerequisite for Flexibility and Actual Interactivity

Modifying existing and generating new information is done by agents (Spirgi, Probst, and Wenger 1990). Each agent knows when to be active because the conditions in the knowledge base that trigger it are part of its definition. Thus, the processes are controlled by the situation in the knowledge base. This approach allows designing applications in which different data constellations induce different processes. Even if new information is added by the user after the system has finished its valuation processes, these data can cause the activation of all the agents that are related to this kind of information. Therefore, new information is treated with the existing processes and can fully be integrated, with the results generated autonomously. This approach leads to actual cooper-

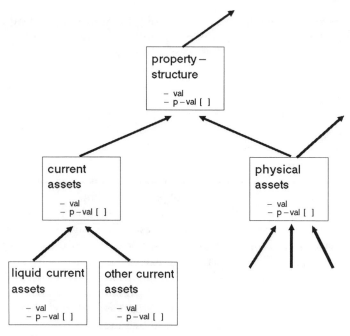

Figure 1. The Generic Task Concept CONDEV.

ation and interaction between user and computer: When the user gives his(her) input to the system, the system's results are affected, and the user's cognitions can be affected by the system results, which might lead to a new user input, and so on. In this sense, a real discussion with mutual influence takes place.

Generic Task Concept

The approach to formulate general agents that are appropriate for a variety of different situations consequently leads to the idea to identify tasks that have to be accomplished in almost all applications (Bylander and Chandrasekaran 1987) and to provide generic techniques (Spirgi, Probst, and Wenger 1991) that can be used when a new application has to be developed. Two of these generic task concepts, which were developed in a separate methodology project, are used in CUBUS: IO-GEN and CONDEV.

IO-GEN is a generic task concept for handling screen input and output information. It is a generic user interface. The most general object class is "screen unit." "Window" and "icon" are object classes that are specializations of "screen unit." The object class "view" consists of one or more windows. A window can appear in more than one view. An icon appears in a window. It can be a simple input field, output field, or a complex table or any graphics. A window can contain many icons, and an icon can appear in different windows. IO-GEN comprises many agents that do all the input-output handling by manipulating the attributes of its object classes. An agent does the window displays, and agents do the handling of the icons, and so on. The CUBUS user interface was designed with minor programming effort by making instances of the object classes "view," "window," and "icon." These instances inherit the attributes and agents of IO-GEN.

The second generic task concept used in CUBUS is *CONDEV* (condensation of valuation information). CONDEV aggregates valuations of a net of hierarchical objects. Assume an object, for example, "liquid current assets," has three partial valuations that are stored in the attribute "p-val" (figure 1). An agent propagates these three partial valuations to the objects that are higher in the hierarchical structure (for example, "current assets" and "property structure"). All partial valuations are propagated to the higher objects. Besides these propagated (indirect) valuations, each object can receive direct primary valuations. A second agent consolidates primary and propagated (secondary) valuations to one resulting valuation for each object (attribute "val").

Truth Maintenance

To guarantee consistent valuations after adding, modifying, or deleting information, the implementation of a truth maintenance mechanism was necessary. The valuations that are no longer valid are retracted, and new valuations are asserted. CONDEV is used to consolidate partial valuations and propagate them to more abstract concepts wherever information changes.

Fuzzy Logic

With each additional partial valuation, the resulting valuation might be modified, and its certainty will increase or decrease according to the level of conformity. A simplified fuzzy logic approach was developed for managing the certainty of the system valuations. This approach allows working with missing and contradictory information (see the Aggregation of Valuations subsection that follows).

Domain-Specific Task: Technology and Basic Algorithms for Solvency Analysis

The application was built by applying CONDEV and IO-GEN and several domain-specific technologies. Input for the CUBUS analyses is the customer's annual account data. Output is the valuation of the customer's solvency and other aspects of his(her) financial situation. The output is presented in the form of a printed report and as an interactive display, which allows the user to consider those aspects of special interest to him(her). We overview the basic algorithms used in the valuation processes in the following subsections (figure 2).

Self-Calibration: Generation of Individual Norms. In the first step, the annual account data are read in, the balance sheet and the profit and loss accounts are created, and the financial ratios are calculated. In the second step, the individual norms (dynamic pattern) that are the base for all valuation processes are defined. In this self-calibrating process, a *normal*, or expected, value is defined for each item in the annual account. Here, implicit assumptions about the branch are taken into consideration as well as some aspects of the company's individual balance sheet as it is.

For example, the financial ratio "capital rotation" is one input that calculates what cash-flow margin can be expected: A company with high capital rotation (trading company) usually has a lower cash-flow margin than a company with lower capital rotation (production company), or a company with many physical assets should have high depreciations. The concrete procedures required for the calculation of each norm are complex because a great number of general parameters have to be linked with many case-specific facts (too numerous to describe here). In this way, a second balance sheet and profit and loss account are defined as an individual norm. In further steps of the analysis procedure, the actual annual account is contrasted with this norm. The knowledge of how to define norms for the single items is not available in published scientific papers and had to be developed by specialists at our bank. The existence of norms for all annual account items allows the definition of valuation scales for ratios that consist of such items. When ratio z $(r\text{-}z)$ is defined as $r\text{-}z = item\text{-}a/item\text{-}b$, then the norm of $r\text{-}z$ is defined as $norm\text{-}r\text{-}z = norm\text{-}item\text{-}a/norm\text{-}item\text{-}b$. In this way, for each financial ratio, i, a value, $norm\text{-}r\text{-}i$, is calculated that is considered normal (not good, not bad), and a valuation scale is defined with $norm\text{-}r\text{-}i$ as middle or normal, $norm\text{-}r\text{-}i + x$ as good, $norm\text{-}r\text{-}i - y$ as bad, and so on.

Credit and Blame Assignment: Passing on the Valuations. On this basis, the company's actual financial ratios can be valuated on a scale of "very bad" to "very good." The next part of this step (figure 3) is the identification of those components of each ratio that make the ratio either too high or too low (for example, when the ratio liquidity I is too low, either the item "extended liquid assets" is too low, or the "current liabilities" are too high). The ratio's valuations are passed on to those

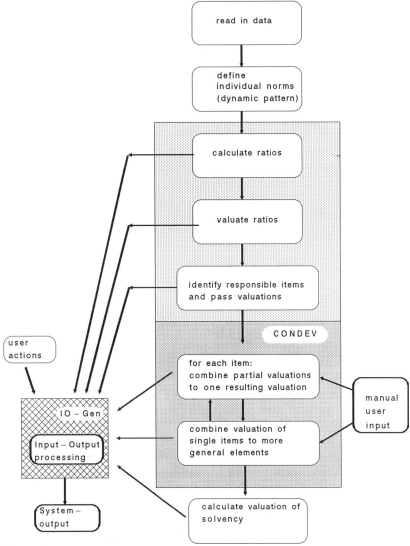

Figure 2. CUBUS Functions.

elements with the most significant deviation from the anticipated values, which are represented in the dynamic pattern. If such a component (for example, "extended liquid assets") itself is an aggregation of further subcomponents ("liquid assets" plus "security holdings"), the valuation is passed on until an atomic target element is found.

Aggregation of Valuations (CONDEV). Each element in the annual ac-

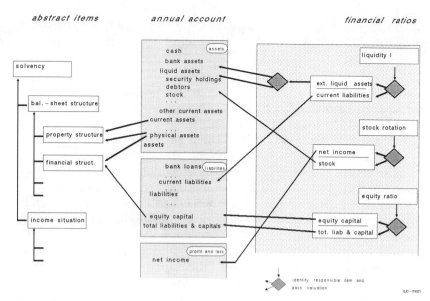

Figure 3. Valuation Model of CUBUS.

count can receive values directly from one or more ratios and indirectly from other elements. Therefore, the final valuation of a component usually has to be combined by several conflicting partial valuations. More than one conforming partial valuation increases the certainty of the resulting valuation, whereas conflicting valuations result in lower certainties. The same principles are applied when the valuations of the basic elements are aggregated to the valuation of more abstract concepts (for example, the valuations of current assets and physical assets are aggregated to the abstract concept "property structure"). The applied algorithm is CONDEV.

Different Views and Graphically Oriented Simulation

In addition to the valuation of the company's current situation, an expectation for the following year is estimated. For each item, the pure system valuations and the combination of manual and system valuations can simultaneously be displayed. Furthermore, the user can switch between two viewpoints at any time: with or without consideration of hidden reserves. All system results are separately calculated by taking these two possibilities into account. Graphically oriented simulation is also provided. The user can simulate changes in the interest rate, the net income, or other factors and obtain a graphic display of the effects on the income situation of the company (what-if analysis). Additionally, s/he can simulate the manual modification of system valuations and analyze how the valuation of other concepts will change. S/he can then decide whether his(her) input has the effects desired.

User Interface and Explanation Component

The user interface is designed as a direct manipulation interface, with the underlying principle of "point and act." The user navigates in the space of well-known concepts. When the cursor is pointed at a screen object, a help line with an explanation or a description of possible ways of action appears for this specific object. This approach makes the application basically self-explanatory. The user is never obliged to do anything. The user is driving the system, not being driven by the system.

The explanation component of CUBUS consists of an elaborate graphic representation of each of the generic or task-specific techniques. Figure 4 shows the valuation scale of a financial ratio and how the static (s) and dynamic (d) valuations are passed through the net of concepts to the items responsible. In figure 5, the aggregation of several partial valuations into one resulting valuation of the item's current liabilities is shown. The aggregation of valuations in the concept net is presented in figure 6 (figures 5 and 6 refer to CONDEV). A comparison between an expected balance sheet (narrow columns) and the actual situation (wide columns) is displayed in figure 7. The user can call these explanations for each item any time s/he wants, which is how an interactive, user-driven explanation component is realized.

Maintenance and Modification

The principle of representing as much information as possible in the data and formulating general rules allows making even fundamental changes (for example, including a new financial ratio, changing the net of concepts, including new concepts, modifying central parameters) without having to modify the rules. The variables that are subject to change are stored in a single file that can easily be edited and modified by a system administrator. Therefore, maintenance and modification can easily be done. The existence of a self-adapting dynamic pattern reduces the necessity of such modifications to a minimum.

Innovations

This section analyzes the innovative elements of the CUBUS system. These innovations include self-calibrating dynamic norms, support of multiperson decision processes, human-computer cooperation, a system development methodology, structured analysis and valuation procedures, and new knowledge management dimensions.

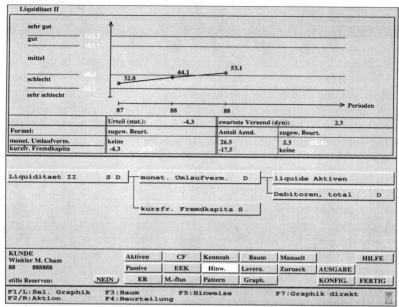

Figure 4. Valuation Scale of a Financial Ratio.

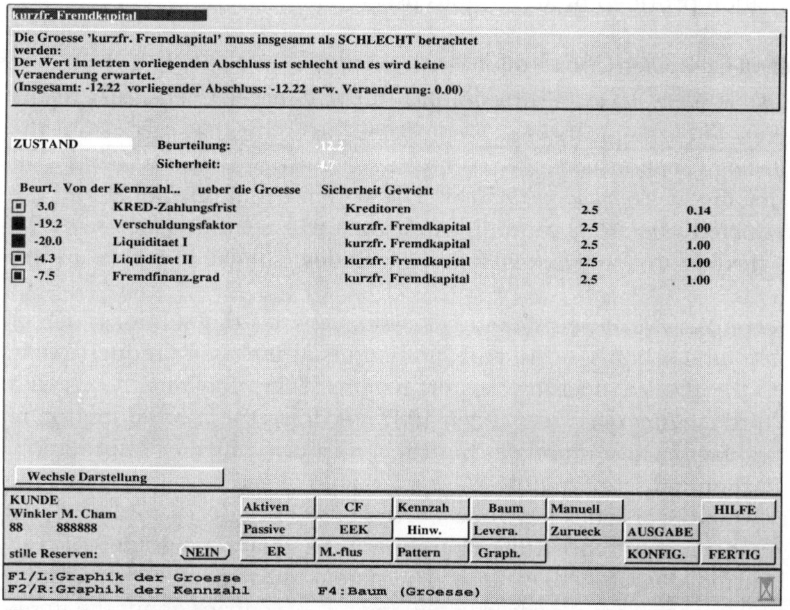

Figure 5. Aggregation of Several Partial Valuations to One Resulting Valuation
of the Item Current Liabilities.

Self-Calibrating Dynamic Norms and Structured Valuation Processes as Basic Requirements for High-Quality Analysis

Fixed norms that are based exclusively on economic branch data are not sufficient for individual solvency analysis. The dynamic pattern approach provides norms that consider a company's specific situation. Avoiding accumulating many heterogeneous heuristics and reducing the whole valuation process to a few types of basic algorithms was a great challenge. The result is a program that can be modified and maintained easily and that is extremely transparent for the developers and the users.

Support of Multiperson Decision Processes

Usually, a credit request must pass more than one department of the bank. CUBUS not only helps a single credit specialist to analyze the annual account data but also allows him(her) to add information. This individually added information is included in the system analysis and is passed to the next department. The next user can then look at this subjective information and make modifications if s/he does not agree. The overwritten elements can be viewed in a history file. This file is how the ultimate user possesses the system valuation as well as the information provided by all previous users.

Human-Computer Cooperation

Flexible interaction is one of the most outstanding characteristics of the system. The system works as a competent assistant that carries out the following functions:

First are *autonomous valuations*: The system produces global and differentiated valuations without requiring any user intervention and offers flexible interactive explanatory facilities (similar to typical expert systems).

Second is *reactive assistance*: The system carries out subtasks such as what-if analysis, prognosis, and simulations at the user's request (similar to the classical decision support systems [DSS] domain).

Third is *active consulting* (Keen 1987): It draws the user's attention to critical factors and stimulates him(her) to provide further information. An elaborated set of questions for each annual account item shows the user which properties might be worth considering in more detail; that is, his(her) search for additional relevant information is guided.

Fourth is *interactive cooperation*: The system integrates the user's input, modifies its own results accordingly, and gives feedback about the implication of this input for the system's valuations. This new constellation might provide new insights that can result in new user activities, for ex-

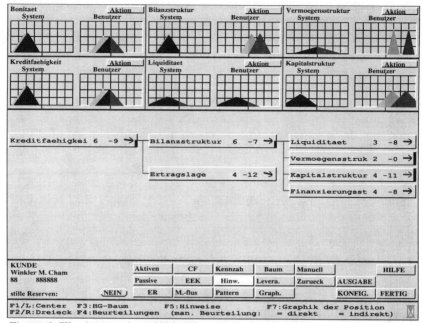

Figure 6. The Aggregation of Valuations in the Concept-Net.

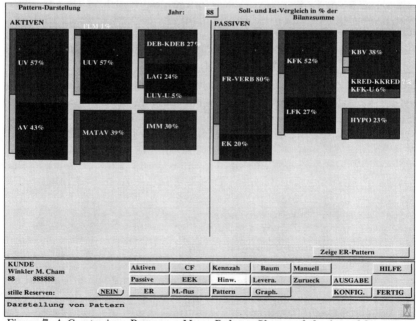

Figure 7. A Comparison Between a Norm Balance-Sheet and the Actual Situation.

ample, carrying out further analysis or providing more information.

Fifth is *presentation of information and knowledge*. This function is de-signed with the following aims: to ensure that the information can easi-ly be integrated into the existing mental models of the user, help him(her) modify or even build his(her) own models of the task do-main, and allow him(her) to reach analyses that are profound and complex and not possible without the system. (See Niva [1986, p. 336]: combining "the human association ability with the logical function of a computer as an explicit cooperative system"; Woods [1986]: joint cog-nitive systems; and Sage and Rouse [1986]: shared mental models.)

System Development Methodology

Application development with data-driven techniques that are based on frames and production rules requires a specific methodology. In Swiss Bank Corporation, an executable methodology for application development was developed, an application that helps to check the consistency of hierarchical relations and define and control the activi-ties of agents in terms of activating constraint and contextual informa-tion and the resulting changes in the knowledge base. This methodolo-gy was built during the CUBUS development. Now, about 10 projects are being developed with the help of this methodology. The integration of our experience in an executable methodology will lead to a tremen-dous growth in productivity and high-quality computer application de-velopment at Swiss Bank Corporation.

Structured Analysis and Valuation Procedures

CUBUS provides a coherent model for the valuation of the solvency of a company and all annual account items. This model consists of a rela-tively small number of generic and task-specific techniques (basic algo-rithms). Through the development of this model, insight into econom-ic relations was gained that was not described in such detail in specific literature. The existence of a general model allows the estimate of the portability of the system to other domains (other countries, other types of companies, purposes other than credit decisions) and the decision of where changes have to be made.

New Dimensions of Knowledge Management

The complete knowledge of how to analyze annual account data was explicitly formulated with the construction of the valuation model. Until this time, most of the knowledge applied was personal and sub-jective. Because the knowledge is now transparent, it can be controlled and criticized by expert committees and can be developed further.

Significant improvements have been achieved this way. New knowledge can rapidly be delivered with new versions of the system, and it is automatically applied. There is no need for the credit specialists to read a lot of papers and change their daily working procedures. Instead, they use the new CUBUS version, and the new norms or valuation procedures are applied. By controlling, improving, deploying, and implementing new knowledge, new dimensions are brought to an organization's knowledge management. Now, even models that are highly complex can be applied because the computer knows how to use them and produces the result within seconds.

Payoff

Since CUBUS was deployed (and as done during the testing periods), a systematic evaluation has been conducted: The quality and acceptance of the system was intensely examined. The profit will also be estimated in collaboration with our controlling division. The numeric quantification of the payoff is difficult because a lot of aspects are qualitative, and many of the financial aspects can only be assessed in several years when the credits have to be paid back.

In regard to *efficiency*, tests showed that the time necessary for analyzing the annual account of a company can significantly be reduced. Today, CUBUS is used by the analysts of 8 local branches. When all SBC credit specialists at all 20 branches can profit from CUBUS (which will be required in 1992), personnel costs will be reduced by approximately US$500,000. The capacity gains will be used for improved customer consultancy and thorough analyses of difficult cases.

In regard to the *increase in the know-how level,* the system's knowledge and analytic capabilities are equivalent to the level of experienced experts. These facilities are now included in the work of less skilled persons when they use the system. When working with the system, the user automatically improves his(her) own knowledge. New staff members can be integrated and become operative in a short time.

In regard to the *improved quality of decisions,* those decisions cooperatively made by persons and the system are superior to the decisions made by a person alone. Even experienced credit specialists often receive hints on aspects they would not have otherwise noticed. Simulations, facilities for prognosis, the immense amount of complex calculations, and the elaborated information presentation help to increase the quality of decisions. It is expected that better decisions concerning new credits and an automatic check of the financial situation of all customers with running credits will help to reduce bank loss by US$1 million each year.

In regard to the *improved understanding of the problem field*, the experts' knowledge of the problem domain has largely been improved by the development of the application. Because this knowledge was structured and made operative in the system, the generation of new approaches and theories (see dynamic pattern) has been possible.

Finally, CUBUS is a management instrument that helps to establish management decisions and guidelines. The system provides standards for fundamental corporate analysis that are automatically applied when the system is used. In contrast to written instructions in manuals, these standards cannot be misinterpreted or ignored. New guidelines and techniques can effectively be introduced through its tutoring facilities.

At least US$1.5 million are expected to be saved each year. In this way, the development costs (less than US$2 million) will be paid back within 1½ years. This calculation does not consider that along with the system development, by-products such as IO-GEN and CONDEV were created and can be used in many other projects. Furthermore, CUBUS versions will be created for special purposes. CUBUS offers completely new possibilities for estimating the solvency structure of the bank debtors that are of growing interest in the asset and liability management of SBC.

Development and Deployment Timeline

CUBUS is now implemented on IBM PS2/70 workstations. The development and deployment time line for CUBUS is as follows:

1987

March: Joint project of German Dresdner Bank, Spanish Banco de Bilbao, and Swiss Bank Corporation started to develop a system for fundamental corporate analysis.

May: Intensive interviews conducted with credit experts. First prototype realized with Prolog by an external firm.

June: Swiss Bank Corporation buys TI Explorer II with Inference Corporation's ART and starts its own development.

October: First ART prototype based on common rules of thumb (for example, IF long-term assets >= 1,2 * (net worth + long-term external fund) AND hidden reserves in fixed assets > 0 THEN the financial structure is ok).

1988

January: Comparative evaluation conducted of the Prolog and ART prototypes. Decision made to further develop the ART prototype as a single Swiss Bank Corporation project. First ideas developed for a deep modeling approach instead of rules of thumb.

July: First deep model prototype finished. Extensive testing started.

September: Different deployment platforms evaluated. Tests on MicroExplorer conducted, and porting to the host under IBM Knowledge Tool started.

1989

March: Development of the prototype on the Explorer continued. Bad experience in search for a convenient deployment platform leads to the evaluation of the personal computer–based ART-IM.

May: ART-IM infrastructure built. Porting the ART-Lisp prototype to ART-IM with integrated further development started.

July: Two systems compared. Decision made to stop development on the TI Explorers.

September: Alpha version operational and installed at a Swiss Bank Corporation branch. Improvements made at the user interface and data transfer from host to personal computer based on the feedback of about 10 users. Further modifications initiated.

1990

January: Beta version operational and released at 3 Swiss Bank Corporation branches. Regular user training started.

May: The dynamic pattern approach makes CUBUS usable for all branches and many countries.

September: Initial production version 3.7 operational. System installation process at the 18 regional Swiss Bank Corporation branches started.

November: Production version 3.9 deployed.

References

Bylander, T., and Chandrasekaran, B. 1987. Generic Tasks for Knowledge-Based Reasoning: The "Right" Level of Abstraction for Knowledge Acquisition. *International Journal of Man-Machine Studies* 26:231–243.

Keen, P. G. W. 1987. Decision Support Systems: The Next Decade. *Decision Support Systems* 3: 253–265.

Niva, K. 1986. A Knowledge-Based Human-Computer Cooperative System for Ill-Structured Management Domains. *IEEE Transactions on Systems, Man, and Cybernetics* SMC-16(3): 335–342.

Sage, A. P., and Rouse, W. B. 1986. Aiding the Human Decision Maker through the Knowledge-Based Sciences. *IEEE Transactions on Systems, Man, and Cybernetics* SMC-16(4): 511–521.

Spirgi, S.; Probst, A. R.; and Wenger, D. 1991. *Generic Techniques in EMA: A Model-Based Approach*. Berlin: Springer-Verlag.

Spirgi, S.; Probst, A. R.; and Wenger, D. 1990. Knowledge Acquisition in a Development Methodology for Knowledge-Based Applications. In

Proceedings of the First Japanese Knowledge Acquisition for Knowledge-Based Systems Workshop, eds. H. Motoda, R. Mizoguchi, J. Boose, and B. Gaines, 382–397. Tokyo: Ohmsha.

Woods, D. D. 1986. Paradigms for Intelligent Decision Support. In *Intelligent Decision Support in Process Environments*, eds. E. Hollnagel, G. Mancini , and D. D. Woods, 153–174. Berlin: Springer.

Government

TIME
U.S. Army, TRADOC & George Washington University

Travel Expense Claim System
State of California, Health and Welfare Agency

Nuclear Test Ban Treaty Verification
*Science Applications International Corporation,
Center for Seismic Studies, & Inference Corporation*

Criticism-Based Knowledge Acquisition for Document Generation

Barry G. Silverman

This chapter describes an AI application called the TRADOC issue management expert (TIME), which was deployed in 1990 for the U.S. Army Training and Doctrine Command (TRADOC). TIME helps generate a document that is part of the system acquisition milestone or decision process. The goal of TIME is to bridge the gap between the headquarters decision makers who know how to write the desired document and the various authors at 17 sites nationwide who know what to put in the document. TIME has several capabilities. In one capacity, it is an expert critiquing and tutoring system that emulates the headquarters decision makers. In this capacity, it communicates good document-authoring rules, heuristics, and practices in real-time (during authoring) mode. In another capacity, TIME is also a knowledge-acquisition system that interviews the author and helps him(her) generate the document. Finally, TIME acts as an intelligent memory that dynamically indexes and collects as many as 600 documents that are produced annually in a corporate memory for later analogical retrieval and illustration purposes. This last capability means that the more TIME is used, the more useful it is.

Significance of the Application to the U.S. Army

The domain for TIME consists of two principal tasks: forecasting and decision problem structuring. The forecasting task is to predict the worst mission a new piece of materiel (for example, tank, helicopter, or gas mask) might have to be taken on. Decision makers can then use this forecast to structure the issues and criteria that must be evaluated to decide whether to purchase or develop this piece of materiel. Accurate forecasts and robust decision issues and criteria are important to the decision to procure the new item and, thus, to the ultimate safety of those who will have to take it into the battlefield. However, this accuracy and robustness are often obscure to the mind of the Army author because of the short schedule for completing the report and all the conflicting demands on the author's time.

Lack of concrete, first-hand information further compounds the prediction-specification tasks. Increasingly, Army experts have less direct experience with current threats (threats are what make a mission difficult to complete) or with what leads to robust performance on the battlefield. Army experts gain much of their insight from interviewing sources and closely studying intelligence reports about the various disciplines (for example, artillery, electronic warfare, or biochemical agents). These experts have little direct experience. That is, except in areas for which they have direct concrete experience, much of the information available for making these forecasts and specifications is abstract data.

In other words, there is a short timetable for completing the overall task as well as delays associated with researching abstract battlefield information. These two features combine in the mind of the expert to create a situation where weak and biased heuristics might replace a more normative form of reasoning. This use of biased heuristics occurs with no loss of confidence on the part of the Army knowledge base preparer.

The system acquisition process in the Army and in the military at large requires hundreds of documents to be generated during the life cycle of each new piece of materiel. The same types of problems occur with other kinds of military documents as occur in the one type of document that TIME helps with. Any success achieved in the TIME project is potentially reusable for solving similar problems in other document preparation efforts.

Significance of the Application to the Field of AI

Helping this domain requires a novel approach. Decision-aiding techniques that might improve the authors' reasoning historically rely on theory-rich but domain knowledge–impoverished approaches. Some examples are decision analysis and multiattribute utility theory. By themselves, such techniques can't solve the problem because domain knowledge is one of the critical missing ingredients leading to bias and error.

Expert systems also are not entirely appropriate. The Army problem requires an interactive decision aid that drives the user to a more theoretically rigorous and normative decision style. However, expert systems are theory poor. Further, expert systems are for replace-the-expert purposes. The domain in this case, however, is too vast (that is, the entire Army is the domain) to replace the human. For the same reason, an intelligent tutoring system also cannot work in this domain.

Although they often are found in support-the-expert roles, expert systems increasingly appear to have poor human factors when applied to decision-aiding settings (for example, see Langlotz and Shortliffe [1983]; Klein and Calderwood [1986]; or Roth, Bennett, and Woods [1988]). More of a "joint cognitive system" orientation is warranted than expert system technology can supply alone. Again, the same human factors concerns apply to intelligent tutoring systems.

Another consideration is that TIME's purpose is to help generate reports or documents in the form of knowledge bases. This tool has to adhere to theoretically correct prescriptions for decision aiding and simultaneously provide knowledge-rich support to its users. These needs require a knowledge-acquisition tool that also uses a form of knowledge-based system technology to critique the validity of the users' input.

Expert critiquing systems that help an expert improve his(her) task performance are not new (for example, see Miller [1983] and Langlotz and Shortliffe [1983]). What is new is (1) the use of deep knowledge of human judgment as a theory of bugs and repairs to guide the design of the critics and (2) the merger of expert critiquing with knowledge-acquisition–system technology. The result is criticism-based knowledge acquisition. This technique offers a judgment theory–motivated, knowledge-rich approach to expert decision supporting, expert problem solving, and other types of human expert–conducted tasks.

This section gives a brief introduction to the theory of criticism (that is, bugs and repairs) of expert intuition. The interested reader can see Silverman (1990, 1991, 1992) for more detail. Readers can also directly consult the bug theories in the literature, such as Kahneman, Slovic, and Tversky (1982). In this literature, it is popular to debias human judgment with the aid of a linear model. Expert critics replace the linear model with a decision network of heuristic critics.

Specifically, a machine critic's heuristics include a decision network of alternative criticism strategies that are triggered when earlier strategies fail to remove the error. As suggested by the rules across the top of table 1, it is useful to have influencers warn experts about biases and explain how to avoid them (prevention is quicker than a cure). Biases,

	THEN: Potential Critic Strategies Are		
IF: Error Category Is	Influencers (Positive, before and during task critics)	Debiasers (Negative, after task critics)	Directors (Task definition adjutants)
OBTAINING INFORMATION (from Memory, Environment, or Feedback) o Availability o Base Rate o Data Preservation o Ease of Recall o Hindsight Bias o Memory Capacity Constraint o Recency of Occurrence o Selective Perception	o Hint & Cue to Stimulate Recall o Show Good Defaults, Analogs , and Other Cut-and-Paste Items to Replace What's Missing From Memory o Explain Principles, Examples, and Referencess (tutoring) to Impart New Insight o Use Repitition	o Test, Trap, and Doubt to See If Memory has Retained the Information Offered By The Influencers o Recognize Memory Failure Modes, Explain Cause and Effect, and Suggest Repair Actions	o Cause the User to Notice More Cues in the Environment and in Memory so he Can Correct the Error Himself o Tell the User How to Follow a Proper Path so He Can Reach a Normative Anchor
HANDLING UNCERTAIN INFORMATION o Adjustment o Confirmation o Conservatism o Gambler's Fallacy o Habit o Illusion of Control o Law of Small Numbers o Overconfidence o Regression Effect o Representativeness o Selective Perception o Spurious Cues o Success/Failure Attribution o Wishful Thinking	o Hint & Cue About Laws of Probability o Show Good Defaults, Analogs , and Other Drag-and-Paste Items to Help User Improve o Explain Principles, Examples, and References (tutoring) to Impart New Insight o Tutor with Differential Descriptions, Probability Models, etc. o Use Visualization Aids	o Test, Trap, and Doubt to See If Info Processing Is Succumbing to the Biases o Recognize Processing Failure Modes, Explain Cause and Effect, and Suggest Repair Actions	o Suggest How the User Can Better Structure the Problem so He Can See the Error Himself o Tell the User How to Follow a Proper Reasoning Path so He Can Reach a More Optimal Outcome
OUTPUT ERRORS o Errors in Difference Between Intended and Actual Output	o Display Visual Depictions of the Output to Give User the 'Big Picture' o Suggest Standard and Useful Responses the User Might Overlook	o Notice Defective Responses o Explain Causes and Adverse Effects o Suggest Repairs	o Provide Proper Format Guidance o Walk the User Through Response Specifications
Knowledge Errors	o Alert User to News and Updates About Knowledge, Constraints, Viewpoints o Disseminate Information not in the User's Purview	o Evaluate the User's Solution From Different Views o Suggest Incremental Improvements	o Tell the User How to Follow Known Normative Procedure and Use Prescriptive Knowledge

Table 1. Types of Strategies Relevant for Critiquing Various Errors.

like perceptual illusions, are often hard to remove even after they have been pointed out. Thus, it is necessary to have debiasers notice that an erroneous judgment remains and steer the experts toward a more correct reasoning strategy. Finally, a formal reasoning director is needed if experts still retain their biased answer. The director requires the user to gather (abstract) data, conduct the steps of a rigorous analysis, and compute the correct answer.

The precise strategy to use for each influencer, debiaser, or director depends on several variables. As the left side of table 1 shows, it depends on the cognitive process and the type of error involved. The critic designer looks down this list to the relevant rows and selects the strategies from the body of the table. The knowledge-rich side of a decision network of critics is domain specific. Individual critics must be instantiated for each new domain tackled. Those built for the Army problem are explained in detail in Case Study: Issue and Criteria Knowledge Base Acquisition and in Description of the Forecasting Task.

In addition to table 1, this application also adheres to the implementation rules of table 2, guidelines for deployment. Table 2 shows the important where, when, and how considerations of critic design. When the conditions on the right side of table 2 exist, the designer implements the critic so that it has the features on the left.

Finally, the TIME critic system is a working application that successfully passed on-site field test in late 1990 . Alpha testing was conducted at 6 sites from January through April 1991. TIME is believed to be one of the largest critic systems ever built. To date, it has over 1,500 rules, 1,500 objects, 2,000 note cards, 300 analogs, and numerous other data structures. This write-up offers only a small look at TIME.

Case Study: Issue and Criteria Knowledge Base Acquisition

The simplest way to introduce the Army case study is to describe a scene that captures the essentials and to which details can and will be added as needed. In illustrating the use of tables 1 and 2, the issue and criteria structuring task appears before the forecasting task even though the reverse takes place in the real TIME system.

Scene

A potential contractor, John, has a new satellite communications component called SATCOM that he hopes organization XYZ will sponsor for further development and, ultimately, for production. XYZ's new communications systems evaluator, Sally, got her graduate degree several years ago in telecommunications engineering and has stayed abreast by regularly reading technical journals and reports and attending short courses on the subject. Sally knows the telecommunications subject fairly well and is impressed with the technical merit of the ideas that John is proposing to incorporate. To stay up to date in the telecommunications technology development field, however, Sally has had little chance to work with the application or operation side of the XYZ organization. She realizes personnel in operations don't have advanced degrees or analytic backgrounds, which is part of the reason that Sally chose technology development as a career, but she doesn't

		THEN These Choices Are Appropriate	IF: These Conditions Exist
WHEN TO DEPLOY DIFFERENT CRITIC TYPES	Types of Applications	Structured	Well-structured task, and intermediate skilled users.
		Semi-Structured	Semi-structured task with existing electronic environment, situated learning is needed, and user errors are likely.
	Timing	Before Task Critic	Commonly recurring errors can be anticipated/prevented and users won't be info overloaded by the preventive measures.
		During Task Critic	Error can be detected before task is finished, users can be safely interrupted, interruption will be beneficial.
		After Task Critic	An error needs correcting and users will correct after the fact.
	Process	Incremental Critics	Suggestions are best given close to time of error.
		Batch Critics	Suggestions can be bunched in a group at specific intervals.
	Mode	Passive Critic	User is best determiner of when to use the critic and the output of the critic is not always desired.
		Active Critic	User is novice/intermediate, suggestions will improve task performance, and user would welcome the interruption(s).
	Knowledge	Shallow Critic	Superficial task and user goal understanding is permissible.
		Deep Critic	Task understanding is required to be precise or user goals and intentions are neede to be non-intrusive.
	Algorithms	Heuristic Critic	Judgment error has replaced a heuristic procedure or missing knowledge must be obtained via heuristic procedure.
		Simple Equation Critic	User error lies in the mis- or non-use of either a qualitative or quantitive equation.
		Formal Model-Based Critic	User error lies in the mis- or non-use of a model-based reasoning procedure.
HOW	Human Computer Interface	Restricted Natural Language Critic	Textual dialogs are the only way to convey information or infrequent use prohibits training of other communication modes.
		Command Language Driven Critic	Frequent users wish to bypass delays of other modes.
		Direct Manipulation Driven Critic	A visual metaphor of the critic can be created, the visual icon is intuitively appealing, and little training is needed to use it.
		Influencer Critics	Positive appeals to the user's intelligence will succeed and reasonable preventive measures can be defined.
	Strategies	Debiaser Critics	Negative condemnations of user's sfforts are needed and after task correction will be heeded by the user.
		Director Critics	Step by step procedures must be explained to either cause the user to see or correct his error.

Table 2. Rules for Design and Deployment of Expert Critics.

see why this deficiency should stop XYZ from keeping technologically apace in the communications technology area.

Sally wrote a three-page report to her manager, Roger, indicating the technical issues, criteria, and thresholds the SATCOM component should be tested against, a set of constraints she had long wanted a component to overcome and that John assured her were achievable.

Within a week, Roger returned Sally's report with a note indicating Sally's assessment needed to be rewritten before he could back it, indicating three basic points: (1) refocus away from technical gadgetry alone and balance the evaluation more squarely on gains in operational performance, (2) stop viewing the component in a stand-alone fashion and instead assess how well it can be integrated with other equipment and operating and maintenance personnel and practices, and (3) summarize the most important issues and criteria only on a level that higher-level management can base decisions on.

Sally stopped by Roger's office later that day to discuss things. Roger said that he was swamped as manager of the Office of Technology Evaluation and that his three written comments to Sally were the same ones he had to write again and again to all the evaluators, no matter what their discipline. Although his evaluators were technically proficient in their respective disciplines, he wished that he had some sort of knowledge-writing aid that would help them to create appropriate evaluation issues, criteria, and thresholds and tests for new technology the first time around.

In the Army domain, as at XYZ, Sally's evaluation report is a knowledge base of the issues, criteria, thresholds, and tests that the new component must pass. That is, the report contains the rules needed to diagnose whether the component should be contracted for (that is, whether it is "healthy"). In this scene, as in the Army, the knowledge-writing aid Roger wants could be an influencer aid, a debiaser, or both. The description of these two classes of critics follows. It addresses each of the task, bias, and strategy levels of a decision network relevant to this domain. It took about two person-years of effort to develop the criticism knowledge bases for the actual U.S. Army version of this case study. This task was achieved in the first six months of 1989.

The Task Level

The case study user community includes individuals skilled in one of about 17 specific disciplines for which the Army buys new combat systems. Sally's telecommunications speciality is analogous to such a discipline. In any given discipline, the responsible individual writes a critical operational issues and criteria (COIC) document, or knowledge base, that defines the conditions under which the Army should proceed (or not) with the purchase-development of the proposed new materiel item. As in Sally's case, COIC is a 5- to 9-page decision paper that is eventually signed off by a headquarters' decision maker. It stipulates what criteria the weapon system must satisfy if the Army is to purchase it. Issues and criteria can be equated to disease hypotheses and symptoms that the weapon system should avoid to be healthy enough to purchase.

Thus, the tasks of writing COIC are to fill in the issue and criteria knowledge base chunks. COIC is a highly structured knowledge base containing primarily logical statements that need to be tested as true or false (or for degrees of belief). Still, this arrangement is just the structural aspect of the knowledge to acquire for a given COIC. Knowing the structure is relatively trivial, the structure is given in a handbook available to all evaluators, and the structure does not provide the answers that are needed in the subtasks just mentioned.

If the structure were all that mattered, this domain could use a traditional knowledge-acquisition system to interview the human to enter another issue or criteria. To the contrary, the cognitive task analysis shows the machine must collaborate with and criticize the human in each of the subtasks of a well-formed COIC. The knowledge-acquisition system needs many critiquing heuristics, first principles, and work package question sets to help in the construction of proper issues and criteria. These needs, in turn, require a number of additional subtasks (for example, the forecasting task) to collect information about the new system, synthesize these data, and think about what is relevant or irrelevant to the COIC document.

The Bias Level of the Cognitive Task Analysis

As with the subtasks, only a sample of the numerous biases encountered in this domain appear in this section. An example bias situation exists in the subtask for developing the criterion measure for a given criterion for a given COIC issue. Figure 1 shows this subtask along with some of the related biases that I now discuss. The strategies plotted on this diagram are the focus of the ensuing subsection. As indicated earlier, the criteria are the dimensions along which the system will be measured so that a procurement decision can be made. In Sally's case, they might include items such as the number of communications successfully processed in a given time interval by SATCOM.

Figure 1 plots Roger's three complaints along with other biases found during the cognitive task analysis of the Army users. The causes of each of these biases are different, potentially unrelated to each other, and often result for different reasons. The individuals interviewed from four separate disciplines react to different organizational influences and exhibit different causes for similar biases. In effect, not all the causes of the bias are known at this point, and it isn't clear whether sufficient study could ever be done to isolate all the causes.

Like the cause, the effect of the errors in the measures varies widely. Where headquarters' personnel catch the errors and send COIC back

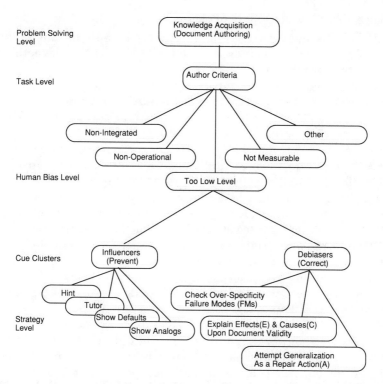

Figure 1. Cognitive Task Analysis Diagram Showing an Actual Set of Biases and Critiquing Strategies for the Criteria-Authoring Task.

for further rewrite, the main effect is a delay in processing the document. If headquarters misses the error, unneeded testing of the item might be done after the document is approved, or insufficient attention might be paid to critical dimensions of the item being procured. The latter effect is, of course, the most serious. In the extreme, it can lead to systems that are ineffective in the battlefield to be fielded, causing needless loss of life.

The process of identifying these biases involved interviewing about a dozen discipline specialists (Sally's) and seven managers (Roger's). Also, in five instances, successive drafts of COICs were chronologically analyzed with the help of one of the headquarters experts who had worked out the bugs on them. Only five could be analyzed because either the files or the relevant experts were no longer available. Thus, the cognitive task analysis covered over 22 cases of biased COIC criteria sets (plus numerous anecdotes from specific interviewees). Each case included anywhere from two to about two dozen specific bias examples.

Implementation-Level Details of the Strategies

What follows is an explanation of one strategy network for one of the biases found when domain experts authored criteria knowledge base chunks, as shown in figure 1. The other biases are subjected to a similar set of strategies; however, space restrictions, as well as readability concerns, dictate that I explain only one illustrative strategy.

The strategies shown in figure 1 implement the two top-level strategies of table 1: (1) influence the user before s/he finalizes his(her) answer (with hints, defaults, analogs, principles, examples, or repetition) and (2) debias and direct the user after s/he gives an answer. Specifically, the domain expert interacts with two separate tools when creating his(her) knowledge base. First, there is a question-asking and critiquing system that includes the influencer and debiaser strategies. There is also a graphic knowledge-level editor that cues the expert to directly edit the knowledge base. For example, s/he sees color cues that indicate incomplete elements of his(her) knowledge base. In the following discussion, I explain the types of interactions found in using tool 1 to generate a first draft of the knowledge base. Tool 2 is then used to refine the knowledge base and further guide the user's visualization of his(her) invention (although it is not described here).

The decision network established for the criteria critics includes many of the strategies in table 1. Specifically, the decision network established for criticizing during the decision problem-structuring task includes the following strategies (figure 2):

The first strategy is *leading question asking*. Many of the influencers or knowledge critics provide leading questions that attempt to place the user in a specific frame of mind to follow the prescribed cues. For example, one leading question is "Would you like to input a criterion for the effectiveness issue?" Other leading questions force the user to study the domain of the weapon system more closely and, thereby, pave the way for collecting a number of terms for the criteria phrase.

The second strategy is *Socratic hinting*. As used here, hinting is a little more direct than leading question asking in that it often states a cue. To continue the example, the question "Would you like to input a criterion for the effectiveness issue?" is accompanied by the following hint: "A good criterion normally factors in the operational and battlefield integration concerns."

The third strategy is *tutoring*. Tutoring makes use of information hiding. It is only invoked when the user fails to understand a hint. When invoked, tutoring exposes the user to a hierarchy of note cards of interlinked principles, good and bad examples, subprinciples, examples of the subprinciples, and references. The user can navigate as deep into

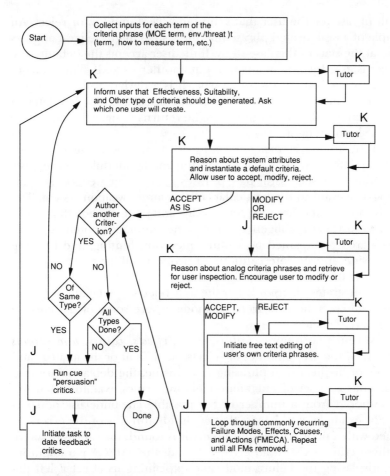

Figure 2. Decision Network of Critics for the Criteria-Authoring Task.

this hierarchy as s/he needs to to understand the associated cue. Tutoring can be set on mandatory mode for novices, which was done (at the first level of note cards) for the Army field test. Part of the first principle note card for our continuing example quotes the handbook on the high-level, operational criteria cue. It gives the decision rules that explain why its important to aggregate and orient away from strictly technical detail. Other principle note cards contain lists of dos and don'ts plus examples and citations.

The fourth strategy is *default reasoning*. When the user selects a type of criteria to input, say, satellite communications, TIME reasons from earlier collected weapon system information and instantiates a good default phrase for the user that s/he can accept, modify, or reject. An example of a well-formed phrase that the system might suggest appears earlier at the start of this case study. If the user accepts the default as is, the user is asked if s/he wants to input another issue. If s/he wants to put in another issue of the same type, it is a deviation from the prescribed cue, and the user is sent to the persuasion critics (see later in this subsection). If s/he is finished, s/he returns to near the top of the network shown in figure 2.

The fifth strategy is *analog reasoning*. If the user wants to modify or reject the default, s/he is first sent to the analog module. There, TIME shows him(her) successful past phrases from other weapon systems (analogs) relevant to the particulars of this target weapon system. The hope is to offer another concrete modify-and-paste anchor that might appeal to his(her) intelligence before s/he commits a potential error. Analogs are accompanied by leading questions, hinting, and tutoring that provide appropriate cautions to properly adjust the analog on transferring it to his(her) knowledge base.

The sixth strategy is *repetition*. If the user rejects the default as well as all the analogs, s/he is in free-text mode, where some of the cue-use cautions are repeated.

The seventh strategy is *failure, mode, effects, causes, and actions* (FMECA). If the user modifies or rejects the default or the analogs and adds any of his(her) own phrasing to the issue, the debiasers are triggered. That is, a set of judgment-debiasing critics examine what the user authored from a number of the possible cue-underuse perspectives. For example, critics exist that could identify any of the errors associated with a poor criterion. If no error is found, the user is unaware that these critics exist. If an error is found, the FMECA paradigm involves displaying the failure mode and explaining its effect if left uncorrected, a cause, and a suggested repair action. Often, this process involves sending the user on a mandatory tour through some of the tutoring note cards s/he earlier overlooked (figure 3). In the tutoring literature, FMECA is often referred to as a theory of bugs (for example, see Wenger [1987]).

The eighth strategy is *persuasion*. If the user appears to violate a normative cue, s/he is sent to a cluster of critics that attempt to find out why s/he is taking these actions. If certain legitimate reasons are missing, the critics attempt to persuade him(her) to use the relevant cue. Persuasion usually takes the form of explaining cause and effect if the cue is ignored.

The ninth strategy is *feedback*. If all the other strategies fail to cause the user to use a given cue, the last resort strategy is to show him(her) what s/he has done and ask him(her) if s/he can bring it more in line with the prescribed cues. For example, if the user creates four communications criteria, s/he is shown the list and asked if s/he can merge and combine any of these to make a smaller set that is more in line with the cue's objectives. The critics assist him(her) in repeatedly looping through the set of criteria until the user feels s/he is done.

Description of the Forecasting Task

The previous task description explains how one can analyze a domain to decide which critic strategies mitigate the biases and commonly recurring expert errors. Without going into the details, it was similarly determined that the following biases prevail in the forecasting subtask: In the information-acquisition stage, the biases are availability biases in the acquisition of distributional information and base-rate biases that promote the attractiveness of the concrete information the forecasters possess in their personal experience base. In the information-processing stage, the biases are habit, nonregressive effects, and adjustment from deficient anchors. In the feedback stage, the bias is the ease of recall.

The purpose of this section is to focus the reader's attention on several of the critic design parameters introduced in tables 1 and 2 but not yet discussed. First, I discuss the human factors of the human-machine interface. Figure 3 contains a listing of the dialogue but omits the actual screens that the user interacts with. Second, the decision network in this section includes a director. This case illustrates how to heuristically handle what analysts often view as a more traditional decision-analytic and quantitative subtask.

The screens, interfaces, and behaviors of the decision network of critics built for the Army problem are shown in figures 4, 5, and 6. These figures follow the strategies for critic rules in table 1 and adhere to the table 2 guidelines for deployment. In each figure, the darkened area is the principal work area. The user types answers into this space after the > sign. The answers are in bold print for emphasis. The white regions hold information the user must read or functions the user can invoke. The functions also appear in the lower-right box of each screen. These functions are primarily of three types: (1) navigational aids that allow the user to leap between different screen layers (help, principle, examples, citation), (2) aids to edit answers or replay earlier sequences (rewind and fast forward, used either to refresh the users memory or undo and update), and (3) commands to save and quit.

The influencers built for the task shown in figure 4 show up just before the task begins. That is, the user has been working in the environment for some time. S/he now reaches the point where s/he must venture a "worst mission" forecast. Five steps are shown in figure 4:

The idea of Critical Operational Issues and Criteria (COIC) is to summarize for decision makers at headquarters. The measures you've selected thus far are:

o Using standard I/O devices, SATCOM must demonstrate a 90 percent probability that it can successfully handle three User Control Interface Devices in use simultaneously operating at data rates up to 4 kbs.

o SATCOM will communicate through the atmospheric conditions produced by a high altitude nuclear burst.

o Receptions successfully completed.

o Successful transmissions sent in a dirty battlefield.

The following are inappropriate:

o Receptions successfully completed.
o Successful transmissions sent in a dirty battlefield.

for the following reason.

These MOEs are often too specific for a COI. A higher level composite MOE which incorporates these MOEs is preferable.

A more appropriate version is:

o Communications successfully completed.

Do you:

I. Accept as is
J. Edit further
K. Reject

> 2

> Communications successfully completed in a dirty battlefield.

What 2 to 3 word name would you like to save this under on the dendritic?

> Receive/Transmit

Figure 3. Example of Epistemological Assessment to Debias Expert Intuition after an Error.

First, the system asks for the expert's forecast of the worst mission. It already knows that the materiel of interest is a helicopter. It also already elicited a list of all missions that the helicopter might be sent on.

Second, before the user is allowed to type his(her) answer, an active influencer attempts to alert him(her) to the potential for biased reason-

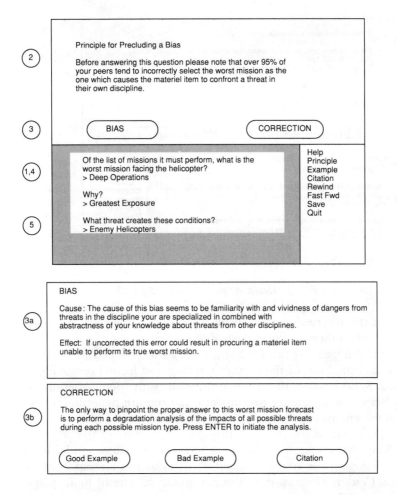

The following content is shown within the figure:

(2) Principle for Precluding a Bias

Before answering this question please note that over 95% of your peers tend to incorrectly select the worst mission as the one which causes the materiel item to confront a threat in their own discipline.

(3)   BIAS   CORRECTION

(1,4) Of the list of missions it must perform, what is the worst mission facing the helicopter?
> Deep Operations

Why?
> Greatest Exposure

(5) What threat creates these conditions?
> Enemy Helicopters

Help
Principle
Example
Citation
Rewind
Fast Fwd
Save
Quit

(3a) BIAS

Cause: The cause of this bias seems to be familiarity with and vividness of dangers from threats in the discipline your are specialized in combined with abstractness of your knowledge about threats from other disciplines.

Effect: If uncorrected this error could result in procuring a materiel item unable to perform its true worst mission.

(3b) CORRECTION

The only way to pinpoint the proper answer to this worst mission forecast is to perform a degradation analysis of the impacts of all possible threats during each possible mission type. Press ENTER to initiate the analysis.

Good Example   Bad Example   Citation

Figure 4. Active and Passive Influencers for a Forecasting Task.

ing. Here, it warns the user that concrete experience in one's own discipline tends to obscure other information. The message is kept short.

Third, two buttons can be pushed to provide deeper explanations of the bias (figure 4, part 3a) and corrective procedure (figure 4, part 3b). These buttons produce passive critics for the user who wants to interrupt his(her) own agenda, having an alternative approach available. The correction note card contains three additional buttons that place the user in an optional tutoring mode. This note card also contains an instruction to select ENTER. By pressing ENTER, the user initiates a director. The director walks the user through a formal reasoning

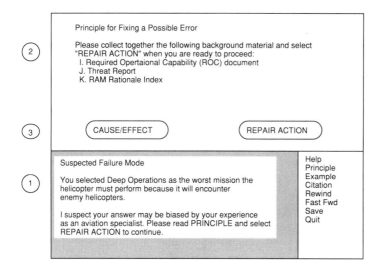

Figure 5. Active and Passive Debiasers for a Forecasting Task.

model of the forecasting task. In all the screens, the users know that ESC will return them to the dark-shaded work area.

Fourth, the user presses ESC and chooses to proceed on his(her) own. S/he opted out of the further tutoring and formal reasoning assistance. S/he answers the original question with "deep operations." This phrase is a designator for missions that require penetration deep behind the enemy line.

Fifth, the system follows with two questions that set the stage for identifying that a cognitive bias leads to a known failure mode. In an earlier dialogue, the system learned that the user is an expert at the Aviation Center. The answer to the last question, "enemy helicopters," is a trigger to the critic that the user relied on concrete information to get his(her) answer. That is, the critic knows the user has experience with aviation threats. Also, its dictionary equates "enemy helicopters" with the aviation domain. Thus, the last question is a trap that the user falls into.

At this point, a debiaser concludes what bias occurred. It also attempts corrective action. Several biases can occur in any given task. Recall that six distinct biases can arise in the Army forecasting task. Each bias might require a different trap and debiaser. For this reason, the critic avoids fixed-dialogue sequences. Instead, a reasoning engine infers the correct set of debiasers to invoke. The engine bases this inference on the facts in working memory about the user and the traps s/he fell into. In the same vein, the reasoning engine branches through a tree of possible traps that might catch the user. Thus, the why question in step 5 of figure 4 yields no trap for the user. His(her) answer is valid; so, the engine branches to a second trap that is successful.

In figure 5, the debiaser adheres to the FMECA method. Here, "failure mode" is a trap checker, or trigger, to verify the bias. EC (effect and cause) explains the error and its associated cause and effect. The action in this case suggests the solution and invokes three director steps:

First, the critic tells the user s/he fell into a common failure mode. It also tells the user its placing him(her) in a temporary machine-directed sequence. The influencer (figure 4, step 2) had only superficial and generic knowledge about types of user errors. This critic (figure 5, step 1) believes it has deeper insight into the user's cognitive judgment processes. For this reason, it is more assertive. The critic uses words such as "suspected failure mode" because it is still conceivable that the user put in the correct worst mission answer.

Second, the critic tells the user to get ready for a formal reasoning procedure (director). There is no simple way to test if the user gave the right answer without doing this analysis. The preparation includes collecting the important sources of abstract information the user previously overlooked.

Third, the two buttons contain active and passive debiasers. The cause-effect button is passive. It serves as motivational information, should the user want it. Selecting it leads to a display of the same bias note card shown in part 3a of figure 4. The repair-action button is no longer passive. It represents the user's only path for proceeding toward the completion of his(her) document (other than selecting "Quit"). Again, it displays the same note card as the earlier correction card shown in part 3b of figure 4. This time the critic deactivates the ESC key.

These three steps cause the user to go through about one hour of computation and literature searches once s/he obtains the proper documents. These computations provide estimates of the degree of degradation experienced by each mission the materiel might be taken on. The director guides the user through a knowledge-rich version of a formal reasoning process. This process consists primarily of following a checklist. The critic runs simple scoring or figure-of-merit equations to compute the type of end results that are depicted in figure 6a. (Purposely falsified data have been used here to avoid any breach of security. However, neither this practice nor the precise meaning of each of the threats and mission list entries is important to understanding how the director works.) In brief, the director gets the user to display the distribution of threats the helicopter will encounter on each mission type. The user then estimates three sets of numbers. These numbers represent the percent of time spent on each mission, the percent of

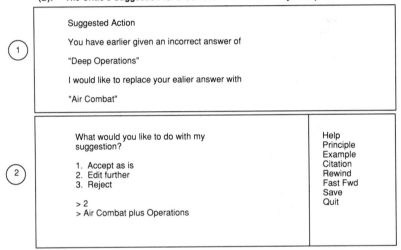

(A): Completed Degradation Analysis Showing Distributional Information

MISSION LIST	Percent of Time on that Mission	THREAT (Exposure % / Degradation)					INDEX
		Tank	DTR	Air	Enemy	Personnel	
Close Operation	30	50/H	40/m	0	10/l	0	72
Deep Operation	25	50/H	30/H	0	20/M	0	70
Rear Operations	15	0	10/H	5/L	85/M	0	0
Air Combat	25	50/H	0	40/M	5/H	5/H	98
Fire Fighting	5	0	0	0	0	0	0

(B): The Critic's Suggestion for a Correct Answer is Usually Accepted

(1)

Suggested Action

You have earlier given an incorrect answer of

"Deep Operations"

I would like to replace your ealier answer with

"Air Combat"

(2)

What would you like to do with my suggestion?

1. Accept as is
2. Edit further
3. Reject

> 2
> Air Combat plus Operations

Help
Principle
Example
Citation
Rewind
Fast Fwd
Save
Quit

Figure 6. Results of Using Critics in the Forecasting Task. (a) A completed degradation analysis showing distributional information. (b) The critic's suggestions for a more correct answer, which is usually accepted.

time exposed to each threat during a given mission, and the amount of likely degradation (high, medium, low, or none for 3, 2, 1, or 0 points) the helicopter will incur from meeting this threat.

Although this analysis is crude, it forces the expert to confront the range of distributional data. It makes him(her) rethink his(her) original answer. In each system run, the Army users experienced an "aha" factor as they realized their own error even before the machine rolled up the numbers into an index and computed the correct answer on its own. For the sake of completeness and for the eventuality that some users might need it, the machine computes the index in the right-hand column of the table shown in figure 6a. A score of 1.0 is a mission of maximum danger—high losses 100 percent of the time. When done, the director returns control to the debiaser. The debiaser performs the following simple operations, which are also listed in figure 6b:

First, the debiaser ranks the list of missions according to the index. It compares the user's original answer with the worst mission from the table. From this information, it concludes a suggested action. It displays the suggestion on the screen.

Second, the user is given three options. Depending on which option is selected, the reasoning engine might need to search for more traps and debiasers. In this case, the user adopts a decision rule that every mission with a high index is bad enough to be the worst. S/he creates a merged name for the worst mission. Because the name includes the machine's opinion of the worst mission in the string, no further reinforcing or debiasing occurs.

How the Application Is Programmed

The TIME application is programmed in a generic language and environment called COPE. COPE is a criticism-based problem-solving and knowledge-acquisition toolbox available on 286- and 386-chip machines under DOS or 68020-based platforms under UNIX. The author and his colleagues created COPE to facilitate research into human-computer collaboration and to act as a criticism-based problem-solving test bed in which numerous applications and experiments could be attempted (IntelliTek 1989b, 1990; Silverman et al. 1987). The COPE architecture supports the life cycle of the development, use, and maintenance of TIME or other applications. This section discusses the development and use steps. Maintenance and Administration of TIME's Knowledge Bases covers the maintenance step.

The developer of a COPE application prepares the necessary objects and rule trees using tool 2, which was mentioned earlier. If s/he is an advanced C programmer, s/he can also decide to extend tool 1's function library in any of a number of directions depending on the analytic, symbolic reasoning, or screen and user interface needs of the application.

The COPE user, in turn, runs tool 1 to construct a case in a given domain (for example, a critical operational issue and criteria case for TRADOC). Tool 1 runs the rule trees that interview the user to collect a new knowledge base or that detect, criticize, and repair problems caused by the user's input. In general, tool 1 reacts to the user's answers to the previous knowledge elicitation questions and fires the proper rule tree objects plus library functions.

The critiquing involves some additional objects of a given rule tree that invoke checking functions: a differential analyzer and a dialog generator. The differential analyzer examines the user's answer to a just-asked question and compares this answer with the target answer stored in an expertise module. This module is often another rule tree or object slot of answers that exemplify what an expert would offer when performing the same task. Differences beyond an acceptance threshold are passed to a file of errors. This file collects biases, opportunities not taken, and so on.

The dialog generator receives the file of errors from the differential analyzer, parses them into user-presentable forms, and displays them on the screen. Often, critics fire canned textual note cards to converse with the users, although these note cards can be organized in a hierarchy, as shown in figures 4, 5, and 6. Critics also include a language instantiation capability that allows them to improve the dialog with the user by binding text variables to context-sensitive strings that are prestored in a database of dialogue utterances. Also, some critics alter what is shown to the user based on insights into the user's skill level collected through direct inquiry.

Using the tool 1 inference engine and a rule tree representation scheme facilitates the creation and experimentation with the critics. Changing an influencer to a debiaser, a debiaser to a director, and so on, is often just a matter of repositioning where the critic is fired in the rule tree sequence (and probably also editing its textual note cards). In this fashion, the decision network of critics is molded into the knowledge-acquisition sequence in the least intrusive fashion.

As the dialogue proceeds, the domain case, or new knowledge base, resulting from the interview is written, piece by piece, into a case database on the computer disk. A transformer module converts this case database into a case tree that can be read by tool 2. Tool 2, the graphic knowledge base editor, allows the user to inspect the new knowledge base constructed by the guided and critiqued interview of tool 1. This process allows the user to visualize what s/he wrote and make any modifications using a direct manipulation interface.

After any editing, the final case can be converted to a hard-copy textual report using WRITER. Alternatively, this case can serve as a new knowledge base for an expert system shell. This new knowledge base can also be passed to an administrator module for assimilation by an analogical reasoning agent that helps COPE learn more about the domain as it is used more (see Maintenance and Administration of TIME's Knowledge Bases).

This overview covered the input, output, and modules and algorithms of the COPE language underlying the TIME application. To program TIME, it was useful to create about 60 rule trees, averaging about 25 objects each, for a total of approximately 1,500 objects. The objects of each tree form on average about 2 dozen rules, hence the estimate of approximately 1,500 rules for TIME as well. Finally, each of the 60-odd trees has about 8 or 9 objects that directly interact with the user; each of these trees has an average of 4 note cards, hence the estimate of 2,000 note cards in the TIME application.

Innovation

Innovation is a relative term that is difficult to judge in the short run. The innovations described here are potential advances, but only time will tell how important they truly are.

Innovation in the Milestone Decision Process

The Army wants to exploit the potential of AI to reduce the heuristic reasoning errors, biases, and foibles, plus the communications obstacles, that traditionally slow system acquisitions. From the perspective of the military, the innovations that AI offers with TIME include the following:

First, TIME successfully integrates and interactively communicates three types of knowledge that were previously difficult to factor into the document-writing process. The previously used hard-copy handbook, which was difficult to read, held many useful principles, good and bad examples, and format instructions that TIME now delivers to the user as needed. The knowledge of the headquarters decision makers of the latest policies, preferences, and decision rules is now delivered by TIME to affect the content and emphases of the material in the document. TIME offers an online, easy-to-access copy-paste-modify library of previously successful issues and criteria phrases from past documents in the domain of the individual authors. TIME brings all three forms of knowledge together—the handbook information, the decision makers' knowledge, and the online library—and shows them to the user at appropriate intervals in the authoring and critiquing process.

Second, TIME persistently refocuses the user away from distractions, selective perceptions, and other potential errors and biases. TIME is the first expert critic system built and deployed for the U.S. military. It not only delivers the knowledge, it also verifies that the author is making maximum use of this knowledge. Thus, TIME serves as a forerunner for similarly transforming the way hundreds of other types of milestone documents are produced in the military and elsewhere.

Third, TIME helps manage knowledge as a corporate asset. Given the mandatory rotation of personnel in the military every two to three years, an important innovation is to capture and retain what is learned so that the next person on the job can easily maintain continuity. The knowledge-acquisition, case-based reasoning, and dynamic memory features of TIME represent an innovative step toward better managing knowledge assets.

Innovation in the AI and Decision Support Fields

This case study illustrates the applicability of COPE to a broad array of reasoning, problem-solving, and knowledge-acquisition subtasks. The TRADOC domain requires that COPE offer criticism-based problem solving in numerous tasks. These tasks cover knowledge base acquisition, report writing, forecasting, and quantitative estimating. The decision network of positive and negative criticism strategies implemented to serve these task requirements cover hinting, default and analogical reasoning, tutoring, debiasing, persuading, and so on. To cover these requirements, TIME synthesizes and extends many ideas from a broad array of AI technologies.

The TRADOC domain also serves as a robust test of COPE's theory of bugs in expert intuition. Numerous cognitive and judgment biases were encountered and successfully reduced or eliminated after extensive field tests. These study results confirm and extend much of the critic design information presented here. Research is ongoing to empirically isolate and confirm additional design insight for the critiquing paradigm.

Finally, this case study demonstrates how TIME and COPE are occupying the space between knowledge-rich, replace-the-expert technology, such as expert systems, and theory-rich, support-the-expert technology, such as decision analysis. Criticism-based problem solving provides a knowledge-rich, heuristic approach to decision-theoretic, support-the-expert situations. This area of investigation is relatively new not only in knowledge acquisition but also in problem solving at large. The TIME case study advances and extends the criticism approach.

Deployment and Use

As already mentioned, the current version of TIME was knowledge engineered in the first 6 months of 1989. In August 1989, 10 Army authors from 4 separate disciplines met in a 4-day workshop to validate the content of TIME's knowledge bases. These participants covered 3 levels of skill in each discipline: novice, intermediate, and expert. This exercise was primarily paper based: A real document was authored by the group while they interacted with a 300-odd–page notebook of the screens they would ultimately see in the finished system. Throughout the workshop, thinking-aloud protocols were recorded, as were user reactions to the screen-by-screen information. After the workshop, the participants returned a detailed questionnaire describing their reactions to many of the system's features.

Also after the workshop, the participants returned to their four installations (one installation for each discipline) and drafted four assessments of the validity and potential usability of the system. Based on these assessments, a follow-up effort was approved, and the construction of the system began in earnest. From September 1989 until November 1990, the equivalent of four full-time people (1) incorporated the improvements suggested by the workshop participants; (2) coded the knowledge bases in the COPE language; (3) optimized and extended some of the COPE features and screen interfaces for the Army-approved Zenith 248 environment; (4) debugged the TIME knowledge bases; (5) prepared training materials; and (6) further refined TIME's knowledge bases, interfaces, user dialogue modes (expert and novice modes are possible), help facilities, and numerous other features.

From June 1990 until the first week of December 1990, a series of field tests were conducted, one at each of the 4 installations that sent participants to the original workshop. The purpose of these field tests was initially to identify bugs that needed to be removed and later to verify the system was ready for deployment. Each field test consisted of the same mix of participants that was sought for the workshop. This time each user tackled a separate, real-world problem and generated his(her) own (COIC) document with the aid of the COPE-TIME system. The field tests began with a ⅔ day of training and user qualification, followed by as many as 3 days of a user running and testing the system. The documents produced during the field tests were evaluated by the participants' immediate supervisors. The supervisor also prepared an installation-level assessment of whether TIME passed the test and should continue being funded. The criteria for evaluating the benefits of the system were documented in headquarters' instructions to the installations:

(1) Can players install the program on the computer using con tractor provided instructions?
(2) Can players clearly understand instructions and information displayed by the program?
(3) Does the program teach/guide the player to make assess ments of the following aspects of the (weapon) system
(A) Operational mode summary/mission profile,
(B) Threat,

     (C) Need,

     (D) Operational characteristics and supporting rationale,

     (E) Doctrine and tactics?

(4) Are error indications and explanations accurate and under standable?

(5) Does the program identify inconsistent player responses and input?

(6) Are the draft COIC (documents) produced essentially in proper format and consistent with current guidance?

(7) Did using the program result in time or effort savings?

(8) Additional comments/observations. (TRADOC 1990, pp. 4–5)

Based on successfully meeting these criteria, TIME graduated from the field-test stage. It was disseminated for use in the four original installations plus two new ones added in late January 1991. During the period of use from January to April, approximately 2 dozen users produced documents with TIME, serving in the "maiden voyage" capacity. All 17 user sites will eventually receive TIME, annually producing as many as 600 reports.

As of this writing (early March), there are only 2 sets of results from the maiden voyage. In both cases, the users found their initial experience with TIME to be slow and painstaking. One user stated, "I used to be able to write a COIC in 2 hours. I've already spent 4 hours with TIME and I'm only half done." This reaction is precisely what TIME should precipitate if it is to reduce the errors, making the user do a more thorough job. The second user indicated that it took him 3 days to produce his first COIC, and he was initially discouraged with TIME. However, he now sees its value and believes he can use it to write a better COIC in under a day. He is now eagerly training all his subordinates to use it.

Payoff

Payoff, like innovation, is another area that is difficult to fully and accurately assess. Also, only preliminary data and expectations are currently available. When measuring payoff, as we must, in terms of the reduction in the frustration of all participants, a lessening of errors in draft documents, and the satisfaction of the eight criteria, then much of the acknowledgment of the system's benefit must come from the sponsors and the users' supervisors. This situation is particularly true given the security and inaccessibility factors that prevent the author from making precise payoff measurements in this environment.

In terms of the payoff, TIME was used to produce 12 documents during the field tests. It is currently being used to create as many as 2 dozen more. Because these documents are passing the eight criteria, they are returning benefits to TRADOC in terms of the originally stated objectives. That is, with TIME, (1) users of all skill levels are receiving error and bias reduction support; (2) novice and intermediate users are being guided and tutored past commonly recurring difficulties; (3) headquarters' personnel are benefitting from reduced workload, higher-quality documents, and faster turnaround; and (4) from a more subjective perspective, the overall morale of the authors has been improved by headquarters' effort to improve their work environment and reduce frustration throughout the organization. The tentative attempts to interview users and their supervisors verify that these items are correct.

For reasons unrelated to the deployment of TIME, the five-person (plus secretarial support) headquarters branch that reviewed all COIC documents was closed in late 1990. The review function (Roger's job) was reassigned to 90 officers stationed elsewhere in the headquarters operation. With this diffusion of expertise, a number of people now view TIME as an increasingly important repository and the place where corporate memory assets can and must be managed. This situation raises a number of interesting and important payoff issues for the maintenance features of the TIME system.

Maintenance and Administration of TIME's Knowledge Bases

After passing the eight criteria for field-test verification and assuring the payoff in terms of these same criteria during initial deployment, a third development-period effort was awarded. This effort is under way and will be concluded by September 1991. In particular, it was decided that development of the TIME maintenance and administrator module should be undertaken after the initial deployment stages were complete. Hooks and interfaces to this module were previously created. However, it was thought prudent to undertake this process as a "backfill" operation to avoid overloading the development team during the earlier phases. This approach also ensures the team members are still around for much of the first year after deployment. Following September 1991, the maintenance and administration of TIME will fully reside with Army personnel. The developer will no longer be under any contractual responsibility to the Army.

To assure the Army can maintain the system on its own, two types of knowledge bases must be able to be updated as easily as possible: the static or fixed knowledge bases, which hold the basic guidance on how to author a good document plus the latest decision maker preferences and heuristics, and the dynamic memory of completed documents, which serves as a cut-and-paste world of cases that can be retrieved and adapted for reuse.

Keeping the fixed knowledge base elements up to date is potentially difficult for three reasons. First, the advice in these elements regularly changes as new decision makers assume office, and Congress passes new regulations. Second, TIME is relatively large sized. As already mentioned, it contains over 5,000 knowledge chunks. Third, the maintainer must learn the COPE language to modify a COPE knowledge base. The goal of the administrator module is to minimize the effort needed to overcome the second and third sources of difficulty. The first item is beyond my purview and is the reason an administrators module is useful. The solution to these problems includes a visual index of the knowledge. This index is supplemented by a hypertext-based online manual, a graphic editor for modifying the rule trees, and a change-control assistant that warns of errors committed and unfinished changes. Even with these aids, it is expected that a TIME administrator will have to spend almost a week of full-time effort to initially learn the COPE language and become adept at update actions.

Maintaining the dynamic memory is far easier than updating the fixed memory. In particular, a previously built and verified case-based reasoning system (IntelliTek, 1989a) is being incorporated into the COPE environment for dynamic memory updating. The 300-odd analogs now available in TIME were all hand coded into databases that are accessed in a context-dependent manner. Each finished document must now similarly be hand coded to add it to these databases. This process is a waste of effort because what the computer collects through knowledge acquisition, it should be able to remember. Also, once the deployment of TIME is complete, and as many as 600 new cases are generated each year, only the computer will be able to keep up with this flow rate in a reasonable time frame.

In concept, TIME can automatically perform this task on its own with the aid of a form of case-based reasoning. Several concerns, however, are being addressed in this final stage of effort, including (1) providing a reasonable scheme by which each of the 17 installations can extend the dictionary of terms in the world model in different directions but simultaneously allow headquarters to keep its version of TIME abreast of all the changes, (2) offering a password-protected function that can be used to delete entire groups of cases (or portions of these cases) that used to be successful examples but now violate the latest approved guidance for the construction of good documents, and (3) assuring that documents aren't assimilated into the case base until they are approved and that their dozens of rules and phrases are properly cross-indexed when they are assimilated. Numerous subtleties are connected with each of these three concerns that are not addressed here.

The goal of this section was to introduce the plan for the final stage of postdeployment effort. The AI and computer science fields, at least in this instance, already have the technologies needed to successfully manage knowledge as a corporate asset. Aside from scaleup, the challenges in applying these technologies are largely organizational rather than technical. They are (1) keeping physically distributed versions in sync when security, budgetary, and organizational factors come into play and (b) balancing the legitimate desire of headquarters to retain control of the knowledge considered acceptable and the equally legitimate need for the field personnel to specialize and advance the precision of the case base residing at their location. Adapting the technology to suit the real concerns of the various interest groups is an important sociotechnical challenge that will be addressed in this final stage of the application.

Concluding Remarks

The TIME application is interesting as an organizational support system. It helps headquarters communicate good job practice information to the field, and it reduces the number of field-created errors and biases that headquarters must deal with. At the field level, TIME reduces the frustration of repeatedly receiving marked-up drafts back from headquarters. It simultaneously supports the field personnel with libraries of examples, principles, analogs, defaults, and so on, that speed their document-authoring task. Finally, for the organization as a whole, TIME serves as a knowledge-capture device that holds the promise of helping to better manage knowledge as a corporate asset.

Technologically, TIME is an example of how a wide variety of hardware, AI, and decision science techniques can be combined to solve the problems encountered in organizations. It addresses the interaction and problem-solving needs of large groups of collaborating employees. From a hardware perspective, much effort was expended to assure TIME could deliver its capabilities into the existing automation environment of low-cost desktop personal computers and local and wide area networks. From the AI perspective, it was necessary to combine expert critiquing systems, knowledge-acquisition systems, hypertext, intelligent tutoring, and case-based reasoning into TIME. From a decision support perspective, it was useful to exploit psychological models of cognitive bias. It was also necessary to adapt math-based, theory-rich decision aids into knowledge-rich, heuristic counterparts that are more natural and acceptable to the users.

Although TIME is the first system of its type in the document generation process of acquiring large-scale systems, it will not be the last. TIME has transformed one step of the process in an operation fraught with difficulty and frustration into a showcase for how the other steps might similarly function. By being innovative and applying new technology, the Army has added a new strategic weapon in the fight to improve the system acquisition process.

Acknowledgments

The financial sponsorship of the U.S. Army Training and Doctrine Command is gratefully acknowledged, as is the contractual assistance of the Defense Systems Management College (PMSS Directorate). When he was at TRADOC, Don Reich showed great vision in starting us down this road. Also, the support of two Small Business Innovative Research Phase II grants (NASA and WSMR/VAL) and several years of Research Incentive Awards from the George Washington University were instrumental in the creation of COPE, the critic test bed used here.

I share the IAAI honor with Greg Wenig, Toufik Mehzer, Bill Rodi, Inhou Chang, and a cast of other helpers too numerous to name here. Also, I thank Mike Donnell who prodded me to write the TIME application in a cogent fashion. All these people and organizations are relieved of responsibility for any erroneous opinions, findings, or conclusions offered here: The author alone bears this responsibility. The Army is also commended for taking a leadership role in admitting where biases occur so that improvement efforts could be attempted. More organizations need to be so forward looking if this field of endeavor is to be advanced.

References

IntelliTek. 1990. COPE User's Guide, IntelliTek, Potomac, Maryland.

IntelliTek. 1989a. ARIEL User's Guide: A Computational Model of Case-Based Reasoning, IntelliTek, Potomac, Maryland.

IntelliTek. 1989b. Knowledge Engineer's Guide to COPE, IntelliTek, Potomac, Maryland.

Kahneman, D.; Slovic, P.; and Tversky, A. 1982. *Judgment under Uncertainty: Heuristics and Biases.* Cambridge: Cambridge University Press.

Klein, G. A., and Calderwood, R. 1986. Human Factors Considerations for Expert Systems. In Proceedings of the National Aerospace and Electronics Conference, 921–925. Washington, D.C.: IEEE Computer Society.

Langlotz, C. P., and Shortliffe, E. H. 1983. Adapting a Consultation System to Critique User Plans. *International Journal of Man-Machine Studies* 19: 479–496.

Miller, P. L. 1983. ATTENDING: Critiquing a Physician's Management Plan. *IEEE Transactions on Pattern Analysis and Machine Intelligence* 5(5): 449–461.

Roth, E. M.; Bennett, K. B.; and Woods, D. D. 1988. Human Interaction with an Intelligent Machine. In *Cognitive Engineering in Complex Dynamic Worlds*, eds. E. Hollnagel, M. Mancini, and D. Woods, 23–70. New York: Academic.

Silverman, B. G. 1992. Building Expert Critics: Unifying Theory and Knowledge to Reduce Expert Error. Unpublished manuscript.

Silverman, B. G. 1991. Expert Critics: Operationalizing the Judgment-Decision-Making Literature as a Theory of "Bugs" and Repair Strategies. *Knowledge Acquisition*. Forthcoming.

Silverman, B. G. 1990. Critiquing Human Judgment Via Knowledge-Acquisition Systems. *AI Magazine* 11(3): 60–79.

Silverman, B. G.; Fritz, D.; Teaque, A.; and Baramvik, S. 1987. COPE: A Case-Oriented Processing Environment. In Proceedings of the European Computing Conference, 399–417. Avignon, France: European Computing Conference.

U.S. Army Training and Document Command. 1990. Memorandum, ATCD-ET, 4–5. Fort Monroe, Va.: U.S. Army Training and Document Command.

Wenger, E. 1987. *Artificial Intelligence and Tutoring Systems*. San Mateo, Calif.: Morgan Kaufmann.

Expert Systems in Data Processing: California Travel Expense Claim System

Allyson Bartman-Gatt

The CALTREC project automated the process of creating travel expense claims for the state of California. This project is a good representative of the types of projects expected to be done by the state. The application is heavily embedded in traditional data processing systems, which added much additional work outside the scope of what is considered to be knowledge engineering.

The Travel Expense Claim Process

The state of California employs about 200,000 people who work for over 200 departments and belong to 20 collective bargaining units. Each year, approximately one third of these people travel on state business and incur expenses in the course of their trips. In addition, while conducting state business, many employees incur a wide range of non-travel-related expenses, including business expenses and overtime meal expenses. Everyone who incurs expenses on state business is entitled to be reimbursed by the state. The vehicle through which the state of California reimburses its employees for state–business-related expenses is a form called the *travel expense claim*, which documents the expenses being claimed. It is completed either by the claimant or a secretary, and until recently, these claims were produced manually. Roughly 400,000 state of California travel expense claims are submitted each year.

Once a travel expense claim is completed by the claimant, it is submitted to the claimant's supervisor for approval, then forwarded for further auditing. Completed travel expense claims are subjected to two levels of audit: The first audit occurs in the department's accounting section, the second at the State Controller's Office (SCO). Once the accounting section approves the claim, the claimant is reimbursed from department funds, and the claim is forwarded to SCO, which audits the claim a second time. Once the claim is approved by SCO, the department is reimbursed.

The rules used to audit travel expense claims are developed by the state of California's Department of Personnel Administration (DPA) and distributed to the rest of the state departments. What is allowed for reimbursement is subject to a number of limitations, depending on such factors as the terms of the employee's current collective bargaining unit contract, the destination and length of travel, and the start and ending dates of travel. In addition, depending primarily on amounts expended for certain items, approvals by various individuals, as well as receipts, can be required.

These rules tend to be confusing and difficult to interpret. Although the rules are documented in a number of manuals, often a person submitting the claim does not know of the existence of such manuals and relies on other sources for the rules governing how to fill out a claim. Even employees who know where to access correct information often do not bother or misinterpret the documentation. To make matters worse, travel expense claim rules change relatively frequently. DPA notifies, by memo, each department's accounting section of changes, but invariably this information does not get distributed to everyone who needs it, and the error rate on subsequent travel expense claims tends to increase. Because people have trouble even remembering or understanding a single version of the travel expense claim rules, to expect them to be able to remember that a change has taken place (if they know about it) and understand how this change should affect the travel expense claim is hopeless.

Given these conditions, it should be no surprise that the error rate of manually produced travel expense claims is staggering; estimates by SCO of the error rates it experiences range from 50 to 80 percent, which suggests that even accounting sections are not correctly applying travel expense claim rules. Because these rates are so high, SCO must audit every single travel claim it receives and is virtually swamped by a backlog of claims to process. Each time an error is detected, the claim is returned. It goes back to the claimant if the accounting section detected an error or to the accounting section and then to the claimant if SCO detected the error. Once the error is corrected, the audit process resumes, but delays result, either in getting reimbursement to the claimant or releasing funds to the department. Although estimates of the exact cost of this process to the state of California have not been made, it is easy to see that given the large numbers of travel claims involved, the cost of the extra handling, along with the delay in the transfer of funds, must be immense.

Travel expense claims can have errors that result in unnecessary cost to the claimant, such as when the claimant is entitled to be reimbursed for an expense but does not claim it because of a lack of knowledge of the rules. The audits performed by accounting sections and SCO are geared to detect cases where reimbursement is being claimed for expenses that are not allowed under the DPA rules, thereby saving money for the state. The auditors assume that the claimant knows the rules and has claimed all reimbursable expenses that were incurred and, conversely, that expenses that were not claimed were not incurred. However, often, the claimant does not fully understand the rules and assumes that an incurred expense is not reimbursable when it really is and does not claim the expense. Because the audit process has no interest in and really no way of protecting the interests of the claimant, the claimant's ignorance of the rules goes undetected. This situation represents another, probably large set of errors that, although not a direct cost to the state of California, is significant nevertheless.

Clearly, the extremely high error rates associated with the travel expense claim process represent a substantial cost to the state of California and its employees. One way to attack this problem would be to implement the travel expense claim rules in a centrally located and maintained computer application. Maintaining all the rules in one place would ensure that the correct rules would always be applied to every claim, thus travel expense claims produced by such a system would be more accurate, consistent, and complete. Equally important, all claims would reflect the most recent rule changes as soon as the changes were added to the software. In fact, several attempts were made to build such an application using traditional software. However, every attempt failed. These applications were no more than data-entry systems; in every case, the software used was inadequate to represent the number and complexity of rules required. Thus, the error rates associated with the attempted travel claim systems were no better than with the manual process. Further, none of the persons involved with these attempts consulted with SCO or DPA in the course of building the applications, evoking the wrath of both entities, which refused to accept the travel expense claim forms produced by these systems.

The CALTREC Project

In 1988, Russ Bohart, the director of the state of California Health and Welfare Agency Data Center (HWDC), became interested in expert systems. It seemed to him that this technology would be widely applicable in state government because much of what goes on in the course of state business consists of judgmental processes based on policies, regulations, procedures, and guidelines, in other words, rules. These processes are continually getting more complex and more difficult for a person to remember and understand, inevitably resulting in errors and inefficiencies for which some cost must ultimately be borne. Furthermore, such processes do not lend themselves well to automation using traditional techniques because of the large number, the complexity, and the changeability of the rules involved. Because expert system technology is directed at just this sort of problem, Bohart decided that his organization should embark on an experiment to evaluate the potential usefulness of expert system technology to the departments that HWDC serves and to the state of California.

HWDC provides computing resources to 10 state departments, supporting about 45,000 employees and 12,000 terminals on a network that extends throughout the state. The data center itself employs a staff of 200 people who run the computer systems and provide technical support to users. The predominant mode of large-scale computing in the state of California is based on IBM System 370 architecture, that is, large mainframes running 1 or more of the 3 IBM 370 operating systems that support many large online and batch applications. Because HWDC is one of the largest IBM installations in the state of California, its expert system applications must run on the available IBM platforms. Thus, the expert system experiment would be conducted using an expert system shell that would run on an IBM mainframe system. HWDC negotiated with the (at this time, 2) vendors that were then offering such shells, and IBM's expert system environment (ESE) was chosen.

Nine volunteers—seven from the data processing divisions of five HWDC-supported departments and two from the data center itself—were selected to participate in an eight-week experiment with expert systems. The volunteers were joined by a project leader and a technical expert from IBM who worked full time on the project and by six other IBM staff members who participated for varying lengths of time. During the course of the eight-week session, the group would spend a week in training on the ESE shell and then build a prototype expert travel expense claim adviser. At the end of the session, the group was to demonstrate the fruits of its labors to the department managers, report on its experiences, and recommend whether to proceed with expert systems.

Automating the travel expense claim process appeared to be an ideal application for a first attempt at building an expert system. First, there was a crying need for improvement in the travel expense claim process, and no other attempts had really succeeded. Although the travel expense claim rules were too complex to automate using traditional languages, expert systems are capable of handling complex problems and, therefore, should be an effective way to automate this process.

Second, virtually everyone who works for the state of California has at some time grappled with the mysteries of filling out a travel expense claim and, thus, would appreciate the benefits of an automated travel expense claim application. Further, the travel expense claim application is considered to be a good example of the kinds of things that ought to be automated in state government, and because the travel expense claim process would be so familiar to many employees, it should readily serve as an inspiration for other expert system applications. Therefore, a working automated travel expense claim adviser would not only have broad appeal statewide but would also serve as a convincing ambassador for expert system technology.

Third, Bohart had the support of DPA, which loaned the state's top expert on travel expense claims, Diane Hachey, to the project. Hachey was (and still is) enthusiastic about the project. She was available full time throughout the course of the eight-week session, has devoted a great deal of her own time in support of the project since this time, and has become one of the most outspoken proponents of the system. Travel expense claim rules are, for the most part, created by Hachey and are set forth in about 50 pages of the *State Administrative Manual.* Because Hachey was involved with the project, any problems with rule interpretation could easily be resolved. With travel expense claim knowledge so easy to access, the knowledge-acquisition phase of the project would be relatively straightforward, therefore reducing the risk of failure. Also, as the recognized expert on travel expense claims, Hachey would lend her unquestioned credibility to the system (in fact, she encourages its developers to promote the system as "Diane in the computer"); this approach would ease the task of selling the system to other departments as well as SCO.

Finally, the overall risk associated with this project was low. First, if the experiment failed to produce a viable application, the loss in terms of time and effort invested would be acceptable. A major goal of the project was simply for the group to learn about the strengths and weaknesses of the technology; if the group had been unable to produce a good system, then the understanding that it would have gained about why would still justify the effort. Second, the application itself was not strategic to the state. If it did not succeed, business could continue as it had in the past; this case did not involve some external factor (such as legislation) that was forcing the development of the application. Third, the technical risk was low: The application did not require access to, or modification of, any other existing automated systems and, therefore, would not interfere with or jeopardize normal operations in any way.

Thus, implementing an expert system to automate travel expense claims was a good choice for a first attempt at building an expert system. The project was highly justified and relatively low risk. If it succeeded, its product would be extremely valuable, and its developers would be heroes, but if it failed, the memory of the attempt could fade quietly into obscurity as everyone returned to his(her) former duties.

The team set to work. Team members divided themselves into two subgroups because it was felt that nine people were too many to be working on the same application. One group continued with the travel expense claim project, and the other group selected another application to prototype. The first action taken by the travel expense claim group was to select a name for their application: CALTREC, which stands for California travel expense claim system. The group then selected a team leader, developed an overall design, and divided the work among the team members. By the end of the eight-week period, a reasonably stable prototype had emerged. Not only did the prototype contain a knowledge base, it also had interfaces to working external programs that printed the travel expense claim produced by the expert system and manipulated start and end dates and times given by the user into forms that the knowledge base could use. Also, the knowledge base interfaced to a DB2 database that stored personal information (name, address, working hours, and so on) about the claimant.

The prototype was demonstrated to management, and despite some rather shaky moments, the system was well received. Bohart considered it promising enough to found a knowledge-based system section at HWDC so that work could continue on CALTREC and (eventually) other expert system projects. One of the participants in the experiment, Jim Henderson, was chosen to lead the new knowledge-based system section, and the IBM technical expert who had been involved in the project (the author) was hired a few months later.

The knowledge-based system section set out to complete CALTREC. Although the knowledge base was substantially complete, there was much work remaining on other aspects of the application. This work predominantly consisted of traditional data processing activities, such as writing programs in traditional languages, writing job control language, and building databases. Both members of the knowledge-based system section have extensive backgrounds in IBM mainframe data processing, and this experience proved to be essential to the completion of the project. About three fourths of the time spent on the CALTREC project was devoted to this work, which is outside the scope of what is considered to be knowledge engineering; these tasks are described later. The fact that so much of the work involved in this project fell outside the bounds of knowledge engineering is significant considering that this application is expected to be typical of expert system applications implemented in the state of California's IBM mainframe environments. This situation indicates that a major amount of traditional data processing effort will probably be required in any expert system project in this kind of environment, not only within the state of California but in any organization that uses this type of hardware and software configuration.

The first effort involved exhaustively testing, debugging, and enhancing the prototype system's interfaces to external routines, which were sketchy, incomplete, and not robust enough to support the release of the system to the general user population. Second, although the knowledge base was complete from the standpoint of containing most of the rules covering travel expense claims, it lacked sufficient control structure to allow the production of claim forms that include more than one trip for each claim (a common occurrence). Implementing this format entailed restructuring the knowledge base and enhancing the print routine used for the prototype.

Third, the system was tailored for delivery under HWDC's office automation system. This system, IBM's PROFS, runs under the VM operating system on a large mainframe and is available to over 3,000 users. Because IBM mainframes are the predominant mode of data processing in the state of California, with PROFS being the major office automation tool, deploying the application under PROFS assures the widest possible exposure to potential users. (Deployment on personal computers was never considered because of the problems anticipated with version control for such a volatile application.)

Integrating CALTREC with PROFS entailed a great deal of thought and some additional nonknowledge-engineering effort. Past exposure to typical users of data processing systems had equipped the knowledge-based system section with a good understanding of the type of person who would use the CALTREC system and what this person's needs would be. PROFS users and, in fact, most of the intended users of the CALTREC system fit into this category. These people are generally not sophisticated computer users; they are accustomed to being guided through the tasks they perform on the computer and do not, in general, learn to use additional commands or functions outside the scope of their normal activities, nor do they wish to learn the underlying structure of the applications they use. Therefore, CALTREC must be simple, easy to use, self-explanatory, and look as much like existing PROFS applications as possible. PROFS is organized as a hierarchy of menus from which the various functions available are selected by using program function keys; so, CALTREC was added as yet another option on a PROFS menu. To further buffer the user from all the steps required to bring up the CALTREC application and to protect the user from possible error conditions, a program was written that is invoked when the PROFS travel expense claim option is selected. It verifies whether the user has sufficient disk and memory space to run the system, then displays screens that offer tutorial information and provide the option to actually invoke the expert system. Once the expert system session is complete, control is returned to the invoking program, which deletes work files that are created during the course of the consultation and returns control to the PROFS system.

The fourth area of effort involved making the CALTREC consultation itself as friendly as possible, which required extensive work on the screens presented by the expert system. Although building screen interfaces is really beyond the scope of implementing the knowledge required for the CALTREC application, effective screen interfaces are essential to the success of the application. No matter how well the system represents the knowledge involved in creating travel expense claims, CALTREC would not be useful (or used) if its audience could not understand how to use it or what it was talking about. The screen-generation facility of the ESE shell was used to provide a user interface that is consistent with other PROFS applications and that provides a great deal of explanation, in familiar language, of what is expected from the user. Now, users feel that they do not have to do anything special to run CALTREC. In fact, most users are completely oblivious to the fact that CALTREC is an expert system or that such things as expert systems even exist; CALTREC is just another tool that helps them do their jobs.

Of all the tasks involved in the CALTREC project, the fifth task, implementing print support for travel expense claims, was by far the most difficult and time consuming. The travel expense claim form is detailed and complex; it must be printed on a laser printer. Clearly, if CALTREC is to be of any practical use, travel expense claims should be printable on whatever laser printer happens to be available at any user's location. However, the various state departments have many different kinds of laser printers; there is no standard for statewide printer use.

Even among HWDC user departments, no standard printer exists. In addition, different brands of printers, even different models made by the same vendor, have unique protocols for receiving, formatting, and printing data. These protocols vary widely, such that there is no standard way to interface with the multitude of printers. This situation meant that a unique interface had to be written to support the printing of CALTREC claims on each type of printer, which would not be easy.

The prototype version of CALTREC interfaced to a printer that happened to be available at HWDC, which, as luck would have it, was the only one of its kind in the state. In the early releases of the system, all output was printed on this one printer and then routed through interdepartmental mail to the user's site. As the project progressed, individual interfaces were built to support what were believed to be the most widely used laser printers, which turned out to be various models made by IBM and XEROX. Then, software was acquired that supports a common interface for IBM and XEROX printers. This software was of great interest to the knowledge-based system group, but it felt that learning the ins and outs of print software was straying too far from its knowledge engineering domain, and by this time, they were too busy to devote the time. Luckily, one of HWDC's technical support groups agreed to attempt, as an exploratory project, to produce a common print interface for CALTREC that allowed printing on both IBM and XEROX laser printers, with the idea that what it learned could be applied to other applications as well. This project was a success, and now, all CALTREC forms are being printed by one interface. The system supports printing on about six IBM and XEROX laser printers, some of which are inexpensive. Potential CALTREC users are required to either acquire one of the supported printers or have their claims printed at a central location and routed to them through interoffice mail.

The final area of effort outside the knowledge engineering domain was a consequence of the use of a technology that was new to the mainframe computing arena at the time. Much time was devoted to the trials and tribulations of using early releases of software, which is simply not, in general, as robust and well debugged as it might be later. The team was forced to devote a great deal of time to resolving problems with the ESE shell and its particular implementation at HWDC, which tended to frequently terminate abnormally and perform inconsistently. These problems were severe enough to delay the deployment of CALTREC and undermine the confidence in expert system technology of at least one department that participated in the original 8-week experiment. IBM worked hard to resolve the problems but had some difficulty responding quickly with fixes. A great deal of the onus for troubleshooting and problem determination was placed on the knowledge-based system group, and there were occasions when applying a fix would cause a whole new crop of problems to arise. This situation was compounded by the fact that both members of the knowledge-based system section were new to HWDC and had to learn the organizational protocols for getting the support they needed to get fixes applied and tested. All in all, 10 months elapsed before all needed fixes were applied and in production, during the course of which over 3 person-months of effort were expended.

The dissatisfaction with the unreliability of the ESE shell, along with the realization that CALTREC's functions were severely limited by the shell's relatively unsophisticated knowledge representation techniques and problem-solving paradigm, led the knowledge-based system group to search for an alternative shell. In October 1989, the KBMS (knowledge base management system) shell was acquired, and the knowledge-based system team immediately set out to reimplement CALTREC in KBMS. This effort was not without its own set of problems; KBMS turned out to be no less bug free than ESE.

In addition to working on the CALTREC project, the HWDC knowledge-based system section has devoted time to various other activities. Among its major goals is to stimulate interest in the use of expert systems by the state and to promote the use of CALTREC. To this end, members of the knowledge-based system section are continually giving presentations, making themselves available to almost anyone who expresses an interest in what they are doing. Their audiences have ranged from informal groups of 1 or 2 people to a group of 400 at a government conference. The most common presentation introduces the CALTREC application to potential users who generally have no interest in expert systems but are involved in processing travel expense claims. A second presentation is directed toward management and potential application developers; using CALTREC as an example, the presentation is an introduction to expert systems and demonstrates why they are important. The knowledge-based system section also presents occasional tutorials that describe some aspect of expert systems in depth. Finally, the section members have consulted with application developers and management on the suitability of potential applications to be implemented using expert systems. Several applications have been identified, and recently, the knowledge-based system section began working with novice developers to facilitate all aspects of building knowledge-based system applications.

Results

Nearly 3 years have passed since the initial 8-week expert system experiment began. Except for occasional minor additions, the CALTREC knowledge base has been complete since early 1989, although only in the last few months have print interfaces been available to allow the printing of CALTREC claims on the major printers used outside HWDC. The ESE version of the CALTREC system has been available to the entire HWDC PROFS user community since August 1989, and about 400 individuals have used it. With the advent of KBMS and the plan to reimplement CALTREC in KBMS, SCO has become involved with the project. As the control agency with ultimate approval authority over travel expense claims, SCO has the greatest interest in the proper functioning of CALTREC. SCO has trained 2 people in the use of KBMS, 1 of whom is now working full time on the conversion project. When the conversion is complete, responsibility for, and control of, the application will be transferred to SCO. This sort of cooperative effort between 2 unrelated departments to produce software that will be distributed statewide is unprecedented in state history. Thus, expert system technology has not only enabled an entirely new set of applications for the state of California but has inspired new ways of building and distributing applications.

The response to CALTREC has been overwhelming, much larger than expected. Word of CALTREC's existence spread from person to person and through an article in an employee newsletter, resulting in many requests for demonstrations of the system. In the beginning, demonstrations of CALTREC were given with the objective of generating interest in expert systems and inspiring members of the audiences to build their own expert system applications. However, to the surprise of the knowledge-based system section, the audiences often became so excited about CALTREC itself that they paid little attention to the topic of expert systems; instead, they clamored for access to CALTREC, even though the knowledge-based system section did not consider the application to be ready for release. In one case, a large department that is not one of HWDC's customers has literally been making a nuisance of itself by demanding access to the system.

Initially, CALTREC was released to about a dozen users at HWDC. These users were administrative staff members, who had been generating travel expense claims for the other members of the department, and managers, who had been passing along the details of their trips to administrative staff members for processing. Interestingly, at first, administrative staff members resisted CALTREC. They were confident that they already knew all the rules of processing travel expense claims and felt that going through the expert system consultation took longer than simply typing the forms. However, they grudgingly used CALTREC. Then, what has come to be a common occurrence began to take place. The knowledge-based system section would cheerfully be notified that CALTREC made a mistake: Such-and-such an expense was or was not supposed to be allowed, and CALTREC was not or was allowing it. The knowledge-based system section would then scramble through its documentation, run tests, and call the expert, only to discover that CALTREC was correct and that the person who identified the so-called mistake was simply not fully aware of the rules. The first few occurrences of this scenario were met by the knowledge-based system section with great excitement (and relief), but it didn't take long before users just accepted the results given by CALTREC. In fact, CALTREC is trusted so highly now that in the event of a question, the burden of proof tends to lie on the accuser; CALTREC's word is taken for granted as correct. However, every time a new group of users is given access to CALTREC, this chain of events occurs again (except that now the anxiety level of the knowledge-based system section is much lower). Recently, a woman who had been doing travel expense claims by hand for a large office for 20 years was surprised to be shown by CALTREC that she had been doing them wrong.

The real benefit of CALTREC is for accounting staff members who must audit travel expense claims. Incorporated into the CALTREC system is an innovation called the "To Do List," which appears as a second page of the claim. This list details all signatures, receipts, and other documentation required for the expenses being claimed to be approved for reimbursement; the lack of such documentation is a major cause for delays in travel expense claim reimbursement. Because of the "To Do List," the claimant now knows exactly what to attach to the claim and is much more likely to submit a complete claim. Likewise, the auditor can now simply verify that the items listed on the "To Do List" are complete without having to remember the rules involved. Auditors no longer have to check for addition and other basic errors and can concentrate on more sophisticated issues. The audit staff at HWDC quickly began to operate under the assumption that CALTREC is always right and subjects CALTREC claims to rather cursory audits. The auditors are also enthusiastic proponents of the system. Other auditors in other departments have also been enthusiastic about CALTREC and often become convinced that they cannot survive another second without CALTREC.

CALTREC's expert, Diane Hachey, has been essential to the acceptance and success of CALTREC. Hachey is highly respected by both the accounting staffs and the travel expense claim audit division at SCO and is in continual contact with accounting staffs in all departments. She also regularly teaches classes to accounting staffs on the travel expense claim process. Hachey is a classic example of the overworked expert. She has a great deal of difficulty getting what she perceives to be her real work done because she is constantly being hounded by people with routine questions, and she immediately saw the potential benefits of an automated travel expense claim system. She uses every opportunity to inform people about CALTREC, and they listen to her: She conveys her excitement about the project with great conviction, and because she is the acknowledged state expert on travel expense claims, her statements bring a degree of credibility that would never be possible otherwise.

Among Hachey's early CALTREC converts was Jeff Braun, manager of the SCO travel expense claim audit division. Braun had reason to be skeptical about CALTREC. There had been attempts in the past to automate travel expense claims, but these products were little more than data-entry devices and, therefore, did not affect the error rates being experienced. Furthermore, it was perceived that the use of these systems actually made the auditing process more difficult because the forms generated tended to be inconsistent with the forms produced manually. Hachey talked Braun into taking a look at CALTREC; he quickly realized that this product was something that could help him tremendously. He is so enthusiastic about CALTREC that he lent his support to the suggestion that the CALTREC application be turned over to SCO and was instrumental in making this idea become a reality. Braun has stated that CALTREC output will be the only form of automated travel expense claim that his office will accept. He expects that his staff members will be able to eliminate most audit procedures for CALTREC claims that are currently being done on manual travel expense claims. Again, this situation will speed the reimbursement process and amount to a great savings of time and effort for Braun's staff.

The knowledge-based system section discovered that the benefits of the CALTREC system are more immediately obvious and understandable to those who must audit travel expense claims than to many of those who submit the claims. If the submitter is a secretary who submits claims for a group of people or is someone who travels frequently, it might actually take longer to run through a CALTREC session than to type the claim by hand. Even in the face of the dismal error statistics with travel expense claims, most frequent claim submitters believe that they already know all the travel expense claim rules, and it can be difficult convincing them that using CALTREC is of any advantage, although, as previously noted, most users of CALTREC discover that their knowledge of the travel expense claim rules is incomplete. The claimant who simply gives his(her) travel data to someone else who then creates a travel expense claim might or might not be willing to use CALTREC, depending on how effective the person actually submitting the claims is as well as how willing the claimant is to try new things. In addition, some people seem to believe that using a terminal is beneath them and will persist in having a secretary produce their travel expense claims. However, CALTREC should be of great use for the average infrequent claimant who must complete his(her) own travel expense claim and is painfully aware that s/he does not know the ins and outs of doing it correctly. This person generally spends a great deal of time trying to find out how to correctly fill out the form and then, because of inevitable errors in the claim, is subjected to many delays before s/he is actually reimbursed. CALTREC will significantly speed the travel expense claim process for this claimant.

Not only is CALTREC viewed as a new way to do an old task better, but it has stimulated some ideas about how to improve the entire travel expense claim process. The CALTREC system was implemented with the objective of simply replacing a process that was being done manually, that is, producing a travel expense claim document, which is a physical piece of paper. CALTREC streamlines the process by formatting and printing the claim and storing personal and claim information on a database to avoid inputting this information more than once. Such information could be used to generate statistics that could be useful in a number of ways, and accounting staffs are interested in this possibility. Also, claims stored electronically could be passed around electronically, reducing the paper flow among destinations. A second new idea inspired by CALTREC is to automatically generate account coding that is assigned by accounting departments to individual expense items on claims. These data are currently being assigned by hand, then input into accounting systems. If CALTREC could produce the account codes, error rates in this area would also be reduced. A number of questions and problems need to be solved before these two ideas can come to fruition, but the fact that CALTREC can not only do its own job well but also inspire new, better ways of doing other facets of the travel expense claim process is encouraging indeed.

Conclusions

CALTREC was implemented in a large, centralized data processing environment (as opposed to using smaller systems) by data processing people for some important reasons. First, incorporating expert system technology into the existing data processing environment is probably the most effective way for state administrative government to make use of expert systems. This approach assures the widest possible user audience and, therefore, the largest possible impact and also affords a great opportunity to leverage existing applications with expert system technology. Second, a major benefit of implementing on a centralized system is that even though there might be frequent updates to the application, every user will be assured of using a current, up-to-date version of the knowledge base. This ability would be unlikely if the application were to run on smaller, more numerous systems. Whenever rules tend to be volatile, the need exists for a centralized control strategy; this characteristic is expected to be common of state expert system applications. (Incidentally, the level of sophistication of these expert systems in AI terms will probably be low, which is not necessarily a problem because these applications have tremendous potential for benefit and relatively low risk and could not have been implemented using traditional tools).

Thus, in this kind of environment, data processing skills are as important (or more so) as knowledge engineering skills. Building the CALTREC knowledge base required only about a quarter of the total time required for the project. Much of the other work that was required must be classified as ordinary data processing activities as opposed to knowledge engineering as such. All this extra effort was required, as previously described, to offer the application in a form that is understandable and palatable to its intended users. The application would have virtually been useless had it not been integrated into the existing user platforms and had it not supported printing on a wide range of printers, no matter how elegant or effective the knowledge base was. In addition, the reality is that the skills required to accomplish these tasks are outside the scope of what is considered to be knowledge engineering work. Thus, given this scenario, the involvement of the data processing staff in the expert system project is essential to its success. However, data processing people are valuable for more than their technical skills because these people are the ones who have been building and maintaining the organization's automated systems; they should be able to offer real insights into opportunities for effectively using expert system technology. Finally, these people are professionals at managing automated system projects: They know what it takes to get a project done and can apply the same skills to knowledge-based system projects.

Despite its problems and pitfalls, the CALTREC experiment unequivocably proved that there is a place in California state government for expert systems. CALTREC successfully automated an application that could not be automated in the past using traditional techniques and is paving the way for other expert system applications: State departments have begun using the technology now that it has been proven by CALTREC. The horizon for expert system use by the state of California looks virtually limitless.

A Knowledge-Based System to Support Nuclear Test Ban Treaty Verification

Gregory Beall, Fred Dashiell, Steven Bratt, and Henry Swanger

The major technical obstacle to the signing of nuclear test ban treaties is the issue of verifying compliance. Since the banning of atmospheric and oceanic testing (Limited Test Ban Treaty of 1963) pushed testing underground, seismic monitoring has been one of the most important technologies available for monitoring compliance with test ban treaties. The goal of these treaties is to progressively reduce the allowed yield of nuclear tests (Threshold Test Ban Treaty) and, possibly, eliminate testing completely (Comprehensive Test Ban Treaty). Increasing the sensitivity of the seismic monitoring requires processing rapidly increasing volumes of naturally occurring background seismicity (earthquakes, mine blasts, and so on) that must be discriminated from nuclear tests. Scientists in the nuclear monitoring community realized that the key to improving the implied search was to bring to bear the rich body of knowledge used by human seismic analysts. This chapter describes a knowledge-based system that was built to apply this approach to the problem.

To address the problem of verification, the Defense Advanced Research Projects Agency (DARPA) has been engaged in an ongoing effort to extend U.S. capabilities to monitor the testing of nuclear weapons throughout the world by analyzing remotely sensed seismic signals. As part of this effort, in 1989, DARPA funded the Nuclear Monitoring Research and Development (NMRD) project for the development of a major system for collecting, organizing, analyzing, and archiving seismological data from many geographically dispersed seismic stations. Science Applications International Corporation (SAIC) is the prime contractor.

Seismic events as energetic as nuclear explosions generate waves in the earth that are frequently detectable beyond national boundaries. A variety of physical processes degrade the information content of the waves as they propagate, however, and the information received by a single station is generally inadequate to firmly identify and locate an event unless the station is close to the event (which is not always possible without the cooperation of the monitored country). It is frequently possible, however, to combine the information received at several dispersed stations to determine the location of an event.

The task of associating signals from a network of seismic stations was originally done manually by human analysts looking at waveforms and features extracted from the waves by signal-processing algorithms. The value of computer assistance to search through the many possible combinations of detections was quickly realized and led to automatic association programs (for example, Elvers 1980; Goncz 1980; Jeppson 1980; Slunga 1980). These programs, however, were not sufficiently flexible to readily incorporate the new expertise that has been uncovered as detection techniques improve. This chapter describes the knowledge-based system called ESAL (expert system for association and location), which, as an integral part of the NMRD project, performs this association task and identifies and locates seismic events from data received by a network of seismic stations.

System Overview

The NMRD project encompasses three separate subsystems with overlapping functions but distinct requirements: the Washington international data center (IDC), the intelligent monitoring system (IMS), and the research and development test bed (RDTB). ESAL is an integral component of the shared functions.

Washington International Data Center

The Washington IDC is one of the four international data centers participating in the United Nations Conference on Disarmament Group of Scientific Experts Second Technical Test (UN/CD GSETT-2). It is located at the Center for Seismic Studies (CSS) in Washington, D.C., and is administered by SAIC.

The Ad Hoc Group of Scientific Experts (GSE) was established by the U.N. Conference on Disarmament to develop and test new concepts for an international system of seismic data exchange for monitoring nuclear explosion testing. In July 1986, GSE, functioning under the aegis of UN/CD, proposed the design and testing of a modern international system based on the rapid exchange of seismic waveform data from a modern global seismic network and the processing of these data at international data centers. The proposed system included national data centers in each participating country that would be responsible for collecting data from designated national seismic stations, processing and analyzing the data, and transmitting results of the analysis and waveform segments to a group of international data centers located in Moscow; Stockholm; Canberra, Australia; and Washington, D.C. Each international data center would be responsible for collecting, processing, and reinterpreting the parameter and waveform data received from the national data centers to produce an optimized global seismic event list, called a *bulletin*. Analysis of the data received from the national data centers involves agreed procedures and is designed to locate as many events as possible. Currently, 28 participating nations provide data from over 50 seismic stations.

GSETT-2 has been conducted in phases, starting in mid-1988, and will conclude with a report to UN/CD on the functional capabilities and relative performance of the different technical approaches in mid- to late 1991. During this period, there has been a series of tests followed by analysis of the results and specification for modifications. A typical day of processing during a test identifies about 25 events out of some 750 detections.

Intelligent Monitoring System

The emphasis in IMS is on automating the collection and interpretation of data. It is structurally similar to IDC but has different data sources and somewhat different processing requirements (Bache et al. 1990).

First, the data currently come from a small set of high-frequency arrays[1] that are tuned to detect regional signals (unlike GSETT, which focuses on signals at global distances).[2] The physics of wave propagation through the earth is different at short (regional) distances than at greater (teleseismic) distances because regional waves largely travel through the earth's crust, and teleseismic waves primarily travel through the mantle. These differences are significant and require the use of different heuristics by IMS than those used by IDC.

A second difference involves the initial identification of phase types, which are essential to the analysis of events. Seismic waves from an event can follow a multitude of paths from the source to the detecting station, for example, crustal, shortest path through the mantle, reflected waves, and diffracted waves. The path of a detected signal, when it can be determined, is denoted by a phase ID, such as Pn or P or PKP. In GSETT, these phases are determined (generally by human analysts) as part of feature extraction performed at the station's national data center. In IMS, this information is not provided, so the task is instead performed by a knowledge-based subsystem of ESAL, referred to as Station Processing.

The third difference is that unlike IDC, which is currently only run during specific GSETT tests and with substantial human interaction, IMS is a fully deployed system running continuously and automatically on data as they arrive at CSS. IMS typically processes 500 to 1,500 detections a day and identifies 20 to 100 events.

Research and Development Test Bed

Despite the significant work done to date in this field, the analysis of seismic signals for nuclear monitoring continues to be an area of active research throughout the world. The goal of a Comprehensive Test Ban Treaty requires ever more sensitive and accurate systems. The data in the CSS database are available to researchers throughout the seismological community who want to examine the merits of different methods of processing the data. Therefore, it is necessary to provide a seismologist-oriented easy-to-use interface to support these researchers, allowing them to graphically alter the heuristics, rerun stored data, and review results.

ESAL Overview

NMRD is a large system that runs on a local area network of Sun workstations at CSS. It includes 7 major modules and 33 major processes plus a relational database. Figure 1 shows the system architecture for IMS, which is representative of the general NMRD system. Waveform data from seismic activity are accumulated at a national or regional data center, where they are signal processed (in IMS at the NORSAR Data Analysis Center [NDAC] in Norway). This processing identifies *detections*[3] in the data and extracts seismologically significant features, such as arrival time, *azimuth* (that is, direction of the incoming wave), phase velocity, amplitude, and frequency content. The features and support-

IMS Architecture

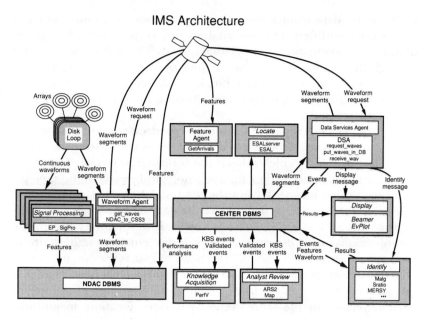

Figure 1. IMS Overview.
The architecture of IMS *is shown by the major groups of processes in* NDAC *(left) and the center's local area networks, which are bridged by a wide-area network connection over a satellite link. The function of the agent processes is to control the data flow. The arrays and disk loops are external to* IMS.

ing waveform data are transferred by satellite link and stored in the CSS database. The knowledge-based system ESAL then attempts to group related detections to identify and locate events. This process provides the essential information of location, depth, and magnitude that is needed for event identification. The results and an audit trail of the analysis are stored in the database and are subsequently reviewed by human analysts who correct the data and conclusions as necessary using the *analyst review station.*[4] A separate knowledge-acquisition tool is being developed to examine the changes made by the analysts, plus ESAL's audit trail, to help identify weaknesses in the knowledge base.

Functional Overview

ESAL is a knowledge-based system that is integrated into the much larger context of the NMRD system. ESAL can run either as part of a real-time pipeline, analyzing data as they become available in the database, or interactively, rerunning historical data from the database on demand. The functional goal of ESAL is to determine and locate all locatable events using data from a network of seismic stations. Once tentative events are identified, humans analysts can review and refine them, drawing on information not available to ESAL. The task of ESAL is to sift through the exponentially large number of potential combinations of detections to find probable groupings, a task that is extremely difficult for human analysts, especially when looking for small events hidden among other events.

ESAL contains two separate knowledge-based subsystems: Station Processing and Network Processing. Figure 2 shows the top-level screen of ESAL's user interface, which reflects the control flow in ESAL. Detection, station, and earth-model data for a seismologically meaningful time period[5] are loaded into ESAL from the NMRD database. The number and types of the stations are unrestricted. The data are optionally processed by the *Station Processing subsystem*, which determines the phase identifications of the detections and provides tentative event groups of detections from a single station. The heart of ESAL is the *Network Processing subsystem*, which examines a set of detections from a network of seismic stations and attempts to determine which groups of detections were generated by the same events. The time, location, magnitude, and composition of these events is the output of ESAL.

In addition, ESAL writes an audit trail of its major decisions, which is stored in the database. When human analysts correct the results produced by ESAL, these changes are also stored in the database. They will subsequently be analyzed by a separate knowledge-based system,[6] which will make deductions about the reason for the corrections and use the audit trail to indicate flaws in ESAL's reasoning. This tool will be important for performance validation and knowledge acquisition.

User Interface

ESAL has a seismologist-oriented graphic user interface that allows a user to graphically examine and modify heuristics, examine the content of solutions, and review details of the reasoning process and evolution of the solutions. Over 200 parameters are available to the user to control ESAL's processing. These parameters and related rules are organized and accessed by module, as seen in figure 3, where the user is examining some of the parameters controlling the Special technique for event hypothesis generation.[7] Figure 4 shows part of the interface available for examining ESAL's solutions. The upper area shows detections along a time line and events (the rectangles) that were constructed from them. The lower area shows high-level information about one of the events and the detections that were considered during its evolution. Selection of an individual detection displays detailed information.

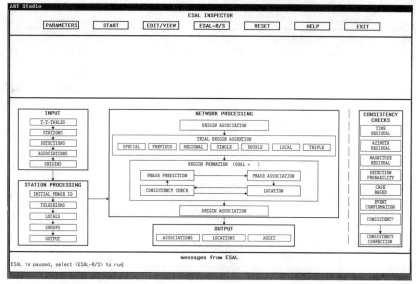

Figure 2. Top-Level ESAL *User Interface.*

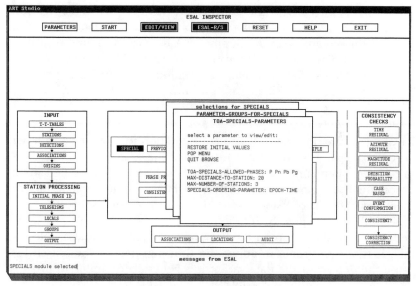

Figure 3. Access to ESAL *Heuristics.*

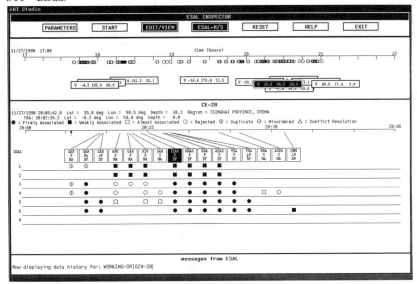

Figure 4. Inspection of ESAL *Results.*

This type of interface is a significant advance over traditional automatic association programs and provides major support for use of the tool for research and development. A user can examine results in detail, adjust heuristics, and then rerun the data. This kind of window into the workings of an automatic association program has not existed before and should provide new insights into its complex behavior.

Design Considerations

Flexibility is the dominant design consideration for ESAL for a number of reasons: First, GSE specifies a number of the seismological heuristics to be used when running GSETT data, which must be modified when processing the regional data in IMS; it might also be desirable to modify them even when processing teleseismic data from other sources.

Second, it is frequently desirable to adjust the search for efficiency depending on the nature of the data, for example, regional or teleseismic. It is also desirable to adjust the thoroughness of the search because the density of the data varies; it is generally desirable to process the data as thoroughly as possible in the available time.

Third, the entire NMRD system is undergoing rapid evolution. ESAL must be able to accommodate data from new stations with new characteristics, new regionally specific earth-model data, and new regionally specific expertise associated with these stations.

Fourth, the field of automatic association itself is an area of active research, especially for regional data. It is essential that seismologists be able to easily examine alternative heuristics.

ESAL must be able to run in a continuous pipeline to support IMS but must also allow the graphically driven interactive reprocessing of data to support RDTB.

ESAL Architecture

ESAL was implemented in ART, Common Lisp, Fortran, and C and is deployed on a Sun workstation. This workstation is part of a local area network of Sun workstations that run the full NMRD system (including the database, telecommunications, signal processing, and analyst review station). The hardware was chosen for smooth integration with the overall system architecture. ART was chosen as the primary programming language after previous experience by SAIC showed that another popular shell was too slow and that a custom inferencing system required too much programming effort and too much focus on the inferencing strategy, distracting effort from the seismological issues. ART was known to have a full set of features, superior performance, and a strong record of successfully deployed systems.

Station Processing

An essential piece of information used by the Network Processing subsystem is the phase ID for each detection. Unlike other data features used by Network Processing, phase IDs cannot be extracted by signal processing alone. During GSETT, phase IDs are determined by human analysts at the various national data centers. In IMS, however, these elements are not provided and are determined instead by Station Processing.

The Station Processing module of ESAL analyzes signals from one station at a time. The features of interest, extracted by Signal Processing before submission to ESAL, include phase velocity, direction of source, wave amplitude, frequency content, and polarization. The principal objectives of this module are to derive the most likely phase type (for example, Pn, Sn, Noise) for each detection and associate detections into groups that are likely to have been produced by the same event to the extent that such conclusions are reliable using information from just one station.

These phase types and groupings are produced for each station being analyzed and are stored in the database. They can then be passed on together to the Network Processing module for more complete location processing. For flexibility, Station Processing can also be used as a standalone module, without also running the Network Processing module.

Currently, Station Processing is most useful for signals produced by events relatively close to the station (local and regional events) because the heuristics are best understood for the closer distances. However, the architecture is designed so that as new stations with more sensitive instruments come online, and new heuristics are developed, single-station treatment of teleseismic data can easily be added to the rules of the module.

There are two major steps in the Station Processing module (figure 2): initial phase classification and event-group association with phase identification. This latter step is divided into special rules for teleseisms, local events, and more generic regional events.

The first step classifies each detection into one of several mutually exclusive categories: regional P-type, regional S-type, teleseism (that is, from a distant event), or noise. This initial phase identification for a detection is based on feature values of the signal without consideration of the relationship it might have with the other detections being considered. The heuristics for this classification are implemented using rules with patterns describing the various categories. The value ranges that delimit the categories in the patterns are parameters that can be modified by the user.

Final phase identification and association into likely event groups is done by considering the detections at the station in time order. The earliest arriving unassociated P-type wave is used as the foundation of a new event group, and the list is searched for following detections that are to be included in the new group. Here, the interrelationships of the detections are used to derive the most likely specific final phase ID (for example, Pn, Pg, Sn, Lg) and decide whether a given detection is consistent with the developing group. The context of a detection within a group, that is, its relationship to other detections in the group, is combined with empirically derived probabilities using Bayesian reasoning to derive a most likely final phase identification.

The reasoning in the Station Processing module is monotonic using a constrained depth-first search. That is, an event group is completely formed, and the phase IDs are affirmatively established and not subsequently revised until additional information is brought to bear during the Network Processing phase. The rules are forward chaining. A major feature is the ability to easily add special heuristics for particular stations or geographic regions to the reasoning.

Network Processing

Network Processing examines detections from a network of seismic stations and attempts to determine which groups of detections were generated by the same events. It consists of an event hypothesis generator

(Trial Origin Assertion in figure 2) and a multilevel loop (Origin Formation) that iteratively adds corroborating detections, relocates the event, and then checks for self-consistency. If this process identifies sufficient corroborating data, the hypothesis is confirmed; otherwise, it is abandoned. The input data used by Network Processing are detection features (for example, arrival time, azimuth, velocity, amplitude, phase ID), station data (for example, location, sensitivity), earth-model information (travel time and amplitude-distance data for the various phases), and user parameters that control heuristics regarding the nature of the events to be formed and the manner in which they are to be formed. It can also include previously formed events and tentative single station groupings that are to be reprocessed using new data or different heuristics. The output are event characterizations (time, location, magnitude) and the set of associated detections. Both are written to the CSS database for subsequent analyst review.

The heuristics used in Network Processing fall into two classes: those controlling the composition of the events that are formed, for example, restrictions on what detections can be used to define an event and the minimum number and character of defining detections, and those controlling how the events are to be identified and formed, that is, control of the search process.

The heuristics in the first class are tightly specified by GSE in IDC. Many of these heuristics are relaxed or modified, however, when running IMS. The heuristics controlling the search have more overlap between IDC and IMS but vary with the type and source of the data.

Network Processing Architecture. Network Processing is implemented as a rule-based forward-chaining system. Detection and station data are stored in ART schemas (also called frames) that allow an object-oriented structuring of the data, pattern matching by rules for the expression of complex conditions, and the use of procedural access and active values for efficient processing when pattern matching is not required. Heuristics are expressed in rules, schemas, and procedures. Some heuristics are encoded in Lisp for efficiency. Many heuristics, however, require a rich pattern-matching language; such as the example in figure 5.

To maintain flexibility, rules are made as generic as possible and frequently represent only the structure of the heuristic. The specifics of the heuristic, such as thresholds, phase restrictions, and minimum requirements for confirmation, are represented in a declarative form that is easily modified by the user. This approach emphasizes the separation of the data from the inferencing mechanism and is a crucial factor in allowing the system to handle multiple seismic domains. Fortran

IF there is ?detection-1 associated-with ?event
  which was detected at ?time-1 at ?station,
    which is at ?distance from ?event
  and which has associated-phase ?phase-1,
    which is a member of ?P-type-phases
AND there is a second ?detection-2 associated-with ?event
  which was detected at ?time-2 at ?station
  and which has associated-phase ?phase-2,
    which is a member of ?S-type-phases
AND (?time-1 − ?time-2) < ?max-P-S-time-for-regional-event
AND ?distance > ?max-distance-to-regional-event

THEN ?detection-1 and ?detection-2 may not be used
  to compute the location of ?event

Figure 5. Complex Conditions Require a Rich Pattern-Matching Language.

and C routines handle a variety of numerically intensive calculations based on the earth model, such as the computation of seismic wave point-to-point travel times.

Complexities in Network Processing. The problem of associating detections with the correct event is more difficult than it might appear because of the large volume of data and the presence of noise. The signals from an event can be detected over a time period that is large compared to the interval between events.[8] Critical discriminating phases can be lost in an overlapping signal from another event. In addition, such strong discriminants as azimuth are frequently unavailable or have large uncertainties. All the detection's features, including the phase ID, carry uncertainties that ESAL must use in its reasoning. Because of these uncertainties, there can be numerous self-consistent ways to combine a set of detections into event hypotheses that ESAL must select between. Furthermore, the number of detections that must be analyzed increases rapidly with the sensitivity of the system (for example, there are roughly 10 times as many magnitude 5 events as magnitude 6 and 10 times as many magnitude 4 as 5 [Bolt 1976]; most of the events located by IMS are below magnitude 2).

Search in Network Processing. An unusual feature of this problem relative to many AI search problems is that ESAL must find as many locatable events as possible within system constraints (for example, acceptable processing time). An exhaustive search is an exponential function of the data density, so the search must be restricted, but it is done in a flexible way so that the extensiveness of the search can be balanced against the amount of data. The search can roughly be described as a *best-first search.* One event hypothesis at a time is generated and allowed to evolve. If the resultant event is considered acceptable, it is retained, and the defining detections are removed from consideration for the construction of subsequent events. If the event is judged to be unacceptable (generally because of an inadequate amount of corroborating data), then it is dissolved, and the associated detections are made available to subsequent events. This process continues until the event hypothesis generator is exhausted.[9]

Hypothesis Generation and Development. A number of techniques are available in ESAL for generating event hypotheses (Trial Origin Assertion in figure 2); the selection and order of the techniques used are under the control of the user and can vary depending on the source and nature of the data. Within each technique, additional heuristics determine the specific order of hypothesis generation and the quality checks that control the minimum requirements for the hypotheses to be considered.

The evolution of the hypothesis (Origin Formation in figure 2) is at the heart of ESAL and is the most complex part of the processing. The loop in Origin Formation has Phase Prediction-Association, Location, and Consistency Check as its main phases. Given an event hypothesis (from Trial Origin Assertion), the set of available detections is examined to identify detections that might corroborate the hypothesis (Phase Prediction-Association). Detections are checked for compatibility with both the location of the event and the composition of the event (for example, the phases detected by a single station must obey various ordering constraints). The new detections are tentatively associated with the event, and the event is relocated using the new information. The solution is then checked for seismological self-consistency (Consistency Check), and detections that are no longer consistent are removed and the event relocated. The hypothesis is then reexamined for additional corroborating detections (Phase Prediction-Association). This refining process continues until no more detections are associated, or a previously examined node in the search space is revisited. This process actually proceeds through a series of stages in an effort to stabilize the convergence of small events, initially using the most reliable data (such as teleseismic primary phases), then adding less reliable data (such as regional and secondary phases) as the solution stabilizes. The number and structure of these stages is under the control of the user.

Network Processing Internal Model. The heuristics that control the association of a detection with an event depend not only on the relationship of the detection to the event but also on the relationship of other detections to the event and of the detection to other events. As previously mentioned, the initial detection and station data are represented by schemas; event hypotheses are also represented by schemas. In addition, as events are formed and evolved, ESAL maintains a dynamic solution model of these relationships in the form of a semantic net. The links between detections and events are themselves objects (schemas) of a single type with many attributes (such as associated phase, type of association, phase and association confidences). This representation allows reasoning about complex aspects of the structure of the net, not just about individual objects. Having a single type of link greatly simplifies the expression of the rules for reasoning about the net, which is essential to the goal of keeping ESAL flexible.

All the data features that ESAL reasons about have uncertainties arising from measurement and the seismological models.[10] These uncertainties are propagated into the event location and are then used to compute confidence levels for the association of detections with events. Confidence levels are uniformly computed throughout ESAL using conventional probability theory and are the basis for determining consistency and resolving conflicts.

Search Control in Network Processing. The search in Network Processing is somewhat unusual in that it is based on the "iterate until convergence" model but must deal with the problem of a minimum discrete step size (adding or removing one detection) that is sometimes large compared to the separation of the local minima of the evaluation function. This step can produce a search that drifts and follows complex orbits and that is difficult to control in numeric models. In ESAL, it is not uncommon to find complex orbits where some detections are added, others are removed, more are added and removed, and the system returns to the same node. ESAL cannot afford to maintain a full representation of the search space, so instead, it records snapshots of significant nodes in the path that it traverses so that it can appropriately terminate these potential loops.[11] At the conclusion of Origin Formation, the event hypothesis is tested against various minimality and validity checks before it is confirmed.

Backtracking and Conflict Resolution. In a conventional automatic association program, the construction of the event would be complete at this point, and the search for the next event would begin. A major innovation in ESAL is the introduction of nonmonotonic reasoning. Programs like that described by Slunga (1980) follow the strict rule that a defining detection cannot be reconsidered by subsequent events. This strategy is correct (and beneficial to the management of the search) if there is a high confidence in the association of the detection with the event.[12] Not all detections can be associated with high confidence, however, because of the uncertainties previously discussed. Therefore, the conventional strategy can erroneously associate a detection with an event, thereby making it unavailable when the correct event is subsequently hypothesized. ESAL introduces the concept of *weak association*, which allows certain associated detections to be considered by subsequent event hypotheses and be temporarily multiply associated. This process allows additional small-event hypotheses to be considered at the processing cost that multiple associations must be resolved before the event is confirmed. The user can control how many detections are weakly associated, thereby trading processing time for expanded search.

Development and Deployment

The overall design of the NMRD system, including a high-level description of ESAL processing, was submitted to DARPA in mid-1988. The detailed design of ESAL started in late 1988. Two Inference knowledge engineers worked full time with periodic input from initially one and eventually four expert SAIC seismologists. The first version of the Network Processing system was delivered to SAIC in the spring of 1989. Station Processing was added at a later stage, the first version being delivered in late 1989. New versions of both systems, containing requested extensions, were released at roughly quarterly intervals. ESAL was first used in GSETT-2 testing in January 1990. ESAL has been fully deployed in the IMS application since November 1990.

ESAL was initially validated by running it with historical GSETT data and having the results accepted by the seismologists on the team. As GSETT testing progressed, the available data increased. These data are now used for regression testing of new releases. ESAL's conclusions in IMS are continuously reviewed by human analysts; however, ESAL is not currently expected to do as well as seismic analysts who have access to the actual waveform data. The following counts indicate an approximate measure of the size of ESAL:

Number of ART rules:	250
Lines of ART code:	12,634
Initial ART schemas:	672
Schemas during run:	~ 1,500
Number of Lisp functions:	1,677
Lines of Lisp code:	35,061
Lines of Fortran and C code:	13,422

ESAL is currently used on a continuous, daily basis within IMS at CSS in Washington, D.C. Within the IMS processing, ESAL has processed all detection data received from the Scandinavian high-frequency arrays

NORESS, ARCESS, and FINESA since 1 November 1990. From this date through 11 January 1991, ESAL processed 64,572 automatically detected seismic phases to form a seismic bulletin of 3,889 local, regional, and teleseismic events. All ESAL solutions are reviewed by an analyst and corrected if necessary. Processing in the IMS application includes both Station Processing and Network Processing. A German array, GERESS, is being added in early 1991, and there is a plan to add two Polish three-component stations and seven three-component stations in the USSR and China by mid-1991. IMS is the only seismic processing system in the world capable of fully automated processing of local, regional, and teleseismic data.

In addition to IMS, ESAL is used in the Washington IDC during GSETT-2 testing. Nineteen days of data between 16 January 1990 and 4 December 1990 were processed as a part of GSETT-2. For these days, ESAL located 487 events using 13,878 reported detections. As in IMS, all ESAL solutions were reviewed by an analyst and corrected if necessary. The final operational exercise of GSETT begins in April 1991, covering 42 continuous days of processing. As part of the technology transfer encouraged by UN/CD and DARPA, ESAL will be installed in Norway in mid-1991 for the Norwegian Council for Scientific and Industrial Research.

NMRD is still actively evolving with the addition of new seismic stations with different detection capabilities (for example, the three-component stations in Poland, the Soviet Union, and China) and the refinement of seismological heuristics, especially in the areas of region-specific refinements and the station processing of teleseismic data. The flexible design of ESAL allows the seismologists to make many adjustments without altering any source code. Alterations that require source code changes are made by the original developers. The audit trail mentioned earlier provides automated support for knowledge acquisition, but the knowledge base update is a manual process.

Innovations

ESAL's innovation is mainly seen in comparison with other automatic association programs. Innovations include the following:

First is the flexibility to process data of diverse quality and type; support multiple seismic domains; alter the reasoning process at run time; control the search, particularly with regard to the concept of weak association and revision of previous hypotheses; and easily add new heuristics.

Second is the ability to automatically assign phase identification to regional and teleseismic phases (Station Processing). Few existing automatic association programs include this ability as an automated procedure.

Third is the ability to express much more complex and knowledge-rich consistency checks than conventional automatic association programs.

Fourth is the graphic user interface. Conventional automatic association programs have no capability that is analogous to the ESAL interface for inspecting intermediate processing results.

Fifth is the ability to run either as part of a data processing pipeline or in interactive mode.

Relative to other knowledge-based systems, ESAL is unusual in that it simultaneously supports a fully deployed real-time system and a research and development tool. The search employed in Network Processing is also unusual among typical knowledge-based applications in that the final solution should contain all viable partial solutions (although this kind of search seems to apply to a variety of problems where it is essential to explain all sources of overlapping data, such as fault monitoring in a network of sensors where errors can propagate significant distances from the source).

Summary

NMRD is one of the most sophisticated systems in the world today for the seismic detection of nuclear testing. It was built to test new ideas about the integration and processing of data from a global network of seismic sensors, and it was designed to use knowledge-based system technology to provide the flexibility to evolve along with the seismological understanding of such a system. This flexibility was demonstrated in late 1990 when, in less than a month, the system was modified to process previously unseen data provided by a different branch of the Department of Defense.

ESAL represents a new generation of automatic association programs that take advantage of knowledge-based technology to incorporate the rich and evolving body of knowledge used by human seismic analysts. ESAL is fully deployed in a continuously running real-time system and is also used as a research and development tool to improve the understanding of such systems.

As for acceptance by the customer, DARPA has identified NMRD as one of the outstanding programs within its funding. The value of this system was not envisioned in hours or dollars saved but in the confidence it could provide to policy makers that a nuclear test ban treaty can indeed be verified. In the world's changing political environment, its greatest value might end up being the ability to monitor regions of the world where treaty negotiations have failed.

BEALL

Acknowledgments

ESAL was developed as part of the Nuclear Monitoring Research and Development (NMRD) project funded by the Defense Advance Research Projects Agency (contract number MDA972-88-C-0024). The top-level architecture and heuristics for ESAL were specified by Science Applications International Corporation (SAIC), the NMRD prime contractor. SAIC also provided the numeric routines for earth-model calculations. The ESAL knowledge base was designed and implemented by Inference Corporation as a subcontractor to SAIC. The authors are indebted to the staff members of the Geophysics Division at SAIC, San Diego, including Thomas C. Bache, director, Jeff Given, and Ethan Brown, and to Bradley P. Allen, director of advanced technology, Inference Corporation.

Notes

1. A *seismic array* is a set of seismic sensors dispersed over a relatively small geographic area whose signals are combined and processed together to produce improved signal-to-noise ratios and improve the extraction of certain features, such as signal azimuth. A variety of new data sources and data types will be added to the IMS network in the near future.

2. Regional distances are within about 2,000 kilometers; teleseismic distances are larger.

3. A detection is determined by a significant increase in the signal over background noise and is interpreted to be an arriving wave front from a seismic event.

4. The *analyst review station* provides the analyst with an extensive graphic and procedural interface to review ESAL's conclusions. This interface includes waveform data, regional maps, and satellite photos that were not available to ESAL. Analysis of the corrections that are made reveals that analysts make use of information in the waveform that is not contained in the current feature set. This analysis might lead to an improved feature set for future processing.

5. It is desirable to have all the detection data for an event, which implies a minimum time interval of about 1 hour. In practice, the interval varies between 3 and 24 hours depending on the density of the data.

6. A performance validator, PerfV, is currently under development.

7. The user typically loads an initializing set of parameters that characterize the data to be run, for example, GSETT data, and then optionally modifies a few of them interactively.

8. Distinct events can occur minutes apart, yet the various waves received by a station from a single event can arrive over a period of tens of minutes because of the different paths taken through the earth.

9. One might expect the search to end when all the detections are associated with an event. Experience has shown, however, that generally about half of the detections are never associated with an event and represent either noise or disturbances too small to be detected at multiple stations (detection at multiple stations is generally a requirement for confirming an event hypothesis).

10. Some of the uncertainties arising from the seismological model might eventually be overcome with sufficient observational experience; measurement uncertainties caused by noise in the seismic signals are unavoidable.

11. It is not adequate to simply record the node. Because reaching a previous node does not indicate an invalid solution, it is also necessary to record information about how to proceed from the node.

12. A detection can only have come from one event; consequently, it is not physically meaningful to have one detection associated with two events.

References

Bache, T. C.; Bratt, S. R.; Wang, J.; Fung, R. M.; Kobryn, C.; and Given, J. W. 1990. The Intelligent Monitoring System. *Bulletin of the Seismological Society of America* 80B: 1833–1851.

Bolt, B. 1976. *Nuclear Explosions and Earthquakes.* New York: W. H. Freeman.

Elvers, E. 1980. International Seismological Data Center: Procedures to Check Events through Dynamic Information and to Estimate Magnitudes, FOA Report C20368-T1, National Defense Research Institute, Stockholm, Sweden.

Goncz, J. H. 1980. Present Status and Dynamic Planning for Automatic Association Programs, Seismic Data Analysis Center Report SDAC-TR-80-2, Teledyne Geotech Co., Arlington, Virginia.

Jeppson, I. 1980. International Seismological Data Center: Automatic Association of Long Period Surface Wave Data, FOA Report, C 20385-T1, National Defense Research Institute, Stockholm, Sweden.

Slunga, R. 1980. International Seismological Data Center: An Algorithm for Associating Reported Arrivals to a Global Seismic Network into Groups of Defining Seismic Events, FOA Report, C20386-T1, National Defense Research Institute, Stockholm, Sweden.

Index

customer premise equipment, 213, 215, 222, 225
customer service, 18, 67-72, 75-82, 269
customized letters, 67-68, 70-71, 75, 77-81

DARPA, 124, 337-338, 351-353
Dashiell, Fred, 337
data processing, 3-5, 7-9, 11-19, 22-23, 27-31, 35, 40, 44-45, 49, 55, 57-58, 60-62, 64, 70-72, 75-76, 80-83, 87, 89-91, 93-96, 101, 108-109, 112, 116-118, 135, 137, 140, 148, 153, 196, 198-201, 207, 212, 216-217, 220, 223-224, 228-229, 233-235, 237, 239-242, 246-249, 252, 255-259, 261-263, 265-268, 273-274, 276-277, 280, 282, 284, 287, 292, 294-295, 298-299, 307-308, 314, 319, 321, 324, 327, 329-331, 333-335, 337-342, 344-355
De Fazio, T. L., 135, 151, 154
DEC, 207, 260, 264-265
decision rules, 249, 261, 301, 311
DECtree, 208
default reasoning, 301
Defense Advanced Research Projects Agency, see DARPA
deregulation, 4, 246-247
derivational adaptation, 127, 130
Development of Syllabus—An Interactive, Constraint-Based, 39
DFMA:
diagnosis, 88, 90-91, 95, 101-103, 105-106, 108-109, 117, 216-217, 220, 224, 229-230
differential analyzer, 310
Digital Equipment Corporation, see DEC
discriminator, 113
double dispatches, 215
Dun & Bradstreet, 255

Ebersold, Brian, 11
Edsall, A. C., 135
engineering, 75, 77-78, 121, 123-124, 131, 135, 150-151, 154-155, 158-160, 164, 172, 174, 198, 210, 295, 319, 321, 327, 329, 335
engineering knowledge, transfer of, 158-160, 164-165, 168, 170, 172, 174, 176, 321, 323, 325-330, 333, 335
ESAL, 338, 340-345, 348-354
Euchner, Jim, 213

Evertsz, Rick, 39
Expert Auditing System for Airline Passenger Tickets, 3
expert system, 3, 7-9, 12-13, 15-19, 22, 58-59, 64, 71, 77, 87, 90, 103, 107-108, 112, 115, 146, 157-158, 160, 198, 212, 216-218, 227, 230, 233-235, 240, 242, 243-244, 251-252, 255, 257-260, 264-265, 268-269, 293, 310, 324-331, 334-335, 338
Expert Systems in Data Processing: California Travel Expense Claim System, 321

fabrication, 135
false dispatches, 215, 217, 223-224
fare audit, 3-9
fare commission audit, 3-9
Federal Deposit Insurance System, 244
Flamholz, Jack, 213
flight operations system:
forecasting, 292, 295, 298, 303, 305-306, 308, 312
Fortran, 345, 347, 351
forward chaining, 220, 261, 346
FOS, 22-25, 27-30, 34
FOXGLOVE, 201, 206
frequent flyer, 11-13, 15, 17-19
fuzzy logic, 274, 276

Golden Common Lisp, 160
GoldWorks, 123, 160
Grammatik, 76
GSE, 339, 344, 347
GSETT, 339-340, 344-345, 351-352, 354
Gupta, Ajay, 87, 95, 103
Gustavson, R. E., 135

Hernandez, J. A., 135
heuristics, 17, 19, 27, 32, 91, 144, 147, 151, 204, 207, 209, 274, 282, 291-293, 298, 315, 318, 340, 342-347, 349, 352, 354
Hood, Steve, 157
HP Labs, 87-88, 99-103
Hutchins, P. M., 135
HWDC, 324, 326-327, 329-332
hypothesis generator, 346, 349

I-DEAS, 118, 124, 137-138, 140, 160, 217, 286, 295, 312, 334, 353

Colophon

Editorial and Production Management by
The Live Oak Press, Palo Alto, California.

Copyedited by Elizabeth Ludvik.

Cover design by Spectra Media.

Composed in New Baskerville and Futura by
The Live Oak Press

Output on a Linotronic 300 by G&S Typesetters,
Austin Texas.

Printed offset on 60 lb. Finch Opaque Smooth by
McNaughton Gunn, Inc., Saline, Michigan.